Y0-AAG-936

Dissertations
in
American Economic History

This is a volume in the Arno Press collection

Dissertations in American Economic History

Advisory Editor
Stuart Bruchey

Research Associate
Eleanor Bruchey

See last pages of this volume for a complete list of titles.

THE AMERICAN COLONIAL WINE INDUSTRY
An Economic Interpretation

David Joel Mishkin

Volume I

ARNO PRESS
A New York Times Company
New York – 1975

First publication in book form, Arno Press, 1975

Reprinted from a copy in
The University of Illinois Library

DISSERTATIONS IN AMERICAN ECONOMIC HISTORY
ISBN for complete set: 0-405-07252-X
See last pages of this volume for titles.

Manufactured in the United States of America

Library of Congress Cataloging in Publication Data

Mishkin, David Joel.
The American colonial wine industry.

(Dissertations in American economic history)
Originally presented as the author's thesis, University of Illinois, 1966.
Vol. 2 consists of an annotated bibliography and indexes for the bibliography.
1. Wine and wine making--North America--History. 2. Mercantile system--History. 3. Wine and wine making--North America--History--Bibliography. 4. Mercantile system--History--Bibliography. I. Title. II. Series.
HD9375.3.M57 1975   338.4'7'663200973   75-2589
ISBN 0-405-07208-2

THE AMERICAN COLONIAL WINE INDUSTRY: AN ECONOMIC INTERPRETATION

BY

DAVID JOEL MISHKIN
B.A., Queens College, 1958
A.M., Columbia University, 1960

THESIS

Submitted in partial fulfillment of the requirements
for the degree of Doctor of Philosophy in Economics
in the Graduate College of the
University of Illinois, 1966

Urbana, Illinois

Preface

This dissertation was conceived and executed as a capital intensive venture. Duplicative and manipulative operations were farmed-out to clerical help, manual and mechanized. The author's responsibilities were limited to the decision operations of research, to the drafting of the dissertation, and to the supervision of clerical help.

Capital intensive techniques were employed in the location, identification, and recall of information sources relating to the vineyard in schemes of American colonization.[1] Bibliographies, the shelf lists of major libraries, and secondary source citations were culled to locate information sources. Clerical help was employed to retrieve these source materials, to construct their bibliographic entries, and to keep track of the flow of materials in use, a task including Xerox copying, photostating, or direct hand-copying of critical portions of source materials. The author alone was responsible for all bibliographic annotations and for the selection of the final content of the bibliography.

---

[1] A Preliminary survey of this disseration was presented under the title "The Vineyard in Schemes of American Colonization" at the 25th Annual Meeting of the Economic History Association, at Yale University, September 1-3, 1965. For an abstract of this invited dissertation address see the _Journal of Economic History_, Vol. 25, No. 4 (December, 1965), pp. 683 to 685.

Identification of information sources was achieved by means of a bibliographic annotation scheme devised by the author.[2] The tasks of information recall and queuing were assigned to computers which were instructed to produce instantaneously from memory units, in words and in coded form, any desired author, title, or subject information.[3]

The economic rationale for this capital intensive approach was the opportunity cost of the author's time and the anticipated value of his earnings at the project's completion. The author, therefore, gladly exchanged anticipated earnings for the current credit of friends, family, and the New York State Higher Education Assistance Corporation. Funds from these sources supplemented fellowship awards from H. B. Earhart Foundation (1965-1966), the Lilly Endowment Inc. (1964-1965) and the National Science Foundation (Summer 1963), and research grants from the Subvention Fund of the University of Illinois Department of Economics and from the Statistical Services unit at the University's Graduate College. The author remains indebted to these benefactors financially, and morally, respectively.

---

[2] Infra, Vol. 2, pp. iv to xiv renders a detailed account of this annotation scheme.

[3] Three such information listings compromise the Index to the Bibliography (Infra, Vol. 2, pp. 211 to 630). The computer techniques employed are reviewed Infra, Vol. 2, pp. xiv to xl.

Bottlenecks were inevitable in the drafting of the dissertation. One production constraint was the dispersion of research materials. The author, thereby, is grateful to the Folger Library, the William Clements Library, the Newberry Library, the Cushing Medical Library, the Columbia University Law Library, and the University of Illinois Libraries for the use of materials in their collections. The Arents Collection of the New York Public Library, the Harvard Libraries and the Massachusetts Historical Society also graciously welcomed the author.

A second production constraint was the dissertation reading committee, Dr. Donald L. Kemmerer chairman. Their attentive supervision and exhaustive review significantly enhanced the style and content of the dissertation. Notwithstanding, the author acknowledges his sole responsibility for this final draft.

Table of Contents

Introduction

This dissertation is three distinct writings: the first a statement of hypotheses and findings; the second a bibliography, annotated according to an original numeric code system; and the third, an index to the bibliography -- computer-produced by application of a modified Keyword-In-Context (KWIC) data processing technique.

The thesis reexamines the commodity trade motive in the colonization of America. The text demonstrates that attempts to promote or to retard the development of a colonial American wine industry played a significant role in the Spanish, French, English, and Dutch colonial policies of the sixteenth, seventeenth, and eighteenth centuries. It further affirms the primacy of economic motives in the viticultural schemes of American colonization -- a hypothesis in opposition to accepted climatic, socio-political theories.

The text, too, develops the concept of Commodity Mercantilism. This new approach stresses the ready availability of commodities -- of naval stores, raw materials, and even wine, the maintenance of a favorable commodity balance and the fiscal solvency of the realm as means for the attainment of mercantile ends. The following synopsis of early colonial ventures to establish vineyards for wine production in the Americas demonstrates of this Commodity Mercantilism concept:[1]

1. The Spanish attempted viticulture in the West Indies prior to 1516 and in New Spain in 1524. The latter attempt was so successful that in 1595 Spain forbade the planting or renewal of vineyards in both the West Indies and in New Spain in order to protect her Spanish wine trade.
2. The French, at about the same time, contemplated establishing vineyards in Florida and in New France. A century later viticulture in New France and in Louisiana was to be outlawed. The French, like the Spanish, feared the competition of colonial wines.
3. These French and Spanish restraints on wine production led the English to develop viticulture in America. There were, as well, three other important stimuli.
    a. A 1567 French statute ordered that two thirds of French lands be earmarked for grain, that land suitable for <u>prairie</u> not be given over to vines, and that the excess planting of vines be forbidden. All these measures were directed

---

[1]The assertions of this synopsis are documented <u>Infra</u>, Vol. 1, pp. 73 to 299.

at achieving higher wine prices and a readily available supply of grain.

b. Enthusiastic reports of explorers and early colonists who were enraptured by the abundance of wild grapes growing on the Florida and Virginia coasts stimulated the development of a colonial wine industry.

c. England hoped that she could redress her unfavorable commodity trade balance in wine by cultivating French, Spanish, and Madeira vines in her colonies. She planned to substitute at home, as well as, in her colonies, colonial wines of these grapes, for the wines of France, Spain, and Madeira.

In each of these instances of Commodity Mercantilism, the mother country -- Spain, France, England -- sought a readily available supply of a commodity, wine. In each case a commitment to maintain a favorable commodity balance at home determined the fate of the colonial wine venture. Spain and France restricted colonial viticulture whereas England sought by diverse means to encourage her own ventures.

The desire for commodity availability continued to motivate later attempts to establish vineyards and later edicts to thwart such ventures in colonial America. Other incentives were the hope of gains from commodity trade, and considerations of royal finance. Even the popularity of gin and distilled spirits in the eighteenth century did not dampen the enthusiasm of English colonizers for viticultural projects. French and Spanish anxiety continued unabated. Throughout the entire period of American colonization, these nations continued to fear the possible success of English ventures and the competition of their own clandestine colonial vineyards.

The opening chapter of the dissertation introduces the hypothesis of Commodity Mercantilism. This concept stresses the ready-availability of commodities, and the maintenance of a favorable commodity balance as criteria of successful mercantile policy. It emphasizes, as well, the importance of fiscalism -- expediency in royal finance -- in determining the commercial practices of the European states. The Commodity Mercantilism hypothesis, a theory of the <u>means</u> of mercantile practice, is contrasted, in a critical review, to the power and wealth-power theses, both theories of mercantile policy <u>ends</u>.

Chapter two develops the rationale of Commodity Mercantilism outlining trade and colonization policies of the European states. It illustrates this rationale with respect to the fishing trade, naval stores, drugs, spices and silk.

Chapters three, four and five demonstrate that attempts to promote or retard a colonial wine industry played a significant role in the Spanish, French, English and Dutch colonial policies of the sixteenth, seventeenth and eighteenth centuries. Chapter three deals with the Spanish ventures; chapter four with the Dutch and French role. Chapter five introduces England's experience. Throughout chapters three, four and five, the Commodity Mercantilism hypothesis is documented.

Chapter six details the actual English attempts at viticulture and wine production in the North American colonies. This chapter reviews the motivations behind these ventures and suggests the reasons for their failure. It affirms the primacy of economic motives in the viticultural schemes of American colonization -- a hypothesis in opposition to accepted climatic, socio-political theories.

* * * *

The _Annotated Bibliography_ and _Index to the Bibliography_ were the first completed parts of this dissertation. The plan was to read and compile all obtainable information before formulating any statements of findings. A desire to increase operational efficiency and to insure the objectivity of historical research motivated this approach.

The topic of efficiency was considered first. Would techniques efficient for writing term papers, articles, and short manuscripts be equally efficient in writing works of far larger scope? Could economies of scale be achieved in historical research? Analysis of the research process revealed two opportunities for scale economies: first, the routinism of decision operations, that is, the design of the uniform numeric code system for the purpose of bibliographic annotation; and, second, the substitution of capital for labor in duplicative and manipulative operations.

This substitution of capital for labor was achieved by using a computer to perform all tasks of information recall, retrieval, and queuing. The computer, given as _input_ over 1200 bibliographic entries and their annotations, and instructed by a modified Keyword-In-Context program, produced as _output_ an author-title-subject index signaling the location of the entire information content of the dissertation, that is, the location of some 30,000 major information statements. The task of compiling the _Annotated Bibliography_ and producing the _Index to the Bibliography_ was completed within two months which suggests the achievement of important economies of scale.

Economics of scale, however, were not the only purpose behind the annotation and indexing schemes. The ability of these schemes to bolster the objectivity of historical research is also important. No longer need the scholar limit his research, nor need he attempt to formulate his finding before _all_ sources have been consulted. Thus, he can be freer of prejudice -- liberated from unintentionally overlooking material contrary to the hypothesis of his work. A less biased survey of his information _input_ is assured if he instructs the computer to perform the tasks of information recall and retrieval and to order this information according to his topic outline. Thus, the job of the researcher is further specialized -- he now may devote himself to the objective review of findings and to the formulation of hypotheses by inductive and deductive techniques. Such hypotheses indicate his evaluation of all the information *input* gathered and queued for him by the computer. This is the research technique developed for this dissertation.

The information *input* collected and recorded in the *Annotated Bibliography* is primary and secondary sources depicting the role of Commodity Mercantilism in the colonization of the Americas. It records, as well, virtually all primary and secondary sources relating to colonial American attempts at viticulture and wine production. This information *input*, once gathered, queued and printed by the computer, is the *Index to the Bibliography*. It offers the scholar, not only the information sample of the text and footnotes, but a proximate information universe of materials relating to the commodity trade motive in American colonization.

CHAPTER I

The Hypothesis of Commodity Mercantilism

> Mercantilism, as this commercial policy came to be called, was not a theory but a condition, an experience in practical form of the experience of those concerned directly with trade and commerce, and indirectly with coinage, credit, interest, and exchange, with banks, customs, and excise, with the naturalization of aliens and the treatment of the poor, the vagrant, and the criminal, that is, with all that had to do with the agricultural, commercial, financial, and social life of the realm. It was the inevitable accompaniment of a state of society in which foreign trade and commerce were rapidly attaining an ascendancy and were determining the attitude of states- and merchant alike toward the other material interests of the nation.[1]

This description of England's commercial and colonial policy characterizes, as well, other European states. It suggests the practices by which the states resolved "a common European problem."[2]

The relative wealth-power position of each European state moved over a wide range; in the sixteenth century Spain dominated the European economic scene, the Netherlands

---

[1]Charles M. Andrews. The Colonial Period..., (938 1270950), Vol. 4, pp. 2-3. The meaning of the code symbol (938 1270950) and of similar symbols is detailed Infra, Vol. 2, pp. iv to vi.

[2]Eli Heckscher. Mercantilism, (935$1270922), Vol. 1, p. 13.

in the seventeenth century, and France in the eighteenth century.[3] England assumed the prominent position in European affairs with the signing of the Treaty of Paris (1763). The relative position was determined by the ability of the state to enlarge domestic production through trade and colonization, augmenting thereby its wealth-power position.[4] By affecting the level of national welfare and the efficacy of the state, political,[5] religious,[6] social[7] and demographic[8]

---

[3] Andrews. The Colonial..., op. cit., Vol. 4, pp. 5 to 8.
E. Lipson. The Economic History..., (961 1271270), Vol. 2, pp. lii to liv.
Henry Chapin and F. G. W. Smith. The Ocean River, (952$1270010), pp. 302 to 304.

[4] Heckscher. Mercantilism, op. cit., Vol. 2, pp. 23 to 26.
Lipson. The Economic..., op. cit., Vol. 2, pp. xcv-xcvi; Vol. 3, p. 4.
Klaus Knorr. British Colonial Theories 1570-1850, Toronto: University of Toronto Press, 1944, pp. 19 to 21.
Charles Cole. Colbert and a Century of French Mercantilism, New York: Columbia University Press, 1939, Vol. 2, pp. 551-552.

[5] Knorr. British Colonial..., op. cit., pp. 19-20.
Arthur Newton. The Colonising Activities..., (914 1270897), pp. 14 to 19.
A. W. Ward. Shakespeare..., (919$1270004), pp. 18-19.
Thomas J. Wertenbaker. Virginia Under the Stuarts..., (914$1270745), pp. 29, 30.
John Parker. Van Meteren's Virginia..., (961$1270480), pp. 3 to 16.

Other source materials relating to the influence of politics on the relative wealth-power position of the state are listed under code numbers 101303 to 113303 and 116303 to 120303. Infra, Vol. 2, pp. 504 to 509. An interpretive key for this coded material is found Infra, Vol. 2, pp. vi to xiv

factors also influenced the state's relative wealth-power position.

Commodity Mercantilism theory is a synthesis of economic practice conducted within the framework of ideas called "mercantilism." It demonstrates the uniformity of mercantile

---

[6] Salvador de Madariaga. The Rise of the Spanish..., (947$1270015), pp. 129-130.
Louis B. Wright. Religion and Empire..., (943 1271269), passim.
________. The Atlantic Frontier...,(947 1271232), pp. 44-45.
Cole. Colbert..., op. cit., Vol. 2, pp. 136, 185, 465-466.
________. French Mercantilism 1683-1700, New York: Columbia University Press, 1943, pp. 6, 64, 68, 113 to 115, 166-167, 251.

Other source materials relating to the influence of religion on the relative wealth-power position of the state are listed under code numbers 101302 to 113302 and 116302 to 120302. Infra, Vol. 2, pp. 502-503.

[7] Albert J. Schmidt. The Yeoman in Tudor and Stuart England, Washington: The Folger Shakespeare Library, 1961, pp. 1 to 12.
Wright. Middle-Class Culture in Elizabethan..., (935$1270467), passim.
________. The Atlantic Frontier..., op. cit., pp. 12 to 18.
Cole. Colbert..., op. cit., Vol. 2, pp. 472 to 511.
Chapin and Smith. The Ocean River, op. cit., pp. 298 to 301.

[8] Knorr. British Colonial..., op. cit., pp. 41 to 51.
George L. Beer. The Origins..., (922$1271268), pp. 32 to 52.
Earl J. Hamilton. War and Prices in Spain 1651-1800, Cambridge: Harvard University Press, 1947, pp. 35, 65, 134, 174-175.
Cole. French Mercantilist..., (931$1270952), pp. 118-119, 216-217.
________. Colbert..., op. cit., Vol. 1, pp. 86-87; Vol. 2, pp. 463 to 472.
________. French Mercantilism 1683-1700, op. cit., pp. 63, 80,81.

practice and the uniformity of the means employed by states to improve their strength and value through trade and colonization.[9] While the theory acknowledges wealth and power as the "ultimate ends"[10] of mercantile policy,[11] it suggests

---

[9]The term "strength and value" is descriptive of the broadest conception of state well-being located within mercantilist literature.

> We understand that to be wealth, which maintains the prince and the general body of his people, in plenty, ease and safety.
> We esteem that to be treasure which for the use of man has been converted from gold and silver, into buildings and improvements of the country; as also other things convertible into those metals, as the fruits of the earth, manufactures, or foreign commodities and stock of shipping.
> We hold to be riches, what tends to make a people safe at home and considerable abroad, as do fleets and naval stores.
> We shall yet go farther, and say, that maritime knowledge, improvement in all kind of arts, and advancing in military skill; as also wisdom, power and alliances, are to be put into the scale when we weigh the *strength and value* of a nation. [The italics are mine.]
> [Charles d'Avenant. "Discourses on the Public Revenue...," (698 1271246), p. 381.]

[10]Knorr. *British Colonial*..., *op*. *cit*., p. 10.

[11]Jacob Viner has asserted that "in particular circumstances it may be necessary...to make economic sacrifices in the interest of military security." [Jacob Viner. "Power versus Plenty...," (958 1270954), p. 271.] Given these circumstances, i.e., war, or threat of war -- the sacrifice of current goods (wealth) for future goods (power and wealth) relegates the current goods to a role of means. Hence, when wealth and power are acknowledged as "ultimate ends" of mercantile policy, there is implied a recognition of the logical inconsistency of a doctrinal theory of *ends*, and its corrollative inadequacy in describing mercantile practice.

that studies of a more critical nature on mercantile thought and practice may be achieved if the *means*, rather than the ultimate ends, of mercantile policy are reviewed. Commodity Mercantilism provides a more consistent explanation of "mercantilism" than the ultimate *ends* of wealth and power.[12]

Within the broadening concept of wealth and power colonization evolved. It developed as an expedient to extend the scope of trade and to control trade flows. As a national undertaking, colonization mirrored the major aspects of Portuguese, Spanish, French, Dutch and English trade, and distinguised the differing attitudes of these nations toward precious metal accumulation.

Colonization reflected the approach of European states to their economic and political objectives. This approach emphasizes *provisionment* and *fiscalism* as the primary objectives of mercantile policy and, therefore, of colonization,

---

[12] The notion of power and wealth as ends of mercantile policy was met, fought and resolved on the field of mercantilist ideas, despite the general admission that the mercantilist's "practice might not rise to the level of his principles," [Viner. "Power versus Plenty...," *op. cit.*, p. 293.], i.e., that the *means* of mercantile policy were not always in accord *with* theoretical *ends*. Discussion of the divergence between mercantile doctrine and practice, however, seldom materialized for such criticism would have violated the ground rules of doctrinal argument:

> In human affairs, moreover, there is always room for divergence between dogma and practice, between principles and the actual behavior of those who profess them. It is doctrine, and not practice, which is the main concern here.
> [*Ibid.*, p. 295.]

as well. Provisionment requires a favorable balance of trade and the ready availability of commodities. It relates to the ready accessibility of critical and strategic tangibles and their position in a balance of trade model. Fiscalism expresses the fortuitous financial solvency of "short-sighted impecunious governments,"[13] domestic and international. While it initially denoted royal finance, it later encompassed all public finance. By observing the provisionment and fiscalism aspects of Commodity Mercantilism, each European state sought to maintain or increase its "strength and value" relative to other states and thereby to insure its military and fiscal viability.

Bullionism, within the context of Commodity Mercantilism, is the preference for greater liquidity in royal (public) finance, and for greater liquidity in the composition of imports. It connotes a preference for a lesser level of commodity availability. States implementing bullionist policies prefered to maintain extensive gold and silver balances relative to total assets and to maximize bullion imports relative to the constraints of fiscalism and commodity availability. These states limited commodity imports to items essential for the fiscal and military survival of the realm.

---

[13]R. H. Tawney. (ed.). Studies..., (958 1270953), p. lxiv. Tawney is expressing George Unwin's sentiments in this quotation.

The willing surrender of bullion in exchange for provisionment was an accepted practice of the European states despite repeated references to the pervasive importance of precious metal accumulation.[14] With the epocial changes in warfare during the sixteenth century,[15] the exchange of bullion for instruments of provisionment deepened, reflecting the increased preference of states to acquire or to equip themselves with the "sinews of war" rather than with bullion.[16]

The bullionism-provisionment trade-off, however, is not limited exclusively to military procurement. Mercantilist

---

[14]Numerous primary sources supporting this statement are quoted In:

Knorr. <u>British Colonial</u>... <u>op</u>. <u>cit</u>., pp. 15, 16.
Viner. <u>Studies</u>..., (937 1270951), pp. 17 to 31.
Cole. <u>French Mercantilist</u>..., <u>op</u>. <u>cit</u>., pp. 214, 215.
Hamilton. "Spanish Mercantilism Before 1700," (932$1280930), p. 223 to 235.
Lipson. <u>The Economic History</u>..., <u>op</u>. <u>cit</u>., Vol. 3, pp. 98 to 102.
Philip Buck. <u>The Politics of Mercantilism</u>, (942$1270944), pp. 22 to 27.
Beer. <u>The Origins</u>..., <u>op</u>. <u>cit</u>., pp. 54, 55.

[15]Knorr. <u>British Colonial</u>..., <u>op</u>. <u>cit</u>., p. 16. Other secondary sources are cited <u>Ibid</u>., footnote 58.

[16]Primary sources supporting this statement are quoted or cited in:

<u>Ibid</u>., p. 14.
Cole. <u>French Mercantilist</u>..., <u>op</u>. <u>cit</u>., pp. 1 to 27.
Hamilton. "Spanish Mercantilism...," <u>op</u>. <u>cit</u>., pp. 226-227, 234-235.
Lipson. <u>The Economic History</u>..., <u>op</u>. <u>cit</u>., pp. 182 to 186.
Buck. <u>The Politics</u>..., <u>op</u>. <u>cit</u>., pp. 27 to 31, 56 to 58.
Beer. <u>The Origins</u>..., <u>op</u>. <u>cit</u>., pp. 72 to 77, 242 to 249.

tracts consistently lament the existence of luxury and consumption-good carrying trades that appear to drain the nation of its bullion supply.[17] In fact, the maintenance of critical and non-critical commodity balances even at the expense of recognized bullion losses is a more uniform, consistent element of early mercantile policy than is bullionism itself. This consistent preference by European states is termed the provisionment bias of Commodity Mercantilism. It unifies elements of mercantile theory that appear antithetical. Specifically, it joins under one theoretical framework both thesis and "the *antithesis* of mercantilism,"[18] *viz*., both Spanish and Dutch commercial policy.

---

[17] A few citations of primary sources are found in:

Knorr. *British Colonial*..., *op*. *cit*., p. 18.
Viner. *Studies*..., *op*. *cit*., p. 30.
Cole. *French Mercantilist*..., *op*. *cit*., pp. 83 to 91, 215, 216.

Characteristic primary sources *not* included in the above secondary sources are:

[Thomas Mun]. *A Discovrse of Trade*..., (621 1271260), p. 56.
[Edward Misselden]. *Free Trade*..., (622$1271259), pp. 11-12.
Gerard Malynes. *The Maintenance of Free Trade*..., (622 1271256), pp. 22 to 25.
Thomas Mun. *England's Treasure by Forraign Trade*..., (664 1271261), pp. 16-17, 21-22.
[Daniel Defoe]. *An Essay*..., (713 1271245), pp. 12 to 14.
Joshua Gee. *The Trade and Navigation*..., (729 1271251), pp. 63 to 69.

[18] Heckscher. *Mercantilism*, *op*. *cit*., Vol. 1, p. 353.

Spanish policy serves as the clearest example of the preference of provisionment over bullionism. No state strove more in its trading and colonization to preserve a closed flow of bullion than did Spain.[19] Yet, no country was as prodigal in dissipating her bullion hoards by trade designed to fulfill schemes of military preparedness and aggrandizement of the ruling class.[20]

---

[19]Adam Smith. An Inquiry...Wealth of Nations..., (776$2270256), pp. 400, 404, 478 to 480, 508, 542-543, 572.
Mun. England's Treasure..., op. cit., pp. 34-35.
Andres V. Castillo. Spanish Mercantilism..., (930$1210931), pp. 33, 34.
Hamilton. "Spanish Mercantilism...," op. cit., pp. 224, 225.
Shepard B. Clough. The Economic Development..., (959$1271239), pp. 225-226.
Herbert Heaton. Economic History..., (948$1271238), pp. 247 to 250.
Clarence H. Haring. The Buccaneers in the West Indies in the XVII Century, New York: E. P. Dutton and Co., 1910, pp. 13 to 24, 31, 38-39, 49, 96, 103, 109.
________. The Spanish Empire in America, New York: Oxford University Press, 1947, pp. 324 to 327, 335 to 337.

[20]Two brief quotations from primary sources highlight this statement:

> In exchange for treasure Spaniards gave the Indians goods and trinkets of much or little value but through the purchase of manufactures [made] from her own [raw] materials Spain was enriching other countries and becoming the laughstock of nations.
>
> [Luis Ortiz. Biblioteca Nacional, Mss. 11,042, fol. 247. (1558). Quoted in Hamilton. "Spanish Mercantilism...," op. cit., p. 231.]

> Thus it is that Spain, that holds onto life only because of France, being constrained by unavoidable force, to take from here grains, cloths, linens, crayons, tanners' sumach, paper, books, indeed woodwork and all hand-work, went

Dutch policy, considered as the "antithesis of mercantilism," also is explained handily by the Commodity Mercantilism thesis. The Dutch approach to provisionment and fiscalism reflected a small liquidity preference and favored higher than average commodity balances and commodity availability. The utility of this position to the Dutch was apparent from the structure of their investment operations.[21]

> to find for us gold, silver and spices at the ends of the earth.
> [Jean Bodin. The Response..., (568 1271242), p. 29].

Documentation from secondary sources include:

> Hamilton. American Treasure..., (934 1271265), pp. 74, 75, 291 to 293, 302.
> Hamilton. "Spanish Mercantilism...," op. cit., pp. 229 to 234.
> Castillo. Spanish Mercantilism..., op. cit., pp. 30, 31, 35.
> Smith. An Inquiry...Wealth of Nations..., op. cit., pp. 572, 575-576, 591-592.
> Gee. The Trade..., op. cit., pp. xi-xii.
> Heaton. Economic History..., op. cit., pp. 266, 267.
> Mun. England's Treasure..., op. cit., p. 91.

[21]Eli Heckscher envisioned the Dutch as the "antithesis of mercantilism" in that "the development of the Dutch cities proves that unprecedented commercial progress was possible without state authority..." [Heckscher. Mercantilism, op.cit., Vol. 1, p. 353.] He did not suggest, however, that the greater size and simplicity of Dutch commercial organizations, themselves, may have been responsible for the ability of the Dutch companies to exercise a degree of control comparable to that of an external political organization. The pegging of commodity prices by the Dutch East India Company during the 17th and 18th centuries, [Heaton. Economic History..., op. cit., p. 278], for example, is comparable to the contemporary commodity price stabilization attempts by the European states.

Jacob Viner ["Power versus Plenty...," op. cit., pp. 295 to 298] suggests, but does not explore in detail, the significant role of commercial interests in formulating Dutch trade policy.

The structure called for capital employment (turnover) in low-risk ventures, or the utilization of loans from foreign persons, businesses or governments.[22] The concept of idle balances in bullion form was not common to the Dutch.

* * *

Commodity Mercantilism as a unifying theory of mercantile policy incorporates significant elements of prior theories into its theoretical approach. As such, its heritage and innovations are revealed in a critical review of mercantile policy concepts.

In 1948, Jacob Viner attempted to resolve the wealth vs. power controvery involving the "end [goal] of foreign policy"[23] by documenting the interdependence of wealth and power in mercantilist writings. He concluded that

> ...practically all mercantilists, whatever the period, country, or status of the particular indiv idual, would have subscribed to all the following

---

[22]Etienne Laspeyres. Geschichte der Volkswirthschaftlichen..., (863 1270274), pp. 56, 57, 117 to 121.
Clough. The Economic..., op. cit., pp. 211, 212.
Andrews. The Colonial..., op. cit., Vol. 4, pp. 22 to 49.
R. W. K. Hinton. "The Mercantile System...," (955$1280893), pp. 286 to 288.

A detailed description of the differences between England and "Hollander" investment, in one particular industry, the herring trade, is found in Thomas Jenner. London's Blame..., (651 1261197), pp. 3 to 9. Differences in investment in 17th century merchant shipping, generally, are touched upon in Violet Barbour. "Dutch and English Merchant...," (930 1280872), pp. 261 ff.

[23]Viner. "Power versus Plenty...," op. cit., p. 271.

> propositions: (1) wealth is absolutely essential to power, whether for security or for aggression; (2) power is essential or valuable as a means of the acquisition or retention of wealth; (3) wealth and power are proper ultimate ends of national policy; (4) there is long-run harmony between these ends, although in particular circumstances it may be necessary for a time to make economic sacrifices in the interest of military security and therefore also of long-run prosperity.
>
> The omission of any one of these four propositions results in an incorrect interpretation of mercantilist thought...[24]

To these four propositions Dr. Viner affixed a significant rider

> It is to be noted that no proposition is included as to the relative weight which the mercantilists attached to power and to plenty, respectively. Given the general acceptance of the existence of harmony and mutual support between the pursuit of power and the pursuit of plenty, there appears to have been little interest in what must have appeared to them to be an unreal issue. When apparent conflict between these ends did arise, however, differences in attitudes, as between persons and countries, did arise and something will be said on this matter later.[25]

The "something...said on this matter later" was little more than an elaboration of proposition (4), above. No explanation was advanced for "the differences in attitudes, as between persons and countries" in the trade-off between wealth and power. Perhaps as Dr. Viner inferred, it was the different roles played by commercial interests of

---

[24] Ibid., p. 286.

[25] Ibid.

different states in the formulation of their foreign policy.[26]

Klaus Knorr, a student of Jacob Viner, in reviewing the work of his teacher, accepts the wealth-power thesis,[27] but affirms that it was not absolute wealth and power that were the ultimate ends of mercantile policy, but, rather, relative wealth and power.[28] Dr. Knorr also heightens the identification of wealth with power. He asserts that the majority of mercantilists not only assumed that wealth bred power, but that, power, through the control of trade, begot wealth.[29] Yet, for all this, Dr. Knorr does not explain the differences over a period of time in the wealth-power trade-off of different states, or of any particular state.

Commodity Mercantilism assesses and explains these differences in terms of the divergent policies toward

---

[26]The influence of commercial interests on European territorial state policy probed by Jacob Viner [Ibid., p. 296], relates primarily to issues of private vs. public gain and commercial interests' quests for peace vs. their quests for war. Professor Viner suggested that the influence of the merchant class on mercantile policy varied between countries, i.e., Dutch merchants exerting the greatest influence, French merchants the least. He did not, however, relate this material directly to differences in the composition of the wealth-power balance in these countries. Thus, it is not certain how strongly, if at all, Dr. Viner meant to imply a connection between these issues.

[27]Knorr. British Colonial..., op. cit., p. 10.

[28]Ibid., pp. 16-17, 20 to 23.

[29]Ibid., pp. 10, 11.

provisionment and fiscalism assumed by each of the European states. It proposes that particular, characteristic trade-off opportunities and needs existed for each of the European states based upon each state's production capabilities and its ability to prosper through trade, and later, through colonization. It stresses the uniformity with which the European states pursued policies of provisionment and fiscalism, despite their differing definitions of the constituents of wealth and power.

It suggests that fiscalism, promoted expediency in royal (public) finance and fathered many policies instituted ostensibly for territorial unification, or for the regulation, protection or promotion of industry.[30] Further, it

---

[30]Herbert Heaton outlines and documents the importance of fiscalism. ["Heckscher on Mercantilism," (937$1280924), pp. 375 to 380]. Discussing Eli Heckscher's five aspects of mercantilism (money, protection, unification, power, and "Mercantilism as a unifying System"), Professor Heaton suggests "Mercantilism had <u>six</u> aspects, not five; the sixth was public (or royal) finance, and one might with great cogency maintain it was the most important of the lot."

Other secondary sources discussing the importance of fiscalism are:

Heckscher. <u>Mercantilism</u>..., <u>op</u>. <u>cit</u>., Vol. 1, pp. 162, 178 to 184, 253 to 256, 261, 301 to 310, 439 to 447.

Castillo. <u>Spanish</u> <u>Mercantilism</u>..., <u>op</u>. <u>cit</u>., pp. 37 to 39.

Curtis A. Wilgus. <u>Colonial</u> <u>Hispanic</u> <u>America</u>, (936 1270671), pp. 306 to 309.

Hamilton. <u>American</u> <u>Treasure</u>..., <u>op</u>. <u>cit</u>., p. 297.

Cole. <u>Colbert</u>..., <u>op</u>. <u>cit</u>., Vol. 1, pp. 65, 76, 107, 205, 256, 257, 260 to 263.

________. <u>French</u> <u>Mercantilist</u>..., <u>op</u>. <u>cit</u>., p. 192.

Raymond De Roover. <u>Gresham</u> <u>on</u> <u>Foreign</u> <u>Exchange</u>,

proposes that provisionment policies engendered pragmatic threat systems: threat systems[31] characterized by military preparedness, political game theory and non-military schemes of national aggrandizement.

Uniform practices advanced provisionment and fiscalism among the European states. Eli Heckscher rightly emphasized this uniformity of means employed in implementing state mercantile policy. He asserted that mercantilist writers followed two main methods in designing policies to further the external power of the state.

> In the practical application of the principles of the policy of power, mercantilism followed two different methods; the first consisted in deflecting economic activity directly towards the particular ends demanded by political, and more especially military, power; the second in creating a kind of reservoir of economic resources generally, from which the policy of power could draw what it required.[32]

(949 1270942), p. 280.
Lipson. The Economic History..., op. cit., Vol. 3, pp. 21-22.
John U. Nef. Industry and Government..., (940 1280756), p. 19, footnote 19; pp. 141 to 148.
Beer. The Origins..., op. cit., pp. 101ff.
Hinton. "The Mercantile System...," op. cit. pp. 288-289.
Frederick C. Dietz. "English Government Finance 1485-1558," (920 1280714), pp. 209 to 212, 213-214.
________. English Public Finance 1558-1641, (932 1270729), pp. 306-307, 324 to 331.

[31]These systems of countervailing power are outlined by Kenneth Boulding. "Needs and Opportunities in Peace Research and Peach Education," in Our Generation Against Nuclear War, Vol. 3, No. 2, (1964), pp. 22 to 24.

[32]Heckscher. Mercantilism, op. cit., Vol. 2, p. 31.

Analyzed from an economic standpoint, Eli Heckscher saw the following distinction between these two methods of flow and stock, respectively:

> The direct use made of the policy of power was deliberately to influence the supply and the accumulation of stores of goods in the desired direction and to cause corresponding changes in prices. The import of goods necessary for war was directly ordered or encouraged by premiums, while their export was forbidden or burdened with dues... By similar... regulations, the number of ships or sailors, the rural population or the total population, could be increased. This was the first [flow control] method. If the second method [stock enhancement] were adopted, the total national income, not the supply of particular goods or services, was taken as a starting-point. It was then considered that taxation would be the state's weapon for accumulating the particular means required... If the problem was tackled in this second way, considerations of power became a motive for stimulating the general economic prosperity of the country, for this was considered the best guarantee for ensuring a powerful state.[33]

This assertion of two methods in policy formulation is not extensively documented. Eli Heckscher, rather, relied on theoretical analysis, describing economic life based upon the ideal of power.[34] Examining this conception in

---

[33] Ibid.

[34] Herbert Heaton rightly challenges this approach:

> Instead of telling us what was done, Heckscher tells us that what men did was determined by the general ideas which they held on the working of the economic system.
> [Heaton. "Heckscher on Mercantilism," op. cit., p. 380.]

terms of the Commodity Mercantilism thesis, the two methods of mercantilism become one -- <u>provisionment</u>.[35]

The detailed documentation of <u>provisionment</u>, and the introduction of <u>fiscalism</u> as a major determinant of mercantile policy, are key innovations of this dissertation. They are, as well, the important differences between the approach of Eli Heckscher to the means of mercantile policy and the approach of this writing.

---

[35]Commodity Mercantilism theory suggests that from the point of view of <u>means</u>, the stock and flow aspects of policy may be fused profitably. Thus, Dr. Heckscher's first method is incorporated within the availability concept of Commodity Mercantilism. His second method supposes a favorable commodity balance approach to enhance the "strength and value" of the state.

CHAPTER II

Arguments of Commodity Mercantilism

It is the thesis of Commodity Mercantilism that the European states employed uniform practices to improve their strength and value. To support this argument, the hypotheses of provisionment and fiscalism are illustrated with respect to fisheries, naval stores, drugs, spices and silk. This material presents the framework for later arguments relating to viticulture and wine production.

A primary explanation for the relative strength-value positions of the European states is price movements. Earl Hamilton, for example, suggests that the 1520-1650 price revolution explains why capitalistic enterprise developed more rapidly in England than in Spain. Dr. Hamilton asserts that the rapid increase in prices stimulated the growth of capitalism by cheapening English labor costs, and thus making possible exceptionally large profits for many decades.[1] Such profits accelerated the accumulation of wealth by English merchants who invested in large-scale enterprises with the expectation of abnormally high returns. In Spain,

---

[1]Earl J. Hamilton. "American Treasure and the Rise of Capitalism," Economica, Vol. 27 (1929), pp. 338 ff.

rising wages did not lag behind prices during the sixteenth century, as they did in England. The greatest contrast between the advance in Spanish and English prices appears from 1600-1640 when Spanish wages advanced more rapidly than did prices.[2]

By 1640, when the advance of wages again equaled that of prices in Spain,[3] wages in England lagged further than ever behind prices. English wage workers were able to buy only half as much with their money as they had at the beginning of the sixteenth century.[4] The fall in the standard of living was part of the cost the English laborer paid for great national progress.[5]

John U. Nef takes issue with Earl Hamilton and J. M. Keynes in his comparison of the growth of industrial capitalism in France and in England during the 1540-1640 period. While he agrees with Professors Hamilton and Keynes[6] that the inflationary effects of treasure inflow from America helped to keep down the costs of labor and land needed for

---

[2]Ibid., pp. 253-254.
Hamilton. American Treasure..., (934 1271265), pp. 272, 273.

[3]Ibid.

[4]Ibid., pp. 350 to 352.

[5]John M. Keynes. A Treatise on Money, New York: Macmillan and Co., 1930, Vol. 2, p. 163.

[6]Ibid., Vol. 2, pp. 152 to 163. The Keynesian discussion of relative prices relates to his profit inflation concept.

mining and manufacturing, he demonstrates that the real earnings of French and English wage workers did not decline as severely as had been supposed.[7]

Dr. Nef also asserts that the prolonged decline in the real wages of labor in France, while undoubtedly an incentive to enterprise, was not by itself a sufficiently powerful influence to cause any industrial expansion, or even to prevent industrial depression.[8] In sum, he affirms the importance of price movements on the industrial development of the European states, but warns "against the tempting assumption that the remarkably long period of rising prices, common to all European countries, was of compelling importance for the rise of industrialism."[9]

---

[7]John U. Nef. "Prices and Industrial Capitalism...," (940 1280756), p. 184.

Dr. Nef utilized a number of new complete series for money wages and the preliminary food-price findings of Sir William Beveridge to improve the accuracy of prior price estimates. These prior estimates were based upon the wage data of Thorold Rogers and Georg Wiebe and the commodity price data of Vicomte d'Avenel and Thorold Rogers. Dr. Nef demonstrates that wage rates apparently rose appreciably more than Rogers' data indicated and that the prices of prepared foods rose far less than did those of commodities [*Ibid*., pp. 164 to 169, 171].

[8]Nef. "Prices and Industrial Capitalism...," *op. cit.*, p. 184.

[9]*Ibid*., p. 183.

Commodity Mercantilism theory views the importance of price movements, not in terms of promoting industrialism, but, rather, in determining relative commodity values and, hence, the value of particular commodities as items of trade and as sources of royal revenue. The theory demonstrates a link between mercantile practice and commodity prices. This link reflects the Crown's awareness of trade as a source of royal revenue and its insistence on fiscalism even in the face of acknowledged bullion and balance of trade losses. It reflects, too, the influence that trade practices exerted on Crown legislative decisions and the occasional subservience of royal policy to the trade practices of the merchant class.

Commodity Mercantilism theory, as well as emphasizing the importance of price movements, stresses the changing complexion of trade which evolved with the discovery of the sea route to India and the acquisition of America. It recalls that greater costs in fitting out expeditions, longer retention of capital for extended commercial ventures, and higher fixed capital outlays[10] resulted in an increased demand for capital, and, more importantly, in capital

---

[10]Capital was required for permanent uses in support of trade and colonization. These uses included setting up business establishments and defense works, and providing military forces, diplomatic representation, and the machinery of administration.

scarcity. The theory seconds Eli Heckscher's conclusion that, "this turn of events was not particularly welcome to any of the new sea-faring nations, and, in fact, they attempted as far as possible to escape the consequences -- the Portuguese and Dutch with the greatest success, Spain and England with the least."[11]

Apart from the problems associated with the increased demand for capital, the European states became enmeshed in the political problems of trade to distant lands. The simplest solution was for the state to assume absolute control over the new trade. This form of state activity was most marked in the overseas commerce carried on by Portugal with India and the intermediate ports on the African coast. Until 1577, the colonial trade of Portugal was carried on almost entirely under a pure state monopoly.[12] The dishonesty of the state administration, the illicit trade of the participants in state trade ventures,[13] and the state's preference not to assume complete control of trade[14] invited

---

[11]Eli Heckscher. Mercantilism, (935$1270922), Vol. 1, p. 340.

[12]*Ibid.*, Vol. 1, p. 341.

[13]Sir William Hunter suggests that Portugal's illicit trade was greater than her sanctioned state trade prior to 1577. [William W. Hunter. *A History of British India*, Vol. 1, pp. 104f., 175 to 181, 236f. cited in Heckscher, *Mercantilism*, *op. cit.*, Vol. 1, p. 342.]

[14]*Ibid.*, [Heckscher], Vol. 1, p. 341.

cooperative ventures in which profit and risk would be shared by the merchant class and the Crown.

Spain originally modeled her methods of trade with "the Indies" (America), on the East Indian fleet trade of Portugal.[15] Spain experienced greater difficulties with this form of trade than did Portugal, because the Spaniards were trading with a newly colonized continent, a continent whose trade centers were both numerous and highly dispersed. Spain, therefore, soon limited the state's function as a matter of principle. She permitted private trade, though she strictly regulated, controlled and organized it by a system of state shipping.[16]

---

[15]Prior to 1577, Portuguese royal-merchant ventures were undertaken on the condition that merchants assign themselves to the royal fleet and sail their ships in the fleet when in pursuit of trade. Merchandise purchased during these joint ventures was to be sold under strict state supervision to Portuguese merchants.

[16]The Spanish fleet method, initiated to protect ships and cargo, was designed, as well, to control the flow of specie and commodities. Fleets were to include armed ships provided by the state; private trading vessels were allowed to accompany the royal fleet only in such number as the state permitted.

As the regulation of the fleet was governed by detailed rules which multiplied from year to year, a special department, the *Casa de Contratacion*, was set up in 1503 and assigned the task of regulating colonial trade. As the burden of such regulation increased *Consulados*, merchant guilds' courts, were organized. The *Consulados* advised the *Casa de Contratacion* and assumed some of its duties, serving at once as a board of trade, a commercial court, and a clearing house for American traffic.

The fleet method is discussed in sources cited *Supra*,

This system excluded foreigners from trading with the New World.[17] Spain interpreted literally the rights granted to her in the papal bull Inter Caetera of 1493 and therefore, restricted her colonial trade to Spanish subjects.[18] She excited the jealousies of other European states who envied her monopoly of newly-discovered commodities and precious metals and her "Silver Fleet"[19] which transported enormous wealth to Spain.

Vol. 1, p. 9, footnote 19.

The institutions regulating Spanish colonial trade are described in:

Heckscher. Mercantilism, op. cit., Vol. 1, p. 344.
Clarence H. Haring. Trade and Navigation..., (918 1270735), pp. 4 to 19.
A. Curtis Wilgus. Colonial Hispanic America, (936$1270671), pp. 324, 325.
Andres V. Castillo. Spanish Mercantilism..., (930$1210931), pp. 94 to 96.
Salvador de Madariaga. The Rise of the Spanish..., (947$1270015), pp. 60-61.
Haring. The Spanish Empire in America, New York: Oxford University Press, 1947, pp. 317 to 323.

[17]Colmeiro. Historia de la economia politica, Vol. 2, p. 397, quoted in Castillo. Spanish Mercantilism..., op. cit., p. 95.

[18]The Inter Caetera strictly forbade "all persons of no matter what rank, estate, degree, order, or condition," to dare without their special permit "to go for the sake of trade or any other reason whatsoever to the said islands and countries after they have been discovered." [Quoted in Irene A. Wright. (ed.). Spanish Documents..., (929 1270098), p. 3.]

[19]Heckscher. Mercantilism..., op. cit., Vol. 1, p. 343.

Foreign trade ventures,[20] and the participation in Spanish ventures by foreign merchants[21] were the first attempts to wrest away the abundance of the Spanish colonies. Commencing with the successful pirate venture of John Hawkins in 1562, states sought to strip Spain of her wealth by illicit trade,[22] piracy and plunder.[23] These

---

[20] Lewes Roberts. The Merchants Mappe..., (637$1271191), Bk. 2, pp. 21-22.
Jean Bodin. The Response..., (568 1271242), p. 29. See also Supra. Vol. 1, pp. 9-10, footnote 20.
Thomas Mun. England's Treasure..., (664 1271261), pp. 90 to 93.
Haring. Trade and Navigation..., op. cit., p. 19. (A brief discussion of the 1538 permission to the Bristol merchants for traffic with the English in the Canary Islands).
William Foster. England's Quest..., (933$1270744), pp. 5 to 7.

[21] Guilhelmi Powell. "The Decades of the Newe World...," (555 1260064), p. 211.
Franklin T. McCann. English Discovery of America..., (952$1270068), pp. 140 to 142.
Gustav H. Blanke. Amerika Im Englischen Schriftum..., (962 1270468), pp. 283-284.
Klaus Knorr. British Colonial Theories 1570-1850, Toronto: University of Toronto Press, 1944, pp. 57-58; p. 57 footnote 146.

[22] Portuguese slave traders from Guinea were the first illicit traders to Espanola. [Wright. Spanish Documents..., op. cit., pp. 6-7.] The most frequent violators of the sanctity of Spanish trade were the English.
Wright. Spanish Documents..., op. cit., pp. 7 to 11.
Diego de Vallejo. "Diego Ruiz de Vallejo to the Crown...," (568$1260099), pp. 114-115.
C. H. Firth. (ed.). An American Garland..., (915 1270471), pp. xv to xix.
"Have over the Water to Florida," (563$1260472), pp. 7, 8.
Stefan Lorant. (ed.). The New World..., (946 1270443), pp. 121 to 123.

[23] "Privateering was a sordid and prosaic business" for the English commencing with John Hawkins' ill-fated voyage

belligerent actions, climaxing in the 1588 defeat of the Spanish Armada, challenged the Spanish superiority of the seas.

Spain strongly objected to these infringements upon her territorial and navigational rights. She attempted to guard her colonies from the illicit trade of other states by concealing knowledge of her trade sources,[24] by utilizing the fleet method to conduct her colonial trade, by imposing restrictions and prohibitive duties on trade between her colonies,[25] and by establishing a colony in Florida as a

---

of 1567. [Arthur Newton. The Colonizing Activities..., (914 1270897), pp. 14 to 17.]

Newton. The European Nations..., (933$1270912), pp. 80, 81.

Lorant (ed.). The New World..., op. cit., pp. 121 to 123.

Haring. The Buccaneers in the West Indies in the XVII Century, New York: E. P. Dutton and Co., 1910, passim.

[24]As early as 1511, Spain forbade the supply of charts or maps of the Indies to foreigners. In 1527, Charles V decreed that even pictures and descriptions of the Indies should not be sold to foreigners without special license. [Woodbury Lowery. The Spanish Settlements..., (901 1270299), Vol. 2, pp. 6-7, p. 7 footnotes 4, 5.]

McCann. English Discovery..., op. cit., p. 63.

[25]Hamilton. "Spanish Mercantilism...," (932$1280930), pp. 223 to 225.

Wilgus. Colonial Hispanic..., op. cit., pp. 324 to 326.

De Madariaga. The Rise..., op. cit., pp. 58-59.

military outpost to deny the coast of eastern North America to any other nation.[26]

Spain reacted bitterly to the intrusion of the French,[27] Dutch,[28] and the English[29] on her North American territory. Yet, she failed to establish sufficient governmental ties

---

[26]The constant reconnaissance of the eastern shores and the subsequent reports of the Florida garrison to the mother country are outlined in:

David B. Quinn. (ed.). The Roanoke Voyages..., (955 1270115), pp. 717, 718, 772 to 778.
Lowery. The Spanish..., op. cit., Vol. 2, pp. 3, 4, 213-214.
W. R. Jackson, Jr. "Early Florida...," (954$1280768), pp. 77-78, 107-108, 112.
Morris Talpalar. The Sociology of Colonial Virginia, (960$1270494), p. 9.

[27]The French intruded on the Spanish North American territory from 1563 until mid-1565 when Philip II dispatched a fleet under Pedro Menendez de Aviles to clear Florida of the trespassers. Menendez captured Fort Caroline and killed its defenders. The Spaniards also massacred the surviving sailors and soldiers from the tempest-torn fleet.
Lorant. (ed.). The New World..., op. cit., pp. 122, 123, "Notes on this Book".
Boise Penrose. Travel..., (952 1270657), pp. 230, 231.
Haring. The Spanish Empire..., op. cit., pp. 329, 330, 335-336.

[28]Haring. The Spanish..., op. cit., pp. 331, 332, 339.
Herbert Heaton. Economic History..., (948$1271238), p. 278.
John Parker. Van Meteren's Virginia..., (961$1270480), pp. 8 to 35, 37.

[29]A. W. Ward. Shakespeare..., (919$1270004), p. 18, especially footnote 2.
Alexander Brown. New Views of Early Virginia..., (886$1271208), pp. 10 to 12.
[George Abbot.] A Briefe Description..., (599 1271114), folio D8, verso.
Haring. The Spanish..., op. cit., pp. 331-332, 335, 340.

with her colonies[30] and because of inadequate attention to their needs, failed to maintain them.[31]

The demise of Spain's domination of colonial trade and the abrogation of her colonial self-sufficiency policy paralleled her latter seventeenth century economic decline.[32] With the ebbing of precious metal flows from her colonies,[33]

---

[30]Despite colonial protests, Spain maintained laws enforcing her monopoly of the Indies. Colonial officials, civic, military, and religious, identified with the colonists rather than with the home country by long association, intermarriage and similar material interests. Consequently, they exercised little influence in support of the home policy. Covert lawlessness and veniality prevailed. [Wright. Spanish Documents..., op. cit., p. 6.]

De Madariaga. The Rise..., op. cit., pp. 58-59.

[31]Hamilton. "Spanish Mercantilism...," op. cit., p. 238.
De Madariaga. The Rise..., op. cit., pp. 127 to 129.
Wright. Spanish Documents..., op. cit., pp. 5-6.
Haring. Trade..., op. cit., p. 127. No fleet was dispatched from Spain for Peru in the three years prior to the 1569 voyage of Francisco de Toledo. For the importance of the 1569 date see Infra, Vol. 1, pp. 86-87.

[32]The economic decline of Spain is reviewed in:

"Virginias Verger...," (625 1260516), p. 234.
Adam Smith. An Inquiry...Wealth of Nations..., (776 1270256), p. 202.
Roberts. The Merchants..., op. cit., Bk. 2, pp. 21-22.
De Madariaga. The Rise..., op. cit., pp. 128-129.
Wilgus. Colonial Hispanic..., op. cit., p. 306.
Castillo. Spanish Mercantilism..., op. cit., pp. 31 to 37.
Haring. The Spanish..., op. cit., pp. 269, 274, 333-334.

[33]Hamilton. American Treasure..., op. cit., p. 301.
________. War and Prices in Spain 1651-1800. Cambridge: Harvard University Press, 1947, pp. 22 to 26.

Spain lost her primacy to the Netherlands who, through entrepot and trade, emerged as the dominant European state.

The Dutch captured a major portion of all European trade and of the sea-carrying trade to the East and West Indies, the Baltic, Scandinavia, and the Mediterranean. They appropriated the Portuguese spice trade, dominated the Oriental trade, conducted much of the slave traffic, and mastered entrepot, that is, the processing and finishing of products for re-export.[34] Despite their meager domestic endowment, the Dutch became "the most hated and yet the most admired and envied commercial nation of the 17th century."[35]

---

[34]Etienne Laspeyres. Geschichte der Volkswirthschaftlichen..., (863 1270274), pp. 116 to 119.
Heaton. Economic History..., op. cit., pp. 274 to 281.
Charles Andrews. The Colonial..., (938 1270950), Vol. 4, pp. 22 to 31.
Shepard B. Clough. The Economic Development..., (959$1271239), p. 211.
E. Lipson. The Economic History..., (961 1271270), Vol. 2, p. liii.
Charles H. Wilson. Anglo-Dutch Commerce and Finance in the Eighteenth Century, Cambridge: Cambridge University Press, 1941, p. 3.

[35]Heckscher. Mercantilism, op. cit., Vol. 1, p. 351. Professor Heckscher states that during this period "the Netherlands were idealized." [Ibid.]. This conclusion is valid only if the writings of the seventeenth century are taken quite literally.

...

Thus Earth, nor Ayres, nor Fire, nor rumbling Warre,
Nor plague, or pestilence, nor famine are
Of powre to winne, where Water but commands,
As witnesse may the watry Netherlands.
Concerning Merchandise, and transportation,
Commerce and traffique, and negotiation,

The simplicity of the Dutch commercial organization,[36] the superiority of Dutch shipping and shipbuilding (and,

---

> To Make each Countrie have by Navigation
> The Goods, and Riches of each others Nation.
> [Huldricke Van Speagle. Drinke and Welcome..., (673 1261048), folio C verso.]

Beneath the literary flourish of most mercantilist authors, however, were specific and succinct expressions of their jealousy. Charles Andrews [The Colonial..., op. cit., Vol. 4, pp. 48-49; p. 49, footnote 1; p. 323] itemizes sources expressing the fears of English mercantilists from Roger Coke (1670) to John Bennett (1738). He omits the following sources which similarly detail English envy of the Dutch:

Mun. England's Treasure..., op. cit., pp. 24-25, 29, 179-180.

T. M. [________]. A Discovrse of Trade..., (621 1261260), pp. 48, 49.

Roberts. The Merchants Mappe..., op. cit., Bk. 2, pp. 119-120.

Thomas Jenner. London's Blame..., (651 1261197), pp. 3 to 11.

Roger Coke. A Treatise..., (671 1271252), pp. 82-83.

Sir William Petty. Political Arithmetick..., quoted in Charles H. Hull. (ed.). The Economic Writings of Sir William Petty, New York: Augustus M. Kelly, 1899, Vol. 1, pp. 253-268.

Charles d'Avenant. "Discourses...," (698 1271246), pp. 390-391.

"An Essay...," (750 1260141), pp. 215 to 217.

Smith. An Inquiry...Wealth of Nations..., op. cit., pp. 91-92, 354.

French jealousies are detailed in:

Charles Cole. French Mercantilist Doctrines..., (931$1270952), pp. 135-136; p. 142 footnote 1.

________. Colbert and a Century of French Mercantilism, New York: Columbia University Press, 1939, Vol. 1, pp. 87 to 89, 207-208, 211 to 214, 345, 383, 448; Vol. 2, pp. 7-8, 83-84.

Parker [Van Meteran's..., op. cit., pp. 8 to 35, 37] points up Spanish rivalry.

Sources cited above do not include material pertinent to English, French or Spanish envy of Dutch fisheries. These sources are presented and discussed Infra, Vol. 1, pp. 52 to 56.

consequently, the lower Dutch freight and insurance rates),[37] along with the Netherlanders' ability to borrow and finance at lower rates than their foreign competitors,[38] fostered the Low Countries' trade and the extension of the lucrative herring industry in the North Sea. The Dutch maintained their commercial superiority through virtually free trade of precious metals and by maintaining higher-than-average commodity balances and commodity availability.[39] These measures and the control of home industry, banking, and trade by the allied political and commercial interests of the Netherlands, provided the Dutch with a continuous stream of real profits[40] from trade and entrepot and increased

---

[36] Heckscher. Mercantilism, op. cit., pp. 351 to 358. Also, Supra, Vol. 1, p. 10, footnote 21.

[37] John De Witt and other Great Men in Holland. The True Interest and Political Maxims of the Republick of Holland and West-Friesland, London: 1702, pp. 20 to 55.
Hans Hartmeyer. Der Weinhandel..., (905 1270535), pp. 17 to 27.
Violet Barbour. "Dutch and English...," (930 1280872), pp. 264 to 267.
R. W. K. Hinton. "The Mercantile System...," (955$1280893), pp. 286 to 289.
Cole. Colbert..., op. cit., p. 383.

[38] Petty. Political Arithmetick..., op. cit., pp. 264-265.
Smith. An Inquiry...Wealth of Nations..., op. cit., pp. 91-92, 446 to 455 ("Digession on the Bank of Amsterdam").
Heaton. Economic History..., op. cit., pp. 282-283.

[39] Supra, Vol. 1, pp. 10-11.

[40] As Holland's ventures and capital uses were mainly short term, the Dutch were largely insulated from the detrimental effects of the continental price inflation and from

remarkably their relative strength and value among the European states.

The Netherlands' loss of economic preeminence in the eighteenth century was relative, not absolute. Other European states, by copying her techniques and ceasing to use Dutch goods, services, ships, and funds, overtook Holland. As Holland was dependent on importing, processing, and exporting, she was vulnerable when countries supplying her or purchasing from her became industrially mature or politically unfriendly.[41] The Netherlands' virtual lack of raw materials prevented her from establishing a home industry to maintain her commercial dominance.

Holland's greatest deficiency, however, was her limited population. She lacked sufficient military forces to withstand attacks directed against her and she could not muster sufficient numbers to protect her colonial interests.[42] Heavy per capita taxes were required to pay interest and

---

the illusion of inflationary profits.

N. W. Posthumus. Inquiry into the History of Prices in Holland, Leiden: E. I. Brill, 1964, Vol. 2, pp. civ to cviii.

[41]The dependence of the Dutch upon the English was voiced as early as 1436:

> The grete substaunce of youre cloothe at the fulle
> Ye wot ye make hit of our English wolle.

[The Libelle of Englyshe Polycye, quoted in Parker, Van Meteren's..., op. cit., p. 4.] Consult also:

D'Avenant. "Discourses...," op. cit., pp. 437 to 431.
Heaton. Economic History..., op. cit., pp. 283 to 287.
Wilson. Anglo-Dutch Commerce..., op. cit., pp. 18-19.

[42]Henry Chapin and F. G. W. Smith. The Ocean River, (952$1270010), p. 303.

Clough. The Economic..., op. cit., p. 212.

principal on loans incurred in meeting the expenses of wars waged with Spain, Portugal, England, and France.[43]

In the last quarter of the seventeenth century, France advanced to usurp the economic supremacy of the Dutch and to rival England for domination, not only of precious metals and the carrying trade, but of the whole colonial and commercial sphere.[44] In this 150-year rivalry, colonies became increasingly important--governmental policies designed to foster military survival and the financial solvency of the realm, as well as those designed to enhance the relative strength and value of the state, hinged upon colonies as sources for raw materials, as outlets for foreign investment and as markets for manufactures.[45] Hence, both France and England sought to subordinate the interests and advantages of the colonies to those of the mother country, and to restrict the trade of the colonies to their own nationals and shipping interests.

---

[43]D'Avenant. "Discourses...," _op_. _cit_., pp. 390-391.
Smith. _An Inquiry...Wealth of Nations_..., _op_. _cit_., p. 433.
Andrews. _The Colonial_..., _op_. _cit_., Vol. 4, p. 49.
Cole. _French Mercantilism 1683-1700_, New York: Columbia University Press, 1943, pp. 108 to 110.

[44]Cole. _Colbert_..., _op_. _cit_., Vol. 2, pp. 549-552.

[45]_Ibid_., Vol. 2, pp. 1 to 131.
Knorr. _British Colonial_..., _op_. _cit_., pp. 63 to 68, 80 to 105.
Andrews. _The Colonial Period_..., _op_. _cit_., Vol. 4, pp. 7-8.

Between 1540 and 1640 industrial output in France progressed less rapidly than during the preceding century.[46] During the same period, there was a marked increase in the rate of production in England. A large number of new manufactures flourished; the output of older industries increased many fold. England prospered; only in the manufacture of luxury items did France maintain or increase her advantage.[47]

The French realized that the strength and value of their state depended on the full utilization of domestic production possibilities and upon the export of sufficient produce to meet their obligations for imported raw materials and manufactured goods. When Henry IV was assasinated in 1610, France, having just mended the damage of her civil wars, again became embattled, first in civil conflict and then in the Thirty Years' War (1618-1648). France emerged from these involvements a united monarchy, a dominant power in European affairs and a militant parent in the colonies.[48]

---

[46]Nef. "A Comparison of Industrial Growth...," (936$1280757), pp. 661 to 666.
________. "Industry and Government...," (940 1280756), pp. 1 to 11.

[47]Nef. "A Comparison...," op. cit., pp. 289 to 317, 505 to 533, 643 to 661.
________. "Industry and Government...," op. cit., pp. 84ff.

[48][Daniel Defoe]. An Essay..., (713 1271245), pp. 3 to 19, 26 to 31.
Andrews. The Colonial Period..., op. cit., Vol. 4, pp. 354 to 365, 374.
Heaton. Economic History..., op. cit., p. 290.
Lipson. The Economic..., (961 1271271), Vol. 3, pp. 98 to 105.

To Jean Colbert was left the onus of fiscal repair, industrial development, and the revival of a merchant fleet and a navy.[49]

Colbert was a staunch believer in productivity. He sought to build up the entire productive capacity of the state in the name of a "narrow and little principle,"[50] bullionism, and thus to secure for the state power, wealth and prosperity. Colbertism continued after the death of Colbert, although the control of economic matters--once highly and effectively centralized--rested with minor officials who received only sporadic supervision.[51]

Less endowed than France, England stressed the importance of trade to supplant the natural advantages of her rivals. The English searched for Northwest and Northeast passages to Asia and the South Seas, but such ventures were doomed.[52] The English did, however, establish trade

---

[49]A. Dubois. Precis de l'histoire..., (903 1270611), pp. 105f.
Cole. Colbert..., op. cit., Vol. 1, 2, passim.
Heaton. Economic History..., op. cit., pp. 294 to 300.

[50]Shepard Clough [The Economic..., op. cit., p. 218.] quotes Colbert, but he does not cite the source.

[51]Cole. Colbert..., op. cit., Vol. 2, pp. 554, 555.
________. French Mercantilism, op. cit., pp. 3 to 5.

[52]Penrose. Travel..., op. cit., pp. 112 to 176.
Foster. England's Quest..., op. cit., pp. 3 to 13, 31 to 68, 110 to 117, 226 to 234.
E. G. R. Taylor. Tudor Geography..., (930$1270653), pp. 103ff.
R. A. Skelton. Explorers' Maps, (958$1170655), pp. 99

companies[53] in eastern and western countries whose fabulous wealth--known to the English through Spanish and Portuguese trade ventures--seized the imagination of the English merchants. Although these companies supplied England with naval stores, drugs, spices, silks and other desired commodities, they proved unprofitable or untenable as trading ventures.[54]

---

to 125.

Blanke. Amerika..., op. cit., pp. 3 to 12, 131 to 151.

McCann. English Discovery..., op. cit., pp. 56 to 68.

Louis B. Wright. Religion and Empire..., (943 1271269), pp. 57 to 90.

________. The Colonial Search..., (953$1270463), pp. 1 to 19.

________. The Dream of Prosperity,..., (964$1270464), pp. 1 to 20.

[53]McCann. English Discovery..., op. cit., pp. 98 to 137.

A. L. Rowse. The Expansion of Elizabethan..., (955$1271230) pp. 158 to 171.

Hinton. "The Mercantile...," op. cit., pp. 289-290.

Susan M. Kingsbury. "A Comparison of the Virginia Company...," (908 1280046), pp. 161 to 176.

F. J. Fisher. "Commercial Trends...," (940 1281233), pp. 171-172.

Edward P. Cheyney. European Background of American History, (904$1270699), pp. 123 to 139.

R. H. Tawney. (ed.). Studies in Economic History..., (958 1270953), pp. 180 to 186.

[54]William R. Scott. The Constitution and Finance...of Joint-Stock Companies..., (910 1270946), 36 to 65, 76 to 89.

Taylor. Late Tudor and Early Stuart..., (934 1270654), pp. 100 to 113.

Foster. England's Quest..., op. cit., pp. 31 to 50, 68 to 79, 144 to 173.

L. J. Pierre M. Bonnassieux. Les Grand compagnies de commerce, Paris: E. Plon. Nourrit et Cie, 1892, pp. 79 to 89, 132 to 165.

England thus attempted colonization,[55] basing her claim in the New World on the Voyages of John Cabot, the Sorte-Real brothers and others who explored for the English.

Initial English attempts at colonization in the New World were highly unsuccessful. Careful not violate openly the avowed Spanish territorial rights, the English fostered colonization by means of private and company charters; royal commitment to colonization was not undertaken until the reign of James I.[56] With this commitment England enforced practices later called the "colonial system."[57]

---

[55] Merrill Jensen. (ed.). English Historical Documents..., (955$1270311), pp. 59, 60, 315 to 321.
George L. Beer. "The Early English Colonial..., [Pt. 2]" (908$1280786), pp. 242 to 258.
________. The Origins..., (922$1271268), pp. 53 to 77, 241 to 269.
Taylor. Late Tudor..., op. cit., 158 to 176.
Matthew P. Andrews. The Soul of a Nation..., (944$1271175), pp. 34 to 65.
Rowse. The Expansion..., op. cit., 206 to 237.
Blanke. Amerika..., op. cit., 283 to 300.

[56] Beer. "The Early English Colonial...[Pt. 1]," (908$1280785), pp. 75 to 80.
Quinn. (ed.). The Roanoke..., op. cit., pp. 118f., 717f.
Ward. Shakespeare..., op. cit., p. 18; p. 18, footnote 2.
Newton. The Colonising..., op. cit., pp. 13 to 23.
A. D. Innes. The Maritime..., (932 1271229), pp. 81 to 104. Professor Innes' statement "in the complex of attractions to the West, [import] trading of this kind was only a very minor motive." [p. 81] is directly challenged in this writing: Infra, Vol. 1, pp. 40ff.

[57] Andrews. The Colonial Period..., op. cit., Vol. 4, pp. 7, 13 to 21, 50ff.
Knorr. British Colonial..., op. cit., pp. 126 to 151.
Philip W. Buck. The Politics of Mercantilism, (942$1270944), pp. 58 to 61.
Victor S. Clark. History of Manufactures...,

France adopted similar controling measures for her colonies. Her perseverance at colonization, despite failures and tragedies in Brazil (1555-1557), South Carolina (1562-1563), Florida (1564-1565), and Sable Island (1598-1603), was rewarded in 1608 with the successful founding of Quebec. Thereafter, France secured colonies throughout the vast area from the Grand Banks to the headwaters of the Mississippi and south to New Orleans.[58]

(929$1270012), pp. 9 to 31.

Jensen. English Historical..., op. cit., pp. 233 to 235, 351 to 353.

Emory R. Johnson et al. History of Domestic and Foreign Commerce..., (915 1270783), Vol. 1, pp. 35 to 53.

[58] Samuel de Champlain. The Voyages..., (604$1260496), Introduction of Edward Bourne.

Marc Lescarbot. The History of New France, (609$1260721), pp. 29 to 50.

Nicholas Denys. The Description..., (672 1260722), pp. 1 to 7.

Henry P. Biggar. The Early Trading..., (901$1270676), pp. 42ff.

Bonnassieux. Les Grandes compaignies de commerce, op. cit., pp. 347 to 425.

N. M. M. Surrey. The Commerce of Louisiana..., (916 1280634), passim.

George M. Wrong. The Rise and Fall of New France, New York: MacMillan, 1928, Vol. 1, pp. 129ff; Vol. 2, passim.

Gabriel Hanotaux and Alfred Martineau. (eds.). Histoire des colonies francaises et de l'expansion de la France dans le monde. Paris: Societe de l'histoire nationale, 1929 [to 1933], Vol. 1, pp. 38 to 95, 192 to 245.

Penrose. Travel..., op. cit., pp. 229 to 239.

Cole. Colbert..., op. cit., Vol. 1, pp. 73 to 75. [Some of these sources are cited Ibid., p. 75, footnote 90.]

Pierre Boucher. Histoire véritable et natvrelle des moevrs et prodvctions de pays de la Novvelle-France [1663], [ed. G. Coffin] Montreal: E. Bastien et Cie, 1882.

P. F. X. de Charlesvoix. Journal of a Voyage to North-America, London: 1761, passim.

M. Chambon. Traité général du commerce...,

When in the 1750's France pressured England to cede portions of North America and India, the English rejected this demand, took to arms against the belligerent French, and after a costly war, deprived them of Canada and strongholds in India according to the Treaty of Paris (1763).[59] At issue in all the Anglo-French conflicts, beginning in 1689 and including the Seven Years' War, was not only supremacy in the colonies, but also the balance of power on the Continent. Through her losses in this war, France experienced a further diminution of her powers. The Revocation of the Edict of Nantes, continual wars, the neglect of sea power, and the atrophy of Colbertism had accelerated the

---

(783$1271228), Vol. 1, pp. 12 to 16.

Francois-Xavier Garneau. Histoire du Canada, Huitieme edition, Montreal: Editions de L'Arbre, 1944, Vol. 1. pp. 64 to 220.

________. History of Canada, [trans. and ed. Andrew Bell] Montreal: John Lovell, 1862, Vol. 1, pp. 50 to 179. [translation of pp. 64 to 220, French edition].

De Charlesvoix. History and General Description of New France [trans. and ed., John G. Shea], New York: John Gilmary Shea, 1872, Vol. 1, pp. 13 to 65, 67 to 99.

Emile Salone. La Colonisation de la Nouvelle-France, Paris: E. Guilmoto, 1906, pp. vii to xii [a very good bibliography]; pp. 15 to 250, especially 195 to 206, 225 to 250.

Paul Gaffarel. Histoire de la Floride Francaise, Paris: Librairie de Firmin-Didot et Cie, 1875, pp. 3 to 43ff.

________. Histoire du Brésil Francais au seizième siècle, Paris: Maisonneuve et Cie, 1878, passim.

Hanotaux. La France vivante..., op. cit., pp. 95 to 131.

[59]Clough, The Economic..., op. cit., p. 137.

general decline.[60] The one-third increase in the French national debt (a result of retaliatory French loans given the American revolutionaries), the ensuing economic malaise, and a crop failure in 1788, foreshadowed the French Revolution.[61] At the same time England--despite her loss of the thirteen American colonies[62]--pursued industrialization and maritime expansion, ascending thereby to economic pre-eminence in Europe.

The attempt to "increase the quantity of gold and silver in...[the] country by turning the balance of trade in its favor"[68] was common to the economic experience of each European state. This 'commercial' or 'mercantile' aim,[64]

---

[60]Cole. Colbert..., op. cit., Vol. 2, p. 552.
Clough. The Economic..., op. cit., p. 221.

[61]Heaton. Economic History..., op. cit., pp. 291, 304-305.

[62]This loss was not without benefit for England. Consult, for examples:

Smith. An Inquiry...Wealth of Nations..., op. cit., pp. 570 to 583.
Knorr. British Colonial..., op. cit., pp. 175 to 201, especially pp. 182-183, 197, 197 footnotes 70, 71.
John Sheffield. Observations..., (784 1270236), passim.
Tench Coxe. A View of the United States..., (794 1270235), pp. 212ff.

[63]Smith. An Inquiry...Wealth of Nations..., op. cit., p. 418.

[64]Adam Smith, following the usage of the Physiocrats, coined the phrase "commercial" or "mercantile" for the system which the German historical school later adapted into the term mercantilism. [Jacob Viner. Studies...,

was subordinate to the preference by a state to maintain commodity balances of particular goods even at the expense of recognized bullion losses. Statutes enacted to foster these commodity balances[65] and avowed state priorities in imports and exports[66] are evidence of such a bias for provisionment.

(937$1270951), p. 3.]

Consult also, M. Beer. Early British Economics..., (938 1271272), pp. 60 to 81.

[65] These statutes are discussed and cited in:

Haring. Trades and Navigation..., op. cit., pp. 3 to 19, 123 to 129.
De Madariaga. The Rise..., op. cit., pp. 57 to 60, 345-346, especially footnote 8.
Hamilton. "Spanish Mercantilism...," op. cit., pp. 225 to 229.
Gustav Fagniez. L'Economie sociale de la France sous Henri IV 1589-1610. Paris: Libraire Hachette et Cie, 1897, pp. 260 to 277.
Cole. French Mercantilist..., op. cit., pp. 33 to 46.
________. Colbert..., op. cit., Vol. 1, pp. 15, 16, 31, 56, 64, 77, 102; Vol. 2, pp. 320 to 349, 458 to 463.
Nef. "Industry and Government...," op. cit., pp. 83 to 108.
Heckscher. Mercantilism, op. cit., pp. 32 to 40.
Scott. The Constitution..., op. cit., passim.
Lipson. The Economic..., op. cit., Vol. 3, pp. 14-15; p. 14, footnote 5; pp. 21-22; p. 21, footnotes 5 to 7.

Some additional citations to the statutes are to be found in sources relating to particular commodity balances: Infra, Vol. 1, pp. 47 to 50, 57 to 60 (armaments and naval stores); pp. 51 to 56 (fishing trade products); pp. 61 to 63 (drugs and spices); pp. 64 to 68 (silk).

[66] And therefore, as it is most plaine, that proportion or quantitie, must euer be regarded in the importing of forren wares; so must there also be a great respect of qualitie and vse; that so, the things most necessarie be first preferred; such as are

States sought to wrest control of the carrying trade from each other as the benefits of overseas expansion became manifest. This struggle was the dominant economic problem of the sixteenth century.[67] It implicitly involved maritime

---

> foode, rayment, and munition for warre and trade; which great blessinges, when any countrie doth sufficiently enjoy; the next to be procured are wares, fitting for health, and arts; the last, are those, which serue for our pleasures and ornament.
>
> T[homas] M[un]. A Discovrse of Trade..., op. cit., p. 213.

Further discussions of import and export priorities are referred to in:

Cole. French Mercantilist..., op. cit., pp. 33 to 46.

________. Colbert..., op. cit., Vol. 1, pp. 12 to 19, 31, 77-78, 102; Vol. 2, passim.

Heckscher. Mercantilism, op. cit., pp. 32 to 40.

Nef. "A Comparison...," op. cit., pp. 295 to 313, 653 to 666.

Richard Hakluyt. "Notes on Colonization...," (578$260020), pp. 181 to 184.

Jenner. London's Blame..., op. cit., pp. 9, 10.

D'Avenant. Discourses..., op. cit., pp. 346, 347.

Andrews. The Colonial Period..., op. cit., Vol. 4, pp. 85 to 107, 336 to 340.

Beer. The Origins..., op. cit., pp. 55 to 57, 65 to 77.

Knorr. British Colonial..., op. cit., pp. 50-51.

Clark. History of Manufactures..., op. cit., Vol. 2, pp. 9 to 12.

[67] Raymond de Roover. Gresham on Foreign Exchange..., (949 1270942), pp. 282-283.

Abbott P. Usher. "Spanish Ships and Shipping in the Sixteenth and Seventeenth Centuries," in Facts and Factors in Economic History. Cambridge: Harvard University Press, 1932, pp. 191 to 194, 210, 211, 213.

Hinton. "The Mercantile...," op. cit., pp. 277 to 279.

supremacy and hence the relative strength and value of each realm and the integrality of its defense. It evolved from states having to increase their imports of raw materials and their exports of finished goods in order to accomodate the increased production of staples, and to augment the material requirements of their defense forces.[68]

Through trade, each European state sought, not only to deflect its "economic activity directly towards...particular ends" but to create "a kind of reservoir of economic

---

[68] De Madariaga. The Rise..., op. cit., pp. 127 to 130.
Robert Smith. Seventeenth-Century Spanish Anti-mercantilism, (940$1280926), pp. 403 to 411.
Castillo. Spanish Mercantilism..., op. cit., pp. 33 to 35.
Bodin. The Response..., op. cit., pp. 29, 30, 49-50.
Antoine de Montchretien. Traicté de l'oeconomie politique, [1615], pp. 323 to 325, quoted in Cole. French Mercantilists..., op. cit., pp. 156, 157.
Gerrard de Malynes. England's Vievv..., (603 1271254), pp. 136-137.
W. Crashaw. A Sermon..., (610 1261168), folio [D4 recto], quoted Infra, Vol. 1, pp. 59-60, footnote 115.
Nicholas Barbon. A Discourse..., (690$1271248), pp. 1 to 7.
Foster. England's Quest..., op. cit., pp. 5-6; p. 5, footnote 1; p. 6, footnote 1.
Kingsbury. "A Comparison...," op. cit., pp. 171 to 176.
L. F. Salzman. English Trade..., (931$1270713), pp. 450 to 456.
Andrews. The Colonial Period..., op. cit., Vol. 4, pp. 86, 87.
H. J. Wood. Exploration and Discovery, (951$1270651), pp. 79f.

resources generally"[69] which would "stimulate the general economic prosperity of the country and thus build up a large national income as a guarantee for insuring a powerful state."[70] Bullionism arguments directed towards increasing the general wealth and power of the state were ordinarily tempered by state policies designed "to insure...the appropriate necessities of war...especially munitions, ships, naval stores, sailors and money."[71]

When trade alone could not neet the demand for particular commodities, or when normal trade channels were disrupted,[72] states resorted to piracy, plunder, warfare and

---

[69]Heckscher. Mercantilism, op. cit., Vol. 2, p. 31. Professor Heckscher's remark relates to England. His exclusion of other European territorial states is not explained.

[70]Heaton. "Heckscher on Mercantilism," op. cit., p. 380.

[71]Ibid., p. 379.

[72]Prohibitive foreign taxation and alien trade monopolies appear to have influenced the extension of trade far more than the threat of war, or war itself. The disruptive effect of foreign taxation and trade monopolies are reviewed in:

John Rutherfurd. "The Importance...," (761 1260726), pp. 110 to 115.
Eleanor Lord. Industrial Experiments..., (898$1270665), pp. 56 to 61.
Knorr. British Colonial..., op. cit., p. 51.
McCann. English Discovery..., op. cit., pp. 138-139.

The significance of war and pirateering to the trade patterns of the European territorial states is explored by:

Heckscher. Mercantilism, op. cit., Vol. 2, pp. 17-18.
Heaton. "Heckscher on Mercantilism," op. cit., p. 376.
Arthur P. Newton. The Colonising Activities...,

restrictive maritime and trade policies in order to fulfill their expanding commercial and defense needs. States later encouraged colonization ventures to promote royal (public) revenue,[73] commodity availability and favorable commodity trade balances.[74] Mercantilist writers emphasized the

---

(914 1270897), pp. 13 to 17.
J. H. Rose, A. P. Newton, and E. A. Benians. (eds.). The Cambridge History..., (929$1270703), Vol. 1, pp. 9ff., 126 to 128.
Viner. The Long View..., (958 1270954), pp. 297-298, p. 298, footnote 53.
Andre L. Simon. The History of the Wine Trade in England, London: The Holland Press, 1964, Vol. 3, pp. 31 to 34, 67-68, 89 to 93, 110. [The 1964 edition is a facsimile of the original 1905-1906 edition with the addition of an index to Volume 3.]

[73]Royal revenue from colonial ventures was derived from taxes and customs duties, and indirectly from taxation of incremental income generated by colonial investments. Generally, the European states used direct taxation -- they considered the colonies outside the fiscal realm and therefore under the obligation to pay regular customs duties. When, however, new colonization projects were undertaken, tax exemptions and concessions were offered for specified periods to encourage the ventures. In such cases the tax benefit accruing to the realm was a result of indirect taxation.
Brief summaries of tax concessions to companies or accredited persons are contained in:

Edward Bourne. Spain in America..., (904$1270738), pp. 216-217.
Haring. Trade and Navigation..., op. cit., pp. 6-7.
Cole. Colbert..., op. cit., Vol. 1, p. 166 [Exemptions], 178 [item 14], 187-188 [item 5].
Andrews. The Colonial Period..., op. cit., Vol. 4, p. 20, footnote 1.
Mattie Parker. (ed.). North Carolina Charters 1578-1698, (963$1270415), passim.

The fiscalism of direct taxation is noted in:

Hamilton. "The Decline of Spain," Economic History Review, Vol. 8 (1937-1938), pp. 168 to 179.
Cole. French Mercantilist..., op. cit., p. 221.
Andrews. The Colonial Period..., op. cit., Vol. 4,

importance of favorable trade balances and suggested concomitant policies. This optimum path[75] leading to favorable trade balances _in practice_, was abandoned, however, in favor of the more pragmatic aims of military and fiscal viability.

In this writing, fiscalism and availability are demonstrated primarily in the context of the primacy of economic motives in American colonial viticultural schemes. Fiscalism and availability applied not only to wine, but also to all other commodities. The ensuing examination of the fishing trade, naval stores, drugs, spices, and silk, will not only reveal the marked uniformity of mercantile practice among the European states, but also will provide a background for

---

pp. 13-14, 19-20.
Beer. _The Origins_..., _op_. _cit_., pp. 74-75, 101-102.

[74]Other arguments favoring colonization were to increase national pride, to enlarge the realm, to facilitate the search for Northwest and Northeast passages, to spread Christianity, and to search for gold, silver, and pearls. The colonies were envisioned, as well, as an outlet for the surplus population, as a source of raw materials and as a market for the manufactured goods of the mother country. These arguments are summarized in:

Arthur P. Whitaker, "Spanish Contribution...," (929$1270678), pp. 2 to 4.
Cole. _French Mercantilist_..., _op_. _cit_., pp. 154 to 158.
Cole. _Colbert_..., _op_. _cit_., Vol. 2, pp. 70 to 82.
Knorr. _British Colonial_..., _op_. _cit_., pp. 26 to 59.

[75]Adam Smith so well described the path that mercantilists believed would lead to favorable trade balances that his description became the Procrustean bed of virtually all later mercantilist discussion. [Smith. _An Inquiry_..._Wealth of Nations_..., _op_. _cit_., pp. 418-419.]

determining the feasibility of colonial viticulture and wine production for each of the European states and for their colonies.

To support defense efforts, each state acted to maintain at hand the sinews of war. They allowed availability to dominate their commercial practice concerning armaments.[76] They followed practices advancing provisionment for national safety.[77] Maritime practices similarly reflect this provisionment bias; European states, in promoting their naval forces, would encourage domestic shipping, shipbuilding, and fishing even when comparative costs would dictate balance-of-trade gains by the consumption of foreign-caught fish, the purchase of foreign-built ships, and the employ of alien vessels and crews.[78]

---

[76]It was Adam Smith [An Inquiry...Wealth of Nations..., op. cit., p. 431] not the mercantilists, who expressed the maxim "defense is more important that opulence." In policy discussion the mercantilists did not recognize the frequency with which they engaged in this trade-off and hence gave it little attention. Mercantile practice, however, made Smith's maxim an actuality.

The contrast between commercial policy and mercantile practice is further discussed Supra, Vol. 1, pp. 4-5; p. 5, footnote 12.

[77]Hamilton. "Spanish Mercantilism...," op. cit., pp. 235 to 237.

Nef. "Industry and Government...," op. cit., pp. 58ff.

Cole. Colbert..., op. cit., p. 132.

Heckscher. Mercantilism, op. cit., Vol. 2, pp. 32 to 34.

[78]Usher. "Spanish Ships...," op. cit., pp. 202-203.

A. J. Richlieu. Testament politique, Vol. 2, pp. 78-79, 90-91, quoted in Cole. Colbert..., op. cit., Vol. 1,

Early arguments favoring the development of fishing and carrying trades related both to the importance of ships as a "nursery for seamen"[79] and as a "forcible wall" of defense.[80] Just as changes in land artillery "relegated bows and arrows to the museum"[81] so did the "mounting" of ships with heavy ordinance render obsolete the use of fishing vessels for defense. Later proponents of the fisheries thus

---

p. 144.

Cole. Colbert..., op. cit., Vol. 1, p. 383.

_______. French Mercantilist..., op. cit., pp. 180-181.

Barbour. "Dutch and English...," op. cit., pp. 267-268.

Andrews. The Colonial Period..., op. cit., Vol. 4, pp. 22-23, 25-26, 38.

[79]De Montchretin. Traicté..., op. cit., pp. 231-232. Quoted in Cole. French Mercantilist..., op. cit., p. 153.

Cole. Colbert..., op. cit., Vol. 1, pp. 97-98, 347, 472.

Hakluyt. "Inducements...," (585 1270028), p. 107, item 25.

Knorr. British Colonial..., op. cit., pp. 38 to 40.

Beer. The Origins..., op. cit., pp. 269-270.

[80]

> To this realme of England in times past belonged a strong nauie of shippes maintained chiefly by fishing, wherewith the Prince and countrie were compassed for their defence, as with a forcible wall...
>
> [Edward Ieninges [Edward Jenings]. A Briefe Discouery..., (590 1261052), folio B recto.]

> Behold then the true form and worth of forraign Trade, which is, The great Revenue of the King,...The employment of our poor, ...The Nurcery of our Mariners, The Walls [for defense] of the Kingdoms...
>
> [Mun. England's Treasure..., op. cit., pp. 219-220.]

[81]Heckscher. Mercantilism, op. cit., Vol. 2, p. 32.

shifted toward balance-of-trade arguments (lamenting trade losses due to the import of foreign-caught fish),[82] while advocates of shipbuilding and shipping adhered to the original arguments, enhanced by balance-of-trade loyalties.[83]

---

82 London's Blame If not its Shame: Manifested by the great neglect of the Fishery, which affordeth to our Neighbour Nation yearly, the Revenue of many Millions, which they take up at our Doors, whilst with the sluggard, we fold our hands in our bosoms and will not stretch them forth to our mouths.
Or the estimable riches of the British Seas, which do yield a monthly Harvest of several Fish in their season, which being brought into the Land, would make Flesh at a low rate, increase Shipping, Mariners, Trade, and publique Revenue...
Let every Ward in London build a Buss, and Money to do it may be thus raised.
[Jenner. London's Blame..., op. cit., title page.]

This eloquent title summarizes the "new" arguments favoring the fisheries. They are detailed in:

Depping. Correspondance administrative, Vol. 3, p. 866, quoted in Cole. French Mercantilism 1683-1700, op. cit., p. 21.
Colbert. ["...to the intendant at Normandy,"] quoted in Cole. Colbert..., op. cit., Vol. 1, pp. 472-473.
Ieninges. [Jenings]. A Briefe Discouery..., op. cit., p. 15.
Tobias Gentleman. Englands Way..., (614 1261098), folio B3 to [B4].
Edward Sharpe. Britaine's Busse, or a computation of the charge of a Busse or herring ship, London: 1615, passim.
Mun. England's Treasure..., op. cit., pp. 22-23.
Simon Smith. The Herring Busse Trade, London: 1641, passim.
Jenner. London's Blame..., op. cit., pp. 5-6, 9.
An Account of the French Usurpation upon the Trade of England, London: 1679, p. 13.
D'Avenant. "Discourses...," op. cit., pp. 428-429.

83 Hakluyt. "Discourse on Western Planting," 584$1260451), p. 110.
Mun. England's Treasure..., op. cit., pp. 219-

These differences notwithstanding, fisheries, shipbuilding and shipping constantly won approval as an employment for the poor[84] and as an appropriate source of training sailors for war and long trade ventures.[85]

---

220. [Quoted Supra, Vol. 1, p. 48 footnote 80.
Gerard Malynes. The Antient Law-Merchant..., (636 1270939), pp. 168, 171 to 175.
M[un]. A Discovrse..., op. cit., pp. 30 to 32.
D'Avenant. An Essay..., (696$1271247), pp. 105-106.
Smith. An Inquiry...Wealth of Nations..., op. cit., pp. 429-430.

Also material quoted in:

Castillo. Spanish Mercantilism..., op. cit., pp. 123-124.
Cole. French Mercantilist..., op. cit., pp. 150 to 153.
Viner. The Long View..., op. cit., pp. 290 to 294, especially p. 291 footnote 38, p. 292 footnote 42.
Scott. "The Constitution...," op. cit., Vol. 2, pp. 361 to 383.
Beer. The Origins, op. cit., pp. 73, 74.

[84] De Montchretin. Traicté..., op. cit., pp. 232 to 235. Quoted in Cole. French Mercantilist..., op. cit., pp. 152, 153, 183.
Cole. Colbert..., op. cit., Vol. 1, pp. 97, 127, 128.
Heckscher. Mercantilism, op. cit., Vol. 2, p. 38.
Hakluyt. "Discourse on Western Planting" [1584], in C. Deane. (ed.). Documentary History of the State of Maine, Cambridge: 1877, Vol. 2, p. 155.
Buck. The Politics..., op. cit., pp. 34-35.

[85] De Montchretien. Traicté..., op. cit., p. 303. Quoted in Cole. Colbert..., op. cit., Vol. 1, p. 97.
Hakluyt. "Inducements...," op. cit., p. 107, item 25.
________. "Discourse...," in C. Deane. (ed.). op. cit., Vol. 2, pp. 91-92, 155-156.
Mun. England's Treasure..., op. cit., p. 130.
Henry Maydman. Naval Speculations and Maritime Politicks, London: 1691, pp. 251 to 265.

To spur the maritime trades, the European states proclaimed Political Lent or "fysshe dayes";[86] established premiums, bounties, preferential duties; ordered import encouragements and export limitations on naval stores, timber, and masts; and enacted Acts of Navigation.[87] These

---

[86]One result of the Protestant Revolt was a decline in the English fishing trades because of the decreased number of fast days. Under Elizabeth's reign various measures, including the Protestant Lent, were adopted to counteract this tendency. The importance of these "fysshe dayes" was not only "...specially that Fishers...may thereby the rather be set on work..." but, also, that these days alleviated the dearth and high price of meat.

The Protestant Lent Acts are reviewed in Heckscher. Mercantilism, op. cit., Vol. 2, p. 38. He models his discussion after that of Cunningham. The Growth of English Industry and Commerce in Modern Times, Cambridge: University Press, 1903, Vol. 1, pp. 499f.; Vol. 2, pp. 67 to 73. The origin and importance of fish days are recorded in:

A Briefe Note of the Benefits that grow to this Realme by the Observation of Fish Daies, London: 1595, passim.

Jenner. London's Blame..., op. cit., pp. 3, 9, 10.

J. C. Drummond and Anne Wilbraham. The Englishman's Food..., (940 1271079), pp. 60 to 63.

Beer. The Origins..., op. cit., p. 269, footnote 3.

[87]Usher. "Spanish Ships...," op. cit., pp. 193-194.

Hamilton. War and Prices..., op. cit., p. 200.

Cole. Colbert..., op. cit., Vol. 1, pp. 450 to 474.

Heckscher. Mercantilism, op. cit., Vol. 2, pp. 36 to 40.

Smith. An Inquiry...Wealth of Nations..., op. cit., pp. 418 to 446, 466 to 490, 562 to 565.

Lawrence A. Harper. The English Navigation Laws: A Seventeenth Century Experiment in Social Engineering, New York: Columbia University Press, 1939 [Octagon Press, 1964], passim.

Jensen. English Historical..., op. cit., pp. 351 to 357.

Lipson. The Economic..., op. cit., Vol. 3, pp. 181 to 186.

Andrews. The Colonial Period..., op. cit., Vol. 4, passim.

Barbour. "Dutch and English...," op. cit., 262-263,

inducements varied considerably in coverage and intensity among the states.

Despite the exclusion of foreign ships from the Indies, the promotion of navigation by the House of Trade, and navigation acts, governing forces in Spain failed to develop shipping "commensurate with the extension of the Spanish empire."[88] This neglect of her maritime interests[89] was

---

266-267.

Cunningham. *The Growth*..., *op. cit.*, passim.

Knorr. *British Colonial*..., *op. cit.*, pp. 38 to 41, 66-67.

Emory R. Johnson et al. *History of Domestic and Foreign Commerce*..., Vol. 1, pp. 35ff.

W. J. Ashley. "Commercial Legislation...," (889 1281264), pp. 4ff.

Beer. *The Commercial Policy of England Toward the American Colonies*, New York: Peter Smith, 1948 [a reprint of the original 1893 monograph], pp. 27 to 42.

[88] Hamilton. "Spanish Mercantilism...," *op. cit.*, pp. 236-237.

[89] Spanish fisheries, closely allied with the merchant marine,▯ declined with the general decline of trade in the first half of the seventeenth century.▯▯ By the second half of the century the fisheries were "utterly decadent"* --foreigners supplied most of Spain's extensive consumption of fish. Thus the wars between England and Holland in 1652-1654, 1665-1666 and 1672-1674 and between Spain and France in 1667-1668 and 1672-1678 tended to raise fish prices by obstructing imports.** Proposals by Uztariz [1724, 1727] for the development of maritime trade and the fisheries went unheeded.*** Effective decrees supporting the development of the Spanish fisheries were not enacted until 1782;# the industrial and maritime revival of Spain spans that date.##

▯ Hamilton. "American Treasure...," *op. cit.*, p. 3.

▯▯ Castillo. *Spanish Mercantilism*..., *op. cit.*, p. 35.
Haring. *The Spanish*..., *op. cit.*, pp. 333-334.
Usher. "Spanish Ships...," *op. cit.*, p. 213.
Hamilton. *War and Prices*..., *op. cit.*, pp. 218-219.

* *Ibid.* [Hamilton], p. 177 footnote 5.

** *Ibid.*, p. 177.

*** Castillo. *Spanish Mercantilism*..., *op. cit.*, pp. 83 to 94, 123-124.

\# Hamilton. *War and Prices*..., *op. cit.*, p. 200.

\## *Ibid.*, pp. 221 to 225.

Descriptions of the general decline of trade are

reflected in Spain's inadequate attention to the trade and consumption needs of her colonies, a neglect which was an important stimulus to the wine industries in the Spanish colonies.[90]

The French, once an important fishing nation,[91] continually bemoaned the decadence of their fishing industry and of their maritime trades.[92] Not until Colbert forcibly encouraged the French, did they develop as a maritime power and regain their coastal and carrying trades from the Dutch and English.[93] In the interim France lost control of her

---

incorporated in:

Hamilton. "American Treasure...," op. cit., p. 230.
Haring. Trade and Navigation..., op. cit., pp. 113, 122, 213 to 215, 243, 270.
Usher. "Spanish Ships...," op. cit., pp. 195, 203 to 205, 212-213.

[90] Supra. Vol. 1, pp. 27f.; and, Infra. Vol. 1, pp. 84f.

[91] Fagniez. L'Economie sociale..., op. cit., p. 298.
Biggar. The Early..., op. cit., pp. 18 to 21.
Bernard G. Hoffman. Cabot to Cartier..., (961 1270675), pp. 197 to 201.

[92] Bodin. The Response..., op. cit., p. 56.
Fagniez. L'Economie sociale..., op. cit., pp. 295-296.
De Montchretien. Traicté..., op. cit., pp. 249, 307. Quoted in Cole. French Mercantilist..., op. cit., p. 151.
Cole. French Mercantilist..., op. cit., pp. 180-181.
________. Colbert..., op. cit., Vol. 1, pp. 96 to 98, 127-128.

[93] Cole. Colbert..., op. cit., Vol. 1, pp. 343, 344, 383 to 391, 468 to 472.
Barbour. "Dutch and English...," op. cit., p. 262, footnote 2.

wine trade, and saw the Dutch and English adulterate her wines. To compete in foreign markets, she, too, resorted to adulteration,[94] thereby injuring the reputation of her wines and discouraging their use in the American colonies.[95]

William Cecil's decision to encourage fishing trades in preference to the wine trade in England represented a significant attempt to develop the fisheries as a mainstay of English maritime power. In a paper entitled "The Inconveniences of enlargying any power to bryng any more wyne into the realme"[96] Cecil hypothesized the consequences of the excesses and losses implicit in the development of the wine trade[97] and demonstrated that fisheries would share none of these disadvantages. To encourage fishing trades, he proposed a compulsory increase in the home consumption of fish by re-establishing and enforcing fish days.[98]

---

[94]Cole. Colbert..., op. cit., Vol. 1, pp. 413, 414. Techniques of wine adulteration are discussed Infra, Vol. 1, pp. 119-120, footnote 28.

[95]Infra., Vol. 1, pp. 120 to 122.

[96]Calendar of State Papers, Domestic..., (547 1221116), Vol. 1, p. 277; item XLI. 58 [1566?].

[97]William Cecil's position is detailed Infra., Vol. 1, pp. 181 to 184.

[98]A 1549 Statute directed that people eat fish on Friday, Saturday, the Ember days, Vigils, and Lent; in 1559 a proclamation was issued in favor of this political Lent. William Cecil, in 1563, was the chief advocate of a law for the "increase of fish and navy days"; the law added Wednesday to the fish days proclaimed in 1549. [Cunningham. The

The success of the English fisheries under the tutelage of Lord Burghley (William Cecil) was short-lived. Despite its avowed national importance,[99] the industry, as well as much of the carrying trade, fell into Dutch hands during the early seventeenth century.[100] Notwithstanding her comparative disadvantage in the fisheries and maritime trade,[101]

Growth..., op. cit., pp. 68-69, 71 to 73; p. 72, footnote 2, 3.]

Other sources discussing the origin and importance of the fish days are cited Supra, Vol. 1, p. 51 footnote 86.

[99] Ieninges [Jennings]. A Briefe Discouery..., op. cit., folio A4 verso, B recto.

Gentleman. Englands VVay..., op. cit., folio B2, B3, [B4].

[Edward Misselden]. Free Trade..., (622$1271259), pp. 34 to 40.

________. The Circle of Commerce..., (623 1271257), pp. 48-49, 140, 141.

Malynes. The Center of the Circle..., (623 1271258), p. 127.

Mun. England's Treasure..., op. cit., pp. 22, 23.

Jenner. London's Blame..., op. cit., passim.

Some of these sources are cited in:

Beer. The Origins..., op. cit., p. 269, footnote 1.

[100]

> And what their [Holland's] chiefest trade is, or their principall gold mine, is well knowne to all Merchants that haue vsed those parts...namely that his Maiesties Seas is their chiefest, principall, and onely rich Treasury, whereby they haue so long time maintained their warres, and haue so greatly prospered, and enriched themselues.
> [Gentleman. England's VVay..., op. cit., folio B3 recto.]

Consult also the sources cited in footnote 99 (above) and

D'Avenant. "Discourses...," op. cit., pp. 428f.

Beer. The Origins..., op. cit., pp. 62, 63; p. 269, footnote 2.

Andrews. The Colonial Period..., op. cit., Vol. 4, pp. 25 to 27, 48, 49.

[101] Charles d'Avenant, echoing Thomas Mun's popular notion of "fish costing nothing but the catching," [England's

England continued to encourage the training of seamen and to stem her balance-of-trade losses incurred by foreign shipping.[102]

The initial reluctance of William Cecil to promote the carrying and re-export of wine made difficult later control of English wine imports and wine prices. Attempts to discourage imported wines in favor of domestic ale and beer

---

Treasure..., op. cit., pp. 22.] nevertheless recognizes England's disadvantage in the fishing trades:

> And suppose we should fish something dearer than the Hollanders, yet this would be almost recompenced to the body of the people collectively considered, by the very freight which would be gotten by the ships for our northward and East Country Trade, which must otherwise go out empty.
> [D'Avenant. "Discourses...," op. cit., pp. 428-429.]

He argues for the development of a fishing fleet, concluding that "there seems only wanting, (to bring so immense a wealth to England as the herring fishery would produce) but to raise a competent stock [vessels, operating capital] to give the wheels motion at first." [Ibid., p. 430.]

102 "The first object of the navigation acts was navigation not trade; and the building of ships, the breeding and increase of seamen, and the preservation and defence of the kingdom preceded trade, just as trade preceded plantations in the scheme of things."
[Andrews. The Colonial Period..., op. cit., Vol. 4, p. 337.]

This point of view is advanced by Andrew Yarranton in England's Improvement by Sea and Land, London: 1677. It is discussed further in:

Smith. An Inquiry...Wealth of Nations..., op. cit., pp. 429 to 432, 484-485.
Andrews. The Colonial Period..., op. cit., Vol. 4, pp. 21, 108, 287-288, 345-346.
Knorr. British Colonial..., op. cit., pp. 66-67.

failed,[103] and substantial balance-of-trade losses resulted with increased wine consumption.[104] To redress unfavorable commodity trade balances in wine, the English cultivated French vines in her colonies and sought to substitute wines of these grapes for those of France, at home as well as in her colonies.[105] The Navigation Acts unwittingly discouraged this project. The Acts excluded Madeira wine from the restrictions and taxation imposed upon European commodities. Thus, the increased accessibility of Madeira established for it a colonial price differential which favored it over dry Continental wines.[106] These factors diverted colonial preference from dry to sweet wines, and thereby further discouraged planting French vines in the colonies.[107]

Procuring vital defense stocks was another aspect of naval policy. Spain failed to develop the manufacture of naval stores vital to her defense and marine trades. By 1569, colonial production in her hemp and flax factories was ordered curtailed in order to sustain the Spanish monopoly

---

[103] Infra, Vol. 1, pp. 207 to 209; p. 208, footnote 65.

[104] Ibid., pp. 185-186, footnote 21; pp. 193 to 195.

[105] Ibid., pp. 224, 241ff.

[106] Ibid., p. 263, footnote 49.

[107] Later colonization schemes advancing viticulture employed Spanish and Madeira grapes. These projects, while producing wine that satisfied the colonists' newly acquired tastes, could not compete in quality or price with imported sweet wines. [Consult Infra, Vol. 1, pp. 279.]

and to render the colonies wholly dependent on the industries of Spain.[108] Earlier edicts encouraging colonial shipbuilding (1516)[109] and fostering native production of hemp and flax (1545)[110] were set aside. At home, Spain failed to sustain production of naval stores beyond the first decades of the seventeenth century;[111] she later paid dearly for this neglect.

England relied upon the Northern powers, particularly Sweden and Finland, for her maritime supplies. These nations overcharged her and heavily taxed her ships. To overcome the monopoly position of these Northern powers[112] England

---

[108] Haring. Trade and Navigation..., op. cit., p. 127.
De Madariaga. The Rise..., op. cit., p. 128.

[109] Haring. Trade and Navigation..., op. cit., p. 124.

[110] Ibid.
Haring. The Spanish..., op. cit., p. 255, footnote 4.

[111] Usher. "Spanish Ships...," op. cit., pp. 193-194, 203.
Hamilton. "Spanish Mercantilism...," op. cit., p. 227.

[112] England's attempts to free herself from dependence upon foreign-purchased naval stores are discussed in:

Hakluyt. "Discourse on Western...," C. Deane. (ed.). op. cit., pp. 155, 163.
M[un]. A Discovrse..., op. cit., pp. 30, 31.
Rutherfurd. The Importance..., op. cit., pp. 110, 111.
Lord. Industrial Experiment..., op. cit., pp. 1 to 3, 56 to 86.
James Williamson. The Caribee Islands..., (926$1270910), pp. 6-7.
Reba C. Strickland. The Mercantile..., (938 1281206), pp. 160 to 168.
Justin Williams. "English Mercantilism and Carolina Naval Stores...," (935$1280920), pp. 169 to 185.
Knorr. British Colonial..., op. cit., pp. 50 to 56.

encouraged home production of naval stores,[113] enforced restraints on their exportation,[114] and prolloted their colonial manufacture through edicts, bounties and differential duties.[115]

---

[113]For example, the tillage of flax and hemp was mandatory under 24 Hen. VIII. c.4., [*The Statutes of the Realm*. (377$1221136), Vol. 3, pp. 421-422.]. The law required that every person occupying land suitable for tillage "shall for every Sixty Acres sew yearly one Quarter of an Acre of Flax or Hemp Seed." The statute was continued, 28 Hen. VIII. c.9.; 31 Hen. VIII. c.7; 33 Hen. VIII. c.17; 37 Hen. VIII. c.23 §§1,2. It was revived and enlarged touching "certain politic Constitutions made for the Maintenance of the Navy." by 5 Eliz. c.5 §§28,29 [*The Statutes*..., *op*. *cit*., Vol. 4, pt. 1, pp. 422 to 425.] which was repealed by 35 Eliz. c.7., §21. 7&8 W. III. c.39, [*The Statutes*..., *op*. *cit*., Vol. 7, p. 156] revived the act promoting the "bringing Flax and Hemp into, and the Making of Sail Cloth in, this Kingdom."

A statement outlining the importance of flax and hemp to England's provisionment appears in Joshua Gee. *The Trade and Navigation*..., (729 1271251), pp. 145, 146.

[114]Heckscher. *Mercantilism*, *op*. *cit*., Vol. 2, pp. 32-33; p. 33, footnote 2.

[115]Consistency of purpose marked the exhortations for the development of the English colonies as a source of naval stores:

> ...as Pitch, Tarre, Hempe, and thereof cordage, Masts...and other such like without being in any sort beholding to a king of Denmarke, or any other prince or state that shall be in sort able to command our shippes at their pleasure, as those do at this day...
>
> [Christopher Carlile. "A Briefe and Summary...," (583 1260452), p. 139.]
>
> Againe, they may spare vs *timber*, *masts*, *crystall* (if not better stones) wire, copper, *Iron*, *pitch*, *tar*, *sassafras*, *sopeashes* (for all these and more, we are sure the Countrey yeeldes in great abundance) and who knowes not we want these, and are beholden to some for them, with whom it were better for vs if we

To meet France's growing need for naval stores Colbert stimulated home production and attempted to wrest the Baltic trade from the Dutch.[116] This attempt, dictated by Colbert's overwhelming desire to deal a blow at Dutch shipping, sought to re-establish French maritime supremacy-- a supremacy predicated upon the comparative advantage of France in salt, hemp, flax, timber and naval stores. Colbert also attempted to imitate the English by promoting colonial sources for naval stores,[117] but he met with little success.

Defense was not the only area dominated by the availability aspect of provisionment. The arguments for availability extended as well to luxury items including spices, drugs, tobacco, silk, and wine, which were becoming

---

> had lesse to doe.
> [Crashaw. A Sermon Preached in London..., op. cit., folio [D4 recto].]

> ...Norway and Poland affoords Pitch and Tarre, Masts and Yards. Sweathland and Russia, Iron and Ropes. France and Spaine, Canvase, Wine, Steele, Iron, and Oile. Italy and Greece, Silkes and Fruits. I dare boldly say, because I have seene naturally growing or breeding in those parts, the same materials that all these are made of, they may as well bee had here [Virginia].
> [John Smith. The Generall Historie..., (624 1260663), Bk. 4, p. 18.]

The measures enacted in England and in the colonies for the encouragement of naval stores are summarized in the sources cited Supra, Vol. 1, pp. 58-59; p. 58, footnote 112.

[116] Heckscher. Mercantilism, op. cit., Vol. 2, p. 39.

[117] Cole. Colbert..., op. cit., Vol. 1, pp. 127, 128; Vol. 2, pp. 79, 80; p. 79, footnote 85.

necessities to the burgeoning European states. The plethora of writings on the wantonness of consumption, and on debauchery and drunkenness,[118] clearly portray the difficulties that the European states experienced with luxury items in attempting to subordinate availability demands to balance-of-trade considerations.[119]

As early as 1525, Oviedo y Valdez, the Viceroy of Mexico, reported on the medicinal products of the new world.[120] The belief that cures for the ailments and scourges that ravished mankind might be found and that spice might be readily obtained also spurred exploration and trade.[121] England's involvement in this trade is evident

---

[118]Simon. Bibliotheca Bacchia..., (932 1200832).
________. Bibliotheca Gastronomica, (953$1200143).
________. Bibliotheca Vinaria..., (913 1200162).
George Vicaire. Bibliographie Gastronomique..., (954 1200837).
Food and Drink..., (937 1200813).

[119]Even French and English wage earners were purchasing an increasing number of minor luxury items during the 1540-1640 period. Consult:
Nef. "Prices and Industrial...," op. cit., p. 184.
Cole. French Mercantilist..., op. cit., p. 83-84.

[120]Wright. The Dream of Prosperity..., op. cit., p. 42.

[121]

> ...Therefore whereas though shalt reade of the great abundaunce of gold, precious stones and spices, which the Spaniardes and Portugales haue brought from the South partes of the worlde,...
>
> ...The right worshipfull Maister Edvvarde Dier...tooke in hande to translate out of Spanishe into Englishe, the thre bookes of Doctour Monardes of Seuill...that in deede it might bryng in tyme rare profite, to my

from John Frampton's remarks in his translator's Preface to Nicholas Monardes' [Dos libros...][122] Ioyfvll Nevves:

> "...the afore saied Medicines...are now by Marchaunts and others brought out of the VVest Indias into Spaine, and from Spain [sic] hether into Englande, by suche as dooeth daiely trafficke thether."[123]

> Countrie folkes of Englande, by vvonderfull cures of sundrie greate deseases, that othervvise than by these remedies, thei vvere incurable.
>
> [[Nicholas Monardes]. Ioyfvll Nevves ovt of..., (577 1261160), pp. ij [ii] - [iii].].

Richard Eden. "Treatyse of the Newe India...," (553 1260063), p. 7.

Jan Huyghen van Linschoten. Discours of Voyages..., (598 1260172), pp. 218, 219.

Richard VVilles. The History of Trauayle..., (577 1260173), p. 188 recto.

> ...Besides, we have seene what great riches were drawne by the Portugalls, by meanes of their severall plantations in the East-Indies, out of those vast and mighty Princes Territories, that filled the whole Worlde with Spices, and other Aromatique Druggs, and excellent rare curiosities not vulgarly knowne to forreigne and former Ages in these Northerly parts of the World...
>
> [Ferdinando Gorges. A Briefe Narration..., (658 1261105), pp. 71-72.]

The importance of drugs and spices in the sixteenth and seventeenth centuries is sketched in:

Wright. The Colonial Search..., op. cit., pp. 27 to 29.

________. The Dream..., op. cit., pp. 41 to 43, 49.

[122]Agnes Arbor. Herbals..., (938 1270399), p. 278.

[123][Monardes.] Ioyfvll Nevves..., op. cit., folio [iii recto].

The popularity of Monardes' book throughout Europe[124] was indicative of the popularity of the new drugs and spices whose flourishing commerce evidenced the strength of availability doctrines and the disregard of Bullionist maxims.[125]

---

[124]Thomas Hariot in his "Briefe and True Report" [(588 1260448), p. 236] directed to the investors, farmers and well-wishers of the Virginia project detailed sassafras as a marketable commodity in the following manner: "For the description, manner of using, and manifold virtues of it, I refer you to the book of Monardus, translated and entitled in English, The Ioyful News from the West Indies." [[Monardes.] Ioyfvll Nevves..., op. cit., folio 45 verso to 47 verso.]

Eleanour Rohde [The Old English Herbals, (922$1270161), pp. 121, 211] traces Monardes' work translated into Latin, Italian, Flemish, and French; she asserts that Frampton's English translation went through four editions.

English excitement over American drugs and spices is further illustrated by:

> Timothy Bright. A Treatise Wherein is Declared the Sufficiency of English Medicine for Cure of All Diseases Cured with Medicine, London: 1580, passim.
> Ralph Lane. "Ralph Lane to Richard Hakluyt...," (585 1260118), pp. 207 to 211.
> Daniel Price. Saul's Prohibition Staide..., London: 1609, folio F2 verso, F3.

[125]

> ...in any famous commonwealth, which will not consent to the moderate vse of wholesome Druggs and comfortable Spices? Which, haue beene so much desired in all times, and by so many Nations; not thereby to surfeit or to please a lickorish tast (as it often happeneth, with many other fruites and wines) but rather as things most necessarie to preserue their health, and to cure their diseases;...
> M[un]. A Discovrse..., op. cit., pp. 6-7.]

> I would mention the Wines, the Fruits, Spices, and sugars and other unnecessary Branches of Import, but am afraid, both the Merchants, and those concerned in the Government and Customs, will think I have gone too great a length already.
> [David Black. Essay upon Industry and Trade..., (706 1270237), p. 25.]

Silk, too, was prominent in foreign trade. Substantial balance-of-trade losses incurred in its importation as a finished good fostered edicts discouraging silk imports, or promoting domestic silk industries which would utilize colonial and home-cultured raw silk.[126]

Spain attempted silk culture in Florida, New Spain and Peru.[127] Her attempts were not limited to culture alone,

---

[126]Both Nicholas Barbon [A Discourse..., op. cit., p. 8] and Gustav Schmoller [The Mercantile..., (884 1270923), pp. 83 to 85] present capsules of the history of silk in the European states.

George Unwin [Studies..., (958 1270953), p. 232] considered the silk industry as "the apple of the mercantilist eyes."

The different approaches assumed by each of the states in seeking to satisfy its domestic demand for silk, to promote silk manufacture at home, and, thereby, to find employment for their poor are outlined in:

> Haring. The Spanish..., op. cit., pp. 254-255.
> Cole. French Mercantilism..., op. cit., pp. 84 to 90, 94, 130 to 132, 208, 209.
> ________. Colbert..., op. cit., Vol. 1, pp. 35 to 37, 42 to 51, 90, 119; Vol. 2, pp. 187 to 197.
> Nef. Industry..., op. cit., p. 84.
> M[un]. A Discovrse..., op. cit., pp. 7, 26-27, 56.
> Mun. England's Treasure..., op. cit., pp. 23, 27 to 33, 176 to 180.
> D'Avenant. "An Essay...," op. cit., pp. 104 to 112.
> Lipson. The Economic History..., op. cit., Vol. 2, pp. 100 to 105.

As directors, Mun and D'Avenant sought to justify the East India Company's (silk) trade. Andrews [The Colonial..., op. cit., Vol. 4, p. 337, footnote 2] cites others who question the benefit of such trade to England.

[127]W. R. Jackson. Early Florida..., (954$1280768), pp. 102-103.

Oviedo. Historia general, Parte 1, Libro 17, Cap. 24. Tomo 1, pp. 556-557. Quoted in Jackson. Early

but extended to the manufacture and dyeing of the finished product.[128] Religious obstacles,[129] the importation of cheaper Chinese silk by way of the Philippine Islands, and the decline in numbers of the Indian laboring population deterred colonial production.[130] Silk production suffered a general decline after 1580; after 1596, silk culture in the colonies was discouraged officially as interfering with textile imports from Spain.[131] This move stifled the decaying industry. Later attempts of the Bourbons to revive silk manufacture in the colonies failed, and home industry correspondingly faltered.[132]

In France, Laffemas sought new silk production centers in addition to those already established by the Council of

---

Florida..., op. cit., pp. 166-167 (footnote 221).
Joseph de Acosta. The Natural and Moral..., (590$1260782), p. 269.
De Madariaga. The Rise..., op. cit., p. 58.
Bourne. Spain in America..., op. cit., pp. 216-217.

128 De Acosta. The Natural and Moral..., op. cit., p. 269.
Haring. Trade and Navigation..., op. cit., p. 127.

129 De Madariaga. The Rise..., op. cit., p. 58.

130 Haring. The Spanish..., op. cit., pp. 254-255.

131 Ibid., p. 255.

132 Ibid.
Smith. Seventeenth-Century..., op. cit., p. 405.

Commerce.[133] Henry IV (1589-1610) prohibited silk imports, and authorized the manufacture of all imported silk items.[134] By 1610, the raw silk output of France had increased substantially, although the grand object of Laffemas' project was not attained.[135] France continued her dependence upon raw silk imports, even in the period when Colbert strove mightily to encourage silk culture and silk manufacture in France.[136]

Aware of early Spanish and French successes in silk production, the English sought to emulate these states.[137]

---

[133]Fagniez. L'Economie sociale..., op. cit., p. 125.
Cole. Colbert..., op. cit., pp. 35 to 37.

[134]Cole. Colbert..., op. cit., p. 106-107, 260 to 262.
________. French Mercantilist..., op. cit., p. 85.
Fagniez. L'Economie sociale..., op. cit., p. 125.
Nef. "Industry and Government...," op. cit., p. 84.

[135]Cole. Colbert..., op. cit., p. 50; p. 50, footnote 2.
Fagniez. L'Economie sociale..., op. cit., p. 130; p. 130, footnote 1, 2.

[136]Dubois. Précis de l'histoire..., op. cit., pp. 104-105.
Cole. Colbert..., op. cit., Vol. 1, p. 90; Vol. 2, pp. 187 to 197.

[137]D'Oliuier de Serres. The Perfect Vse of Silk-VVormes..., (607 1261099), folio [A4, recto].
Iohn Bonoeil. His Maiesties graciovs..., (622 1261194), title page, folio (a), [(b)], pp. 1 to 3.
[Edward Williams]. Virginias Discovery of Silke-Wormes..., (650 1261193), folio A3, [A4].
Samuel Hartlib. The Reformed Virginia Silkworm..., (655 1271177), folio A2.
Gee. The Trade and Navigation..., op. cit., p. 28.
Analytical Index...Remembrancia..., (878 1250176), pp. 520-521, Item No. III. 61.

To encourage silk culture in her colonies, the English offered bounties and differential duties;[138] to encourage silk manufacture in England, she forbade the importation of foreign-wrought silks.[139] Yet, bounties, differential duties and prohibitions did not advance the English silk industry until late in the seventeenth century[140]--the influence of the East India trade, the failure of colonial silk

---

[138] Alice B. Lockwood. (ed.). Gardens of Colony..., (931 1270869), Vol. 2, pp. 29 to 32.
"Growth and Manufacture of Silk...," (828 1231159), pp. 13 to 18.
Edward Eggleston. "Husbandry in Colony Times," (884 1281205), pp. 431 to 434.
Royal Instructions..., (935 1220883), p. 758 [23 Geo. II, c. 20. (1750)].

[139] Prohibitions of imported silk into England include: State Papers Domestic, Addenda, 1625-1649, p. 313 (Petition against wrought silks, 1628?); Statutes, vi. 173, 443 (Act of 1690 prohibiting the importation of thrown silk except Italian); Statutes at Large, vii. 441, 559, 588 (Acts of 1762, 1765, and 1766 prohibiting foreign-wrought silks); House of Commons Journals, xxx. 210, 725-726, 758; xxxiv. 241.
[Lipson. The Economic History..., op. cit., Vol. 3, p. 14, footnote 5; p. 21].
Leo Stock. (ed.). Proceedings and Debates..., (924 1221132), Vol. 2, p. 164 (March 7, 1695/6 HC).

[140]
> That the Silk Manufacture of the Kingdom, by the Incouragement it hath receiv'd from the Crown, and divers Acts of Parliament, is above twenty times as great as it was in the year 1664...
> ["The Case of the Silk-Weavers...," quoted in [Defoe]. The State of Silk and Woollen Manufacture Considered: In Relation to a French Trade. London: 1713, p. 16.]

> The Silk Manufacture that was hardly known in England Forty Years ago, is, by the Encouragements from the Crown, and Parliament, in Prohibiting the Wearing of East-India Wrought

culture enterprises, and the deficiency of English skill in silk manufacture all impeded development of the industry.

Despite the burgeoning demand for silk, spices, drugs tobacco and other new items of European commerce, states continued to discourage their import from foreign nations and supported colonial and domestic ventures favoring their production. These ventures reflected the states' vested interests in sources of royal (public) revenue. Fiscalism policies thus supplemented those fostering availability: policies designed to promote long-term favorable trade balances were set aside in favor of practices promising not only commodity availability but also immediate royal revenue. Fiscalism worked against viticulture and wine production in all colonies.

Spain and France, as wine producers, restricted colonial production of wine and other commodities that would affect adversely their export trade. They attempted to control colonial trade and to augment royal revenue by taxing the sale of wine and other commodities. To supply the needs of home industry, they promoted the colonial production of naval stores, spices, drugs and silks by exerting pressures to channel colonial manufactures in these directions. They manipulated colonial charters and grants, controlled

---

> Silks, but chiefly from the Interruption of Trade with _France_; now brought to Perfection...
>
> [[Defoe]. _The State of Silk_..., _op. cit._, p. 5. Consult also _Ibid._, pp. 41 to 43.]

differential duties, drawbacks, tax concessions and bounties, and established export price schedules which favored the needed raw materials. Such pressures discouraged viticulture and wine production by employing colonial capital and labor and by promoting imported wine in the colonies.

The Dutch, having a copious supply of wine through entrepot trade, did not encourage colonial attempts at wine production.[141] Similarly, the Dutch colonists had little incentive to promote a wine industry. They turned, rather, to wine imports as a source of colonial fiscalism, finding it convenient to finance almost their entire colonial regime by wine and liquor imposts, excises, and sales taxes.[142]

English practices[143] best reveal how fiscalism curtailed viticulture and wine production in colonial America. In light of availability and balance-of-trade considerations, England stood to gain markedly by encouraging colonial wine industries. This she acknowledged, and included viticulture in her initial colonization projects, promoting it along with other ventures designed to fulfill availability needs. The bounties and encouragements offered to viticulture and wine production, however, were insufficient; other ventures

---

[141] Infra, Vol. 1, pp. 132 to 134.

[142] Ibid., pp. 134 to 137.

[143] These practices are detailed and documented Infra, Vol. 1, pp. 224ff. This text is a synopsis illustrating fiscalism.

gained the attention of the Crown because of their potentially superior public revenue.

Beginning in 1604, tobacco occupied English royal interest.[144] As long as the tobacco market was firm, little was done to advance the drug, spice, silk and wine industries. Only when tobacco prices fell precipitously in glut markets[145] did demand for colonial production of other

---

[144]The 1577 Frampton translation of Monardes' Ioyfvll Nevves..., op. cit., [Supra, Vol. 1, p. 62f., footnote 123, 124] contains an enthusiastic appraisal of tobacco recommending its healing qualities and its benefits as an opiate.* In A Counterblast to Tobacco [London: 1604], King James I expressed his extreme displeasure in the rising English use of tobacco.** Despite this opposition, tobacco was introduced into Virginia in 1606*** or in 1610-1611.# Colonial attempts at tobacco production were explained as curing "the maine decay of trade, and the chiefe cause that hindereth the importation of Bullion out of Spaine."## Fiscal considerations also prevented the Crown from banishing tobacco; both James I and Charles I, despite their vituperative opposition to the plant, farmed patents for tobacco in the interest of royal revenue.###

* Wright. The Dream of Prosperity..., op. cit., pp. 49 to 51.

** Ward. Shakespeare..., op. cit., p. 14; p. 14, footnote 3.
Meyer Jacobstein. "The Tobacco Industry...," (907$1271223), pp. 14-15.
Wright. The Dream of Prosperity..., op. cit., p. 53.

*** Ward. Shakespeare..., op. cit., p. 14.

L. C. Gray. "The Market Surplus...[Part 1]," (927$1281200), p. 231.

[Edward Bennett.] A Treatise deuided..., (620 1261195), folio [B] ([sig. a3]).

Hinton. "The Mercantile System...," op. cit., p. 288.
Jacobstein. "The Tobacco Industry...," op. cit., p. 14.
Beer. The Origins..., op. cit., pp. 91 to 100.

[145]Consult Appendix I and Infra, Vol. 1, pp. 224 to 233.

staples become clamorous. Attention centered on the dire effects of the tobacco glut on the colonial economy and on the royal purse. At the end of each tobacco glut, however, the relative advantage of manufacturing commodities other than tobacco had not improved. The encouragements offered to other staples were insufficient.

In eighteenth-century England, silk manufacture overtook tobacco in economic importance. England voiced increasing concern for a continual supply of raw silk that would free her from competing with the French, Dutch and Spanish. Bounties favoring colonial viticulture and wine production accompanied those encouraging silk culture. The nexus of these bounties, fused during earliest colonization, continued throughout the eighteenth century, although later bounties increasingly favored silk. Hence, the allegience of royal interests in silk manufacture set colonial viticulture at a comparative disadvantage.

Another manifestation of English fiscalism also adversely affected colonial wine production. The Crown developed a vested interest in the manufacture of hard liquors, that is, in the royal revenue derived from them. Thus, Queen Anne revoked the distillers' monopoly encouraging unrestricted gin production to augment royal revenue. With the flowering of the Gin Age the popularity of wine diminished; the Crown was thus less inclined to sponsor wine production for availability, fiscalism or balance-of-trade reasons.

These arguments of Commodity Mercantilism theory outlining trade and colonization policies of the European states found expression in practices relating to all commodities, not only wine. They influenced state domestic and colonial policy relating to luxury items such as spices, drugs and silks, as well as state policies directed toward maintenance of defense and enhancement of trade.

Commodity Mercantilism theory asserts that the economic motivations and consequences of the attempts to establish fisheries and to encourage naval stores, drugs, spices and silk, parallel the economic motivations and consequences behind attempts at colonial wine manufacture. The commercial practices of the Spanish, Dutch, French and English regarding viticulture and wine production illustrate these parallels emphasizing the consistency of Commodity Mercantilism theory.

CHAPTER III

The Spanish Experience

Provisionment and fiscalism policies strongly influenced Spanish practices relating to colonial viticulture and wine production. During the first half of the sixteenth century, provisionment induced the Spanish to promote colonial vineyards. These attempts were initiated to insure the domestic availability of wine, as sizable colonial exports had impinged upon the Spanish wine supply.

This availability aspect of provisionment dominated Spanish viticultural policy until the latter half of the century when the favorable balance of trade aspect was stressed. Thereafter, Spain attempted to restrict colonial viticulture during periods of domestic overproduction when colonial vintages appeared to compete with Spanish wine exports.

The objectives of fiscalism often did not coincide with those of provisionment. Fiscalism restrained the Spanish from the total prohibition of colonial viticulture. It encouraged the colonial governments to ignore or even sanction violations of planting and vintage restrictions in order to achieve revenue objectives.

Throughout the ensuing examination of Spanish viticultural policy, the ascendancy of economic motives is documented. Climatic and socio-political theories are severely modified, if not dismissed. The primacy of economic motives is shown in a review of Spanish colonial viticulture and wine production ventures spanning three centuries.

When Bodadilla arrived in Espanola in 1500, he found only 300 Spaniards on the whole of the island; Columbus had failed as a colonizer of the Indies.[1] The sovereigns of Spain, aware of this failure, appointed Nicolas de Ovando as governor of the Indies, in an attempt to realize the promise of Espanola, which Columbus had so enthusiastically described:

> La Spanola is marvelous, the sierras and the mountains and the plains, and the meadows and the land are so beautiful, and rich for planting and sowing and for livestock of every sort, and for building towns and villages...[2]
> I shall give them [the Spanish royalty] as much gold as they want...besides spices and cotton...and gum mastic...and aloe wood... and slaves. And I believe that I have found rhubarb and cinnamon, and I shall find a thousand other things of value.[3]

---

[1]Arthur Newton. The European Nations..., (933$1270912), p. 17.

[2]"Columbus's Letter to the Sovereigns His First Voyage 15 February 1493," in Samuel E. Morison. Journals and Other Documents on the Life and Voyages of Christopher Columbus, New York: The Heritage Press, 1963, p. 183.

[3]Ibid., p. 186. Dr. Morison does not call attention to the standard misrepresentation of Columbus's opinion of La Spanola. Adam Smith appears to have originated the misconception: "Finding nothing either in the animals or vegetables of the newly discovered countries, which could justify a very advantageous representation of them, Columbus turned his view towards their minerals; and in the richness of the productions of this third kingdom, he flattered himself, he had found a full compensation for the insignificancy

Nicolas de Ovando sailed from Seville in February, 1502, with thirty-two ships, 2500 men, and supplies of domestic animals and useful plants from Spain and the Canaries. Within four years the number of Spaniards in Espanola had risen to 12,000. Immigration to the colony had become so attractive that Ovando had to appeal to the Crown not to permit emigrants in greater number than the colony could absorb.[4]

One goal of colonization was establishing a royal trade monopoly in America: in return for producing raw silk, spices, wood and rice, and for harvesting gold, silver and pearls, Espanola was to be supplied Spanish wines, oils, arms, and finished goods. Accordingly, in 1503, King Ferdinand forbade production of wine in Espanola,[5] an undertaking which began there in 1494 during Columbus's second

---

of those of the other two." [Adam Smith. An Inquiry...Wealth of Nations..., (776 1270256), p. 528.

Arthur P. Whitaker. ["Spanish Contribution...," (929$1270678), pp. 2 to 4], comments upon the misrepresentation of Columbus's report; he does not cite Adam Smith.

[4]Newton. The European Nation..., op. cit., p. 18.

[5]Clarence Haring. Trade and Navigation..., (918 1270735), p. 125.

visit to the islands.[6] The supply of wine from Spain, however, proved either insufficient or not to the liking of Espanola's inhabitants, for, in 1508, they petitioned King Ferdinand not to limit their imports of wine to those grown near Seville.[7]

The Spanish crown soon was forced to concessions as the lure of gold and silver to Mexico and Peru eclipsed the attractiveness of Espanola. In 1518, the Spanish government offered Espanola colonizers free passage, land and livestock, a twenty-year exemption from the burdensome alcabala tax (a turnover tax), and premiums for producing raw silk, spices, woad and rice.[8] The Casa de Contratacion ordered in 1519 that every ship sailing for the islands carry a number of vines to be planted there.[9] The success of Espanola viticultural attempts may be judged from the description of the islands given by Gonzalo de Oviedo in 1526:

---

[6]"Soon, the young vines were set out, the plains smiled with bounteous produce...providing all the grain and all the wine that could be used for two whole years." [Within a year the Spaniards declared they were starving.] "Syllacio's Letter to the Duke of Milan, 13 December 1494," in Morison, Journals..., op. cit., p. 242. The comment in brackets is Dr. Morison's.

[7]Edward G. Bourne, Spain in America..., (904$1270738), p. 218.

[8]Ibid., p. 217.

[9]A. de I., 139. I.6, lib. 8, fol. 138, quoted in Haring. Trade and Navigation..., op. cit., p. 125.
Haring. The Spanish Empire in America, New York: Oxford University Press, 1947, pp. 253-254. Dr. Haring does not explain that the 1519 instruction was a concession to the colonists.

> In the wooded parts of Tierra Firma [Espanola] there are many good wild vines covered with grapes, some bearing single grapes, others in bunches. They are larger, better and not so sour as those that grow in the groves in Spain. I have eaten them many times in large quantities. I want to make it clear that grapes and vines would do well there. All these grapes that I have seen and eaten are black. In Santo Domingo I have eaten very good large white grapes grown on vines on arbors from vine shoots brought from Spain. They are as good as those grown in Spain.[10]

The viticultural concessions to Espanola soon were paralleled in New Spain (Mexico). Hernando Cortes, in 1524, recommended that the Casa de Contratacion require all vessels coming to New Spain to bring over a certain quantity of seeds and plants.[11] He made it a condition of grants of land on the plateau that the proprietor of every estate should plant a specified number of vines on it.[12]

---

[10]Gonzalo de Oviedo. _Natural History of the West Indies_, trans. and ed. by Sterling A. Stoudemire, Chapel Hill: University of North Carolina Press, 1959, p. 85.

[11]Rel. Quarta de Cortes, ap. Lorenzana, p. 397. Quoted in William Prescott. _History of the Conquest_..., (843$1170107). Vol. 3, p. 269.
R. Altamira. _Historia de Espana_, Madrid: 1902, Vol. 3, p. 512.
Arthur Whitaker. "Spanish Contribution...," _op. cit._, p. 4. Dr. Whitaker cites a study by A. S. Aiton [_Antonio de Mendoza_..., Durham, North Carolina: 1928, p. 109; p. 109 note 83] showing that the order requested in 1524 was issued in 1532.

[12]Ordenanzas Municipales, ano de 1524, MS. Quoted in Prescott. _History of the Conquest_..., _op. cit._, p. 269.
Hernan Cortes. _Encrites Sueltos_, Mexico: 1871, Vol. 3, pp. 30-31. Quoted in Welton Sensing. _The Policies of Hernan Cortes_..., (954 1210108), p. 252.
Greyton Taylor. _Treasury of Wine_..., (963$1270109), p. 2.

Nuno de Guman, on being named governor of Panuco in 1525, forced the Indians there to turn from their recently adopted livestock grazing to viticulture. This early promoter of wine-making in Mexico eventually could boast that "the churches in all the villas are using wine from my estate."[13]

Land for vineyards also was granted near Mexico City,[14] where grapes and olives were reported growing in 1531.[15] By 1544, wine also was made in Oaxaca, where, because the land outside the city was reserved for the Indians, residents had to grow their vines, as well as their figs, within the city.[16]

The success of the New Spain ventures, however, was limited. Motolinia, in a treatise written between 1536 and 1541, suggested,

> ...the land they call New Spain...is certainly of greatest value; and it would be still more valuable if they had set it with plants that would thrive very well in it, such as grapevines and olive trees...On many parts...there are very thick wild grapevines. Nobody knows who planted them. They produce very long

---

[13]Epistolario de la Nueva Espana, Francisco Paso y Troncoso (ed.). Mexico: 1942, Vol. 2, p. 47; Vol. 14, p. 185.

[14]Ibid., Vol. 14, p. 233.

[15]A. Curtis Wilgus. Colonial Hispanic America, (936$1270671), p. 320, footnote 62.

[16]Epistolario, op. cit., Vol. 14, p. 233.

> shoots with numerous bunches of grapes. These grapes are eaten green. Some Spaniards make vinegar of them, while others have made wine, although of this wine there has been very little.[17]

here is an undocumented assertion that the Spanish, finding he wines produced from wild grapes unsatisfactory, first mported European vines to Mexico in 1572.[18] Nothwithstand-ng, attempts at wine production on the central plateau of exico generally met with failure. Father Joseph De Acosta, riting in 1590, explained that,

> ...in New Spaine there are some vines which beare grapes, and yet make no wine. The cause is, for that the grape ripens not well, by reason of the raine that falles in the months of Iuly and August, which hinders their ripening, so as they serve onely to eate.[19]

e asserted that, although wine could be made, it would be like that of Lombardy, which is very weak and arsh-tasting."[20]

It is largely to the credit of Viceroy Mendoza of exico and his successors that viticulture and wine produc-ion continued in New Spain. When in December, 1542, nperor Charles V proclaimed the "New Laws of the Indies,"

---

[17]Toribio de Motolinia. Montolinia's History..., 536 1260694), p. 274.

[18]Wilhelm Hamm. Das Weinbuch..., (865 1270771), p. 364.

[19]Father Joseph de Acosta. The Natural and Moral..., 590 1260782), p. 267.

[20]Jose de Acosta. Historia natural y moral de las ndias, Mexico: Fondo de Cultura Economica, 1940, p. 203.

which limited or prohibited Indian forced-labor in the Spanish colonies and which ordered the abolition of the encomiendas at the death of their present owners, Viceroy Mendoza assumed a dispensing power and suspended the operation of the king's edict in Mexico.[21] As late as 1590, the Viceroy of Mexico assigned Indians to work in vineyards.[22] The ordinance of 1601, forbidding the customary employ of Indians for the cultivation of vineyards,[23] was suspended as well. Within a few years the Crown was insisting only that the Indians employed in the vineyards not be payed in wine or chicha.[24]

Spanish viticultural attempts also took place on the Florida and Virginia coasts. The wild vines on the Florida coast "which grew vppon the trees that are next them, bringing forth grapes that are good to be eaten,"[25] were described as early as 1518. Those who returned from the Florida

---

[21] F. A. Kirkpatrick. The Spanish Conquistadores, (963$1270909), pp. 256 to 258. Appendix III, pp. 352-353. Alexander de Humboldt. Political Essay..., (814 1270151), p. 183.

[22] Fuentes para la historia del trabajo en Nueva Espana, Silvio Zavala and Maria Castelo (eds.). Mexico: Fondo de Cultura Economica, 1936, Vol. 3, p. 102.

[23] Recopilacion de leyes de los reynos de las Indias, Madrid: Consejo de las Hispanidad, 1943, lib. vi., tit. xiii, ley 6.

[24] Ibid., lib. vii, tit. xiii., ley 6.

[25] Jan Huyghen van Linschoten. Discours of Voyages..., (598$1260172), p. 218.

explorations of Fernando de Soto in 1537-38 described the land as "fertile, and bountiful in food, grapes, nuts and other fruits in Spain."[26]

In 1565, Petro Menendez de Aviles proposed to the King "the many and great profits that would acrue to Spain from the abundant wine of the country."[27] Juan de La Carrera noted, in 1572, on the coast of Florida (Virginia),

> ...a very beautiful vineyard as well laid out and ordered as the vineyards of Spain. It was located on sandy soil and the vines were laden with fair white grapes, large and ripe. These the Lord had prepared for us and we gave Him many thanks.[28]

---

[26]Lopez de Velasco, Geografia, pp. 179-80. Quoted in J. R. Jackson, Jr. "Early Florida...," (954$1280768), p. 98.
De Soto himself described the grapes of Terra Florida: "In the grapes there is onlie want of dressing: for though they bee big, they have great kirnell." [Don Ferdinando de Soto. "The Discovery...," (539 1260034), p. 169. Consult also "The Narrative of the Expedition...," (543 1260326), p. 271.]

[27]Pedro Menendez de Aviles to Philip II, October 15, 1565, Ruidiaz, La Florida, tomo ii, pp. 98 to 104. Quoted in Woodbury Lowery. The Spanish Settlements..., (901 1270299), Vol. 2, p. 213.

[28]Quoted in Clifford M. Lewis and Albert J. Loomie. The Spanish Jesuit Mission..., (953$1270042), pp. 138-39. Lewis and Loomie consider Juan La Carrera's description of the Florida coast as "a typical pious exaggeration met in his narrative." [Ibid., p. 141, footnote 18.] They identify the land as Strachey's Kecoughtan, an area along the Virginia coast.
Jennings Wise [Ye Kingdome of Accawmacke (911 1270059), p. 6 to 8] suggests that Kecoughtan is identical to the Virginia shore described by Verrazano in 1524. According to Jennings Wise, then, Verrazano's description of Kecoughtan would indicate that Lewis and Loomie erred grossly not only in misplacing the site of Verrazano's landfall, but also in considering Juan La Carrera's account of it an aggrandizement

Several years later, the Spanish cultivated vineyards in Florida. In 1577, Bartolome Martinez planted grape vines in Santa Elena.[29] Pedro Menendez Marques, in his portrayal of St. Augustine, in 1579, pictured abundant harvests of maize and the beginnings of "many of the fruits of Spain, such as figs, pomegranates, oranges, grapes in great quantity."[30] This promising commitment to viticulture was not sustained for two reasons: first, the royal government and missionaries of Florida specified that the soil was the

---

fact. The vineyard which La Carrera believed "the Lord had prepared" was, in fact, a product of Indian viticulture:

> Wee sawe in this Countrey many Vines growing naturally, which growing vp take hold of the trees, as they do in Lombardie, w^c if by husbandmen they were dressed in good order without all doubte they woulds yeelde excellent wines: for wee hauing oftentymes seene the fruite thereof dried, whiche was sweete and pleasaunt, and not differing from ours. Wee doe thinke that they [the Indians] doe esteeme the same, because that in euery place where they growe, they take away the vnder braunches growing rounde about, that the fruite thereof may ripen the better.
> [John Verrazanus [Verrazano]. "The Relation...," (524 1260096), p. 62].

[29]L. C. Gray. History of Agriculture..., (941 1270207), Vol. 1, p. 12.

[30]Marques is quoted extensively in Verne E. Chatelain. The Defenses..., (941$1270328), p. 118, footnote 14.
An interesting contrast to Marques' description is found in a 1575 report on the settlers of Florida. The findings reveal numerous complaints on poor soil quality and climate. No mention is made of viticultural attempts or of wine production. Consult "To the R. C. M. of the King...," (575 1261108), pp. 148, 149, 153, 155, 157 to 177.

inalienable property of the Indian and was not to be taken from him; and second, the encomienda system failed to gain a foothold in Florida.[31]

Royal Spanish provisionment policy and colonial self-sufficiency characterized early Spanish attempts at viticulture and wine production in the Americas. Spanish provisionment policy required that a favorable commodity balance in wine be maintained in Spain, and that its supply to the colonies not impair the availability of wine in the mother country. Wine scarcities in New Castile thus dictated limited wine exportation to the colonies in the early 1530's,[32] and encouraged colonial wine production which might augment the mother country's supply.

Accordingly, the 1503 edict ordering a royal monopoly of the wine trade[33] was set aside in Espanola in 1519.[34] In 1524,[35] viticulture was first encouraged in New Spain. These attempts to promote colonial wine production mitigated, but did not nullify, the wine shortages that persisted

---

[31] Ibid., p. 16. Francis Drake's razing of the San Augustine Spanish colony and his cutting down "the fruit trees, which were numerous and good," also discouraged Spanish husbandry attempts. [Pedro Marques. "Document No. 32...," (586 1260092), p. 164 and "Document No. 48...," (586 1260093), p. 191].

[32] Earl J. Hamilton. American Treasure..., (934 1271265), p. 192.

[33] Supra, Vol. 1, pp. 75-76.

[34] Ibid., Vol. 1, p. 76.

[35] Ibid., Vol. 1, p. 77.

in the Spanish colonies during the entire first half of the sixteenth century.[36] These shortages illustrate the dependence of the Spanish on wine for their daily beverage,[37] for fiestas, for medicinal use,[38] and for celebration of Mass.[39] They, and the burgeoning illicit foreign trade of the

---

[36]The wine shortage is exemplified by Diego Velasquez's reselling wine to Cortes' expedition before it embarked for Mexico. Epistolario..., op. cit., Vol. 1, p. 147.

[37]Earl Hamilton estimated that at least one-tenth of the normal expenses of the Spanish household during this period was for wine. Hamilton. American Treasure..., op. cit., p. 276.

[38]Arturo Chavez. Guadalajara en el siglo XVI, Guadalajara:..., p. 157. For the use of wine for medicinal purposes, particularly as a treacle, see the discussion of herbals Infra, Vol. 1, pp. 190 to 192, footnote 31.

[39]Without wine Mass could not be celebrated, a calamity which befell Valdivia's expedition to Chile, and a need which led the Crown to guarantee the supply of wine to monasteries in the New World. [Enrancisco A. Encina. Resumen de la historia de Chile, Santiago: Zig-zag, 1954, Vol. 1, p. 52. Also, Recopilacion, op. cit., lib. xviii., tit. xvii., ley 4.] The 1603 grant of Philip III, allowing monasteries and convents to produce wines [Recopilacion, op. cit., lib. viii., tit. iii., ley 1], was a relaxation of the Crown policy.

An interesting contrast to the Spanish is seen in the French missionaries of Brazil (1607). When faced with a shortage of wine with which to celebrate Mass, the French decided that "they would have no compunctions in falling back on a substitute," the customary beverage of the country, a drink made of cactus leaves. [Marc Lescarbot. The History..., (609$1260721), Vol. 1, pp. 186-187].

Spanish colonies,[40] reveal the inadequacy of the Spanish "fleet" method[41] in supplying the colonies.

A consequence of these shortages was the sale of wine in the colonies at premium prices, and a correlative inducement to produce colonial wine and to manufacture substitute beverages. The shortages particularly stimulated Peru, Chile and Brazil to produce wines.

It is uncertain when wine production originated in South America. Garcilaso El Inca, in 1538, reported he could not find in Mexico or Peru grapes like those in Spain.[42] A. Curtis Wilgus claims that Peru raised grapes and olives in about 1541; he does not, however, document this assertion.[43] The first vintage in Peru that can be documented was gathered in 1551, for at that time, not only

---

[40]Diego Ruiz de Vallejo. "Diego Ruiz...," (568$1260099), pp. 114-115.
Father Escobedo. "La Florida," pp. 218, 253b-254. Quoted in James W. Covington (ed.), Pirates, Indians..., (597$1260776), pp. 69, 96.
Lewes Roberts. The Merchants..., (637$1271191), Book II, p. 21.
Herbert Heaton. Economic History..., (948$1271238), pp. 269 to 272.

[41]Irene A. Wright (ed.). Spanish Documents..., (929 1270098), pp. 7 to 10.
Eli F. Heckscher. Mercantilism, (935$1270922), Vol. 1, pp. 343 to 345.

[42]Garcilaso El Inca. La Florida, Libro 2, Parte 1, pp. 580-verso, 590-recto. Quoted in Jackson, "Early Florida...," op. cit., p. 100.

[43]Wilgus. Colonial Hispanic..., op. cit., p. 320.

was the harvest legal, but it was reported and taxed for the Crown by local officials.[44] Within three years, the production of wine had spread to Chile, promoted by Pedro de Valdivia, who was inspired by the "obsessive idea of organizing a nation based on agriculture and grazing."[45]

By 1555, the culture of grapes had succeeded in Chile.[46] South Peru was producing wines by 1570;[47] this fact suggests a major expansion of the earlier Peruvian industry localized about Lima. Grapes grew the full year in vineyards of Piratininga, Brazil, "so laden that they bow to the ground...if they cut them everie moneth, they beare everie moneth Grapes successively."[48] These grapes were yielding wine in 1601.[49]

With such bountiful produce, the shortage of wine in the colonies promised to be overcome, not only in South America, but, by means of inter-colonial trade, in other Spanish colonies of the Americas as well. A 1569 directive,

---

[44]Robertson. Some Notes..., (927 1280677), p. 15. Emilio Romero. Historia economica de Peru, Buenos Aires: Sudamericana, 1949, p. 124.

[45]Encina. Resumen..., op. cit., pp. 82-83.

[46]Abiel Holmes. [The Annals..., (829$1270212), p. 79; p. 79, footnote 3], reports that in 1555, Bartholemew de Terrcas sent thirty Indians loaded with excellent grapes to Garcilaso de la Vega who recorded the event.

[47]Wilgus. Colonial Hispanic..., op. cit., p. 322.

[48]Manoel Da-Baya. "A Treatise of Brazil," (601$1260505), p. 502.

[49]Ibid.

secretly issued by Philip II to Viceroy Francisco de Toledo of Peru, forbade both planting new vines and replacing decayed vines.[50] This directive aimed to curtail Peruvian wine exportation to the Caribbean and New Spain markets.[51]

Despite the 1569 ruling, viticulture and wine production continued uninterrupted in Chile and Peru. Father Joseph de Acosta attested to this in his 1590 description of Spanish colonial wine trade:

> They carry wine out of Spaine, and from the Canaries, to all partes of the Indies, except Peru and the realme of Chile, where there are vines that yeelde excellent wine, which increase daily both in quantity, for that it is great riches in that country, and in beauty, for that they are become with time and practise more expert vine growers.[52]

By 1595, when it became clear that a complete prohibition of viticulture was unenforceable in the South American colonies, the clandestine planting in these colonies was made legal in the following royal instructions dispatched to the viceroys:

> The planting of vines in the Indies is prohibited by instructions to viceroys, and other cedulas and prohibitions, and the viceroys are ordered not to give license for new plantings or for the replacement of worn-out vines;

---

[50]Haring. Trade and Navigation..., op. cit., p. 126. Salvador de Madariaga. The Rise of the Spanish..., (947$1270015), p. 59.

[51]Woodrow Borah. Early Colonial Trade and Navigation Between Mexico and Peru, Berkeley: 1954, p. 93.

[52]De Acosta. The Natural and Moral..., op. cit., p. 267.

> nonetheless the inhabitants of Peru have planted many, and we could proceed against their owners for the crime of having violated our orders, and having usurped the lands where they have been planted.
>
> But out of our goodness and clemency, we order and command that all the owners and possessors of vines give and pay to us every two per-cent of the fruit that they take from them...the Viceroys and President-Governors shall give in our name titles giving the owners and possessors the privilege without limit of time...but as far as the planting of new vines is concerned, the old cedulas and instructions which prohibit this remain in force.[53]

Several years later, Philip III reiterated the 1595 directive. The reiteration, modeled after the original 1569 prohibition, was ratified by Viceroys Velazco and Montesclaros, who based their approval on "many reasons of importance, and principally because there is a sufficient supply of them [grapes and olives], which weakens trade and commerce with these regions."[54]

The 1595 prohibition of viticulture in the Indies, and its later renewal by Philip III, had but a temporary restrictive effect on the islands' viticulture and wine production. Contrary to De Acosta's assertion that "there growes no wine nor grapes in the Ilandes, nor in Tierra Firme,"[55] vines flourished in the West Indies. Richard

---

[53]Recopilacion. op. cit., lib. xviii., tit. xii., ley 4, cited in Hubert Bancroft. History of Mexico, (900$1270695), p. 613. Translation by Matthew D. Edel (see Infra, Vol. 1, p. 94, footnote 81).

[54]Recopilacion. op. cit., lib. vi., tit. xii., ley 4.

[55]De Acosta. The Natural and Moral..., op. cit., p. 267.

VVilles, writing about 1577, described the great trees of the West Indies as having entwined about them,

> certayne vynes, whiche were so laden with blacke grapes of pleasaunt taste, that they satysfied more then fyftye persons whiche ate them fyl thereof.[56]

In 1596, George Earle of Cumberland described in detail the wild grapes of the Indies,[57] and, the hiatus in viticulture current in the islands immediately following the 1595 prohibition. He declared:

> ...yet have they good store of wines, indeed brought in from other countries; not that this Iland will not nourish Vines: for I have seene some grow here In Puerto Rico very flourishingly. But I have heard the King will not suffer them to plant and dresse Vineyards, as a matter of policie.[58]

Only a few years later, the "great questionary" on the Indies assumed lawful the cultivation of vines, and the production and trade of wine.[59] The Crown even established a prize "to the first who introduced some fruit of Spain such as corn, barley, wine or oil into the new peoples [the Indians] of America," in 1604.[60]

---

[56]Richard VVilles. The History of Trauayle..., (577 1260173), pp. 205-206.

[57]George Earle of Cumberland. The Voyage..., (596 1260504), p. 94.

[58]Ibid., p. 98.

[59]Coleccion de Documentos Inedites..., Madrid: 1864-1884, (42 vols.) Vol. 9, p. 69, questions 180-184. Quoted in De Madariaga. The Rise..., op. cit., p. 345, footnote 8.

[60]Provisiones Reales para el Gobierno de las Indias, MS J 49, 2989, Biblioteca Nacional, Madrid, and Coleccion de Documentos Inedites, Vol. 6, pp. 487 and 491. These sources are quoted in De Madariaga. The Rise..., op. cit., p. 346, footnote 9.

Crown policy to limit or prohibit the wine industry was reiterated more frequently in New Spain than in any other Spanish colony. The Marques de Casafuerte prohibited the manufacture of liquors which could hurt the consumption of "Caldos de Castilla" [The Wine of Castille]; the Viceroy, Archbishop Bizarron reiterated the prohibition in 1737.[61] In 1761, Viceroy Cruillas circulated an order prohibiting vineyard planting.[62] In Parras, the most productive wine region in Mexico, wine output nevertheless rose from 320 arrobas in 1617 to several thousand arrobas in 1760.[63]

Throughout the yet later colonial period, the prohibition of viticulture was frequently mentioned in Mexico; its enforcement, however, was only sporadic as the private judicial system of the _acordada_ was assigned to the task of prevention. In 1802, the Viceroy of Mexico was barred from granting any licenses for planting or processing grapes for wine.[64] Alexander de Humboldt, visiting Spain in 1814, reported that:

---

[61] Lucas Alaman. _Historia de Mejico_, Mexico: 1849, Vol. 1, Adiciones, 74.

[62] Lillian E. Fisher. _The Background of the Revolution for Mexican Independence_, Boston: Christopher, 1934, p. 145.

[63] Robert C. West. _The Mining Community in Northern New Spain_: The Parral Mining District, Berkeley: University of California, 1949, pp. 80, 127. [An arroba is approximately 16 liters.]

[64] Fisher. _The Background_..., _op. cit._, p. 145.
Alaman. _Historia_..., _op. cit._, Vol. 1, p. 105.

> During my stay at Mexico the viceroy received orders from the court to pull up the vines (*arancar las cepas*) in the northern provinces of Mexico, because the merchants of Cadiz complained of a diminution in the consumption of Spanish wines. Happily this order, like many others given by the ministers, was never executed.[65]

In South America, Chile overtook Peru as the continent's most important wine producer. Chilean exports were shipped to Peru; they were transshipped through Mendoza overland to Buenos Aires and Paraguay. As winemaking had become an economically important Chilean industry,[66] the Spanish government issued a royal decree at the close of the 17th century suspending the prohibition on the planting of vineyards in Chile--a prohibition that appears never to have been enforced.[67] The Crown's Peruvian policy, in contrast, was one of restriction. Examples of such a policy are the 1609 ordinance forbidding the use of *mitayos* (Mita Indians) in the production of wine[68] and the 1614 and 1615 prohibitions on the export of wine or olives from Peru to Guatemala or Panama[69]--a prohibition replaced in 1718 by a 30,000

---

[65] Humboldt. *Political Essay...*, *op. cit.*, p. 469.

[66] Francisco Frias. *Historia de Chile*, Vol. 1, Santiago: Nascimiento, 1947, p. 273.

[67] Miguel L. Amunategui. *El cabildo de Santiago desde 1573 hasta 1581*, Santiago: Imprenta Nacional, 1890, p. 173.

[68] Bailey W. Diffie. *Latin-American Civilization...*, (945$1270692), p. 317.

[69] Romero. *Historia...*, *op. cit.*, p. 170.

botija (short-necked jug) limit on wine export.[70] The decline of the Peruvian wine industry relative to that of Chile, did not, however, represent an absolute decline in Peruvian wine production. This may be surmised from a 1774 order directed to Viceroy Amat commanding the reiteration and enforcement of the prohibition of viticulture in Peru.[71]

Several hypotheses have been advanced concerning the continual violation of Spanish viticultural and wine production prohibitions in the colonies. They seek to explain how colonial wine production thrived despite these prohibitions. The consensus is that the bans on viticulture and wine production were never meant to be enforced uniformly.

Alexander de Humboldt claimed that the Crown tolerated the commerce of wines and indigenous oils in Peru and Chile "only because those colonies, situated beyond Cape Horn, are frequently ill provisioned from Europe, and the effect of vexatious measures is dreaded in provinces so remote."[72] Clarence Haring interprets the relaxation of the 1569 prohibition as a concession to the Peruvian vineyard owners, the vineyards having been "planted with the tacit consent of the king, and to destroy them would have entailed infinite

---

[70]Haring. Trade and Navigation..., op. cit., p. 126.

[71]Diffie. Latin-American..., op. cit., p. 348.
Romero. Historia..., op. cit., p. 126.

[72]Humboldt. Political Essay..., op. cit., p. 469.

hardship and injustice."[73] Haring points to various alternatives that were employed:

> that the Indians be permitted to use wine instead of chicha, and so consume the local product; that all Peruvian wine put up for sale be bought by the royal exchequer; that...in 1614 and 1615 it was forbidden to export oil or wine to Panama or Guatemala regions which could be supplied from Spain.[74]

Professor Bailey W. Diffie presents a more articulated version of Dr. Haring's hypothesis:

> ...it would seem that the ban [on wine production] was never meant to be absolute, but merely to limit such privilege to those holding royal license, and to protect them from competition. The colonial system was one of privilege and licensing. The <u>right</u> to trade did not exist; only the <u>privilege</u> where granted by the Crown.[75]

The wording of the 1595 prohibition[76] suggests that Philip II considered the vineyards of Peru to exist by privilege of the Crown. The suspension of the ordinance of 1601 forbidding the assignment of Indians to cultivate vineyards in Mexico[77] and the character of the ownership of the Parras

---

[73]Haring. <u>Trade and Navigation</u>..., <u>op</u>. <u>cit</u>., p. 126.

[74]<u>Ibid</u>.

[75]Diffie. <u>Latin-American</u>..., <u>op</u>. <u>cit</u>., pp. 316-317.

[76]<u>Supra</u>, Vol. 1, pp. 87-88.

[77]<u>Ibid</u>., Vol. 1, p. 80.

estates,[78] the most important Mexican winemaking estates, support the belief that wine was produced by people in the king's favor. In 1796, a tax of six pesos per barrel was levied upon _aguardientes_ (a grape brandy), despite a prohibition in New Spain against its manufacture.[79] Similarly, in 1802, when the king reiterated his ban on planting or processing grapes for wine, he himself granted licenses to plant vines to several favored applicants.[80]

For each of these affirmations of Dr. Diffie's assertion there are examples to the contrary.[81] An indifference to

---

[78]At Parras the estates passed to daughters who married the governor, or some other important official, in the region, thereby insuring a continuation of royal favor and a reluctance to thwart wine production on the estates.

Vito A. Robles. _Coahuila y Texas en la epoca colonial_, Mexico, 1938, chapter 19.
Pedro Tamaron y Romeral, _Demostracion del Vastisimo de la Nueva Vizcaya_, p. 19, note 25.

[79]Diffie. _Latin-American_..., _op_. _cit_., p. 349.

[80]Atanasio G. Saravia. _Apuntes para la historia de la Nueva Vizcaya_. Mexico: Reveces, 1938, pp. 255-256, 292.
Robles. _Coahuila_..., _op_. _cit_., pp. 143 to 148.

[81]The author is indebted to Mr. Matthew D. Edel, a graduate student at Yale University, who generously made available to him a paper written for Dr. Diffie which challenged Dr. Diffie's assertion quoted above. Mr. Edel's conclusions about the influence of Spanish prices on the enforcement of viticultural and wine production prohibitions in the Spanish-American colonies, parallel those of this dissertation. That fact became known after the author had delivered an abstract of his dissertation at the 25th Annual Convention of the Economic History Association (September 1-3, 1965), a conference attended by Mr. Edel.

The researches of the author and of Mr. Edel were done independently, although the author did revise his writings to include some references to Spanish sources made available to him by Mr. Edel's paper.

privilege is seen in the Crown's 1604 offer to introduce viticulture to the natives of the Indies.[82] The New Spain viticultural prohibitions of 1737 and 1761 were, impartial as well.[83] The 1774 Peruvian order reiterating the prohibition of viticulture[84] did not suggest exclusions by means of royal favor. The most telling counterargument to Dr. Diffie's thesis is that the Viceroy of Mexico withheld royal permission from Hidalgo to make wine.[85] Chilean policy, too, offers no indications of patronage.[86]

Such instances attesting to the insensibility of Spanish policy to claims of privilege suggest the need for a more

---

[82] Supra, Vol. 1, p. 89.

[83] Ibid., Vol. 1, p. 90.

[84] Ibid., Vol. 1, p. 92.

[85] Arthur H. Noll and A. Philip McMahon. The Life and Times of Miguel Hidalgo y Costilla, Chicago: McClurg, 1910, p. 35.

Luis C. Ledon. Hidalgo, Mexico: 1948, Vol. 1, p. 90.

Hidalgo's denial is important evidence supporting the theory that prohibition of wine production in the Spanish colonies was a major cause of the independence movement in the Spanish empire. This theory is proposed by:

A. Stuart Chisholm. The Independence of Chile, Boston: French and Company, 1911, p. 26.

Fisher. The Background..., op. cit., p. 144.

Carlos. M. de Bustamente. Cuadro Historico de la Revolucion Mexicana, Mexico: Navarro, 1854, p. 67.

The material of this chapter portraying the permissiveness of Spanish colonial viticultural policy should hasten the demise of the Chisholm-Fisher-Bustamente theory.

[86] Supra, Vol. 1, p. 91.

reliable evaluation of Spanish colonial wine policies than that offered by Dr. Diffie. The new approach would relate economic conditions in Spain to Spanish colonial policy and its economic implications. It would explain the fundamental causality of the prohibitions, an issue, heretofore, not sufficiently developed. Such an approach is presented in this writing. It is the hypothesis here that provisionment and fiscalism, and not the protection of privilege, were the key motivating factors in Spanish colonial policy.[87]

Fiscalism expressed itself in excises and other taxes foisted upon colonial wine production and upon the shipping and sale of Spanish produce. The distribution of Spanish wine in the colonies was organized, ostensibly, to give the mother country a monopolist's price and to bolster royal (public) finance. Imported wine was held in government warehouses; traders wishing to buy wine for local sale, at fixed prices and in fixed measures, were required to purchase licenses.[88] Fiscalism, rather than the protection of Spanish wine growers, however, was clearly the purpose of taxing local wine production. Thus, in Peru, locally produced wine was taxed from the first vintage in 1551.[89] Mexican officials instituted a _sisa_ (excise tax) on wine

---

[87]The hypothesis of Commodity Mercantilism applies equally to Dutch, French and English colonial policy. Consult _Infra_, Vol. 1, pp. 112ff.

[88]West. _The Mining Community_..., _op. cit._, p. 80.

[89]_Supra_, Vol. 1, p. 86; p. 86, footnote 44.

before 1575.[90] A two percent usufruct on Peruvian viticulture was ordered in 1595.[91] In the eighteenth century, the wine of Mendoza was subjected to a tax of one real per botija.[92] Taxes were levied in 1771 and 1796 on prohibition violators.[93] They demonstrated the increasing importance of fiscalism considerations in later Spanish policy.

Provisionment expressed itself first in its commodity availability aspect, and then later in its favorable balance of trade element. During the first half of the sixteenth century, colonial demand for Spanish wines, coupled with wine shortages in Spain, caused the colonial wine trade policy of the Spanish to hinge more on considerations of

---

[90]Silvio Zavalo and Maria Castelo (eds.). Fuentes para la historia del trabajo en Nueva Espana, 8 vols. Mexico: Fonso de Cultura Economica, 1936, Vol. 1, p. 5.

[91]Recopilacion. op. cit., lib. xviii., tit. xvii., ley 4.

Charles E. Chapman [Colonial Hispanic..., (933$1270018), p. 155] errs in saying that "the Peruvian [wine] industry was allowed to continue, under heavy penalties" following the 1595 edict. There was but one penalty: the two percent usufruct. Its punitive effect was negligible.

[92]Zavalo and Castelo (eds.). Fuentes..., op. cit., Vol. 1, p. 5. [A botija is a squat bottle.]

[93]The 1771 six percent tax on total value of product was levied on violators of the Mexican prohibition on grape cultivation [Infra, Vol. 1, p. 109]. A tax of six pesos per barrel was imposed on violators of the aguardiente prohibition of 1796 [Alaman. Historia de Mejico, op. cit., Vol. 1, Appendix].

The low rates of these and prior taxes on colonial wine and aguardiente production indicate that the purpose of these taxes was local fiscalism. Considerably higher tax rates would have been imposed had the purpose of the taxes been to protect Spanish wine growers.

availability than those of gains through trade.[94] In the latter half of the sixteenth century, and thereafter, it was the favorable balance of trade aspect of provisionment that was stressed. The issue was the effect of clandestine and legalized (Peru post 1595) colonial viticultural attempts on the wine trade of the mother country.

The Commodity Mercantilism theory contends that falling domestic wine prices encouraged prohibitions on the production of colonial wine. It proposes that Spanish grape growers, producers and merchants of wine favored their enforcement in periods of overproduction. In these periods, the wine interests in Spain would induce the Crown to hinder colonial competitors, and thus to further the marketing of Spanish wines in the colonies. As Spanish royalty was generally attentive to such interests, periods of restrictions on colonial viticulture and wine production paralleled periods when Spanish wine prices were not advancing as rapidly as the general price level in Spain.[95] Analogously,

---

[94] Supra, Vol. 1, pp. 75 to 80.

[95] Spanish merchants were probably more sensitive to changes in their total income over time, than to changes in wine prices. Thus, price variation itself need not have signaled discontent on the part of Spanish merchants: high prices accompanying a small vintage or low prices resulting from a bountiful yield, in so far as they produced the same total income, were probably a matter of relative indifference to the merchant. Only the sequence of years in which prices clearly reflect a change in the relative share of national income received by the vendors are, therefore, significant in this study. Hence, peak price years, such as 1549 and 1614--which undoubtedly resulted from crop

periods of regulatory non-enforcement or other concessions to colonial wine interests parallel periods when Spanish wine prices were rising as rapidly or faster than the general price level in Spain.

A chronological comparison of the price movements for wine in Andalusia, New Castile, Old Castile-Leon, and Valencia, and the timings of prohibitions on viticulture and wine production in the Spanish colonies confirm this hypothesis. Several distinct periods are identified in which declining wine prices (relative to the general price level) parallel movements to institute, or enforce prohibitions. The data span the years 1500 to 1800.[96]

---

failure--are dismissed, as are individual low price years such as 1581 and 1602 (New Castile prices).

Individual years of low prices and high prices may reflect, as well, exceptionally high and low quality vintages. Generally, there was a downward price inelasticity in poor vintage years as the demand for wine had always to be met from the production of that year, and virtually no wine was set aside from year to year during the period of this study. Wine was drunk as new wine, or, at best, "racked" only through one winter.

Statutory regulation of the sale of the vintage is discussed briefly by Earl Hamilton in American Treasure..., op. cit., p. 148, footnote 1.

[96]Ibid., pp. 319, 335 to 339, 358 to 369 (Andalusia wine prices 1503 to 1650); pp. 320, 321, 340 to 347, 370 to 375 (New Castile wine prices 1501 to 1650); pp. 322 to 327, 348 to 353, 376 to 383 (Old Castile-Leon wine prices 1503 to 1650); pp. 328 to 334, 354 to 357, 384 to 389 (Valencia wine prices 1501 to 1650); pp. 222, 223 and 224, or in graphic form pp. 226, 228, 230, 232, 235, 237, 241, 273 (General price level 1501 to 1650).

Hamilton. War and Prices in Spain 1651-1800, Cambridge: Harvard University Press, 1947, pp. 238 to 241, 246.

Throughout the first half of the sixteenth century, wine prices in New Castile, Old Castile-Leon, and Valencia advanced more rapidly than commodity prices, and more rapidly than the general price level.[97] Earl Hamilton attributes this to the heavy exports of wine to America which "appear to have been largely responsible for the phenomenal upswing in wine prices."[98] He neglects, however, to recount the Crown's active role in encouraging viticulture in Espanola (1519) and New Spain (1524) to nurture colonial self-sufficiency and to assure the availability of wine in Spain. Thus, he erroneously assumes a dearth of colonial production, ascribing this to "the prohibition of the planting of grape vines and olive trees in Peru...the great length of time required to bring vineyards and olive trees to fruitage, the ineptitude of indigenous labor for the industries, and the engrossment of the early Spanish immigrants in the quest for treasure."[99] This apparent

---

to 249, 254 to 257 (New Castile wine prices 1651 to 1800); pp. 174 to 176 (General commodity index 1651 to 1800).

[97]Hamilton. American Treasure..., op. cit., pp. 226, 228, 230, 232, 235, 237, 241, 273.

[98]Ibid., p. 299, footnote 2.

[99]Ibid., pp. 299-300, footnote 2.
Earl Hamilton's error is threefold: (1) The author finds no evidence of a prohibition of viticulture in Peru during the first half of the sixteenth century; Dr. Hamilton fails to document the existence of any prohibition; (2) The maturation periods for vines and olive trees are not comparable--a vine cutting can bear full fruit in from three to five years, whereas an olive tree requires no less than fifteen years from date of planting; (3) the encomienda

"dearth" of colonial production represented, in fact, the prodigious consumption of the colonists. Spain supplied wine, when available, to meet the extensive colonial demand--a demand which exceeded colonial production.

Additional evidence in support of the Commodity Mercantilism thesis may be adduced by examining fluctuating Spanish wine prices from 1550 to 1650 to each of the four regions[100] for which price data are available:

New Castile: Wine prices, after rising from a low point in 1551 to a peak in 1564, declined steadily until 1572. In 1573, these prices rose, and remained for two decades at higher than pre-1564 levels. Beginning in 1593, they trended downward for a decade, recovering in 1603. From 1603 until 1650, the advance of wine prices exceeded the rise in the general price level. Wine prices advanced slightly behind the general price level from 1650 until the price collapse of 1680;

---

system of Mexico showed the suitability of indigenous labor at viticulture. It was the enforcement in Peru of the 1542 prohibition of encomiendas, [Kirkpatrick. The Spanish..., op. cit., pp. 257, 258], not the ineptitude of the Indians, that prevented the extensive use of the Indian labor.

[100]Although grape growers, producers and merchants of wine in New Castile exercised the greatest influence on royal policy, their counterparts in Andalusia, Old Castile-Leon and Valencia, at times, too, significantly affected Crown policy. The 1609 expulsion of the Moriscos from Valencia (Infra, Vol. 1, p.102), and the 1737 Castilean demands from enforcements of Mexican wine production prohibitions (Infra, Vol. 1, p.108) support this assertion.

Old Castile-Leon: In contrast to New Castile, wine prices did not break at the mid-century. Old Castile-Leon wine prices continued at levels below their 1551 peak until 1562 when a decade of low prices commenced. This decade was followed in 1575 by ten years of relative price stability at high levels and then, from 1585, by rapidly advancing wine prices. Wine prices from 1591 to 1596 were more than a third lower than those of the five previous years. Except for the severe decline during 1615 to 1618, Old Castile-Leon wine prices climbed more rapidly than the general price level until 1650;

Valencia: The prices of wine, moving over a narrower range than those in New Castile, Old Castile-Leon, or Andalusia, continued their gradual trend upward from the mid-sixteenth century to 1564. In 1564, wine prices entered a period of moderate decline which was broken in 1573. Valencia wine prices, thereafter, steadied to 1587, rose to a peak in 1593, and dropped substantially for the years 1594 to 1598. Wine prices again peaked in 1604, but declined steadily for four years thereafter to less than half their 1604 level. This decline may have influenced the decision to expel the Moriscos from Valencia in 1609.[101] The expulsion of those wine producers, however, did not have any noticeable effect on Valencia wine prices which failed to

---

[101] Hamilton. American Treasure..., op. cit., p. 304.

advance at a more rapid rate after the Moriscosian expulsion than they did before 1604;

Andalusia: Wine price data before 1600 are incomplete. They sketch the doubling of wine prices between 1559 and 1567. In 1569, the price plummeted to 1559 levels. In 1571, it was to attain a new high. A similar pattern is in evidence between 1591 and 1602; wine prices rose from 1591 to 1594, fell to less than one-half of their 1594 level in 1595 and 1596, and attained their former highs in 1602, after several years of severe price fluctuation. Wine prices between 1602 and 1650 fluctuated widely. They rose to peak levels in the 1640's, although they declined substantially in the last four years of that decade.

The analysis of wine price data for New Castile, Old Castile-Leon, Valencia and Andalusia offers impressive evidence in support of the Commodity Mercantilism theory.

New Castile wine prices declined steadily from 1564 to 1572; Old Castile-Leon wine prices declined for a decade from 1563; Valencia wine prices declined from 1564 to 1573; Andalusia wine prices hit bottom in 1569. In that year, Philip II issued to Viceroy Francisco de Toledo a directive prohibiting the planting of new vines and the replacing of decayed vines in Peru, and all vine planting in the Indies.

The Commodity Mercantilism hypothesis would indicate that the turnaround of wine prices from 1571 to 1573 (Andalusia--1571, Old Castile-Leon--1572, New Castile and

Valencia--1573) and their subsequent rise during the ensuing twenty-year period were the primary reasons that the 1569 edict was not followed immediately, and consequently fell into disuse.

For the decade 1593 to 1603, wine prices declined, whereas the general price level rose rapidly. Hence, wine interests again appealed to the Crown concerning the intrusion of colonial wine production on Spanish wine markets. By 1593, however, the production of wine in the colonies already had reached sizable proportions. Thus, the 1595 edict, designed to inhibit wine production in the colonies by prohibiting new plantings or replacing vines in decay, was of little immediate consequence. Additional measures were designed to suppress wine production in the Spanish colonies. These included taxes on wine making and wine shipping,[102] prohibiting the use of _mitayos_,[103] prohibiting Peruvian wine shipments to Central America,[104] and prohibiting the making of palm wine in Mexico in 1610 so as to encourage colonial consumption of colonial wines.[105] As Spanish wine prices rose in the second decade of the 17th century and maintained their upward trend until the price

---

[102]_Supra_, Vol. 1, p. 97.

[103]_Ibid_., Vol. 1, p. 91.

[104]_Ibid_.

[105]Diffie. _Latin-American_..., _op_. _cit_., p. 96.

collapse of 1680, the edict of 1595 and the prohibitions of 1601, 1609, 1614 and 1615 gradually became dead-letter. These restrictive measures shared the fate of their predecessor, the edict of 1569. In both instances, the periods of regulatory nonenforcement paralleled periods when Spanish wine prices were rising as rapidly as, or faster than, the general price level in Spain.

Earl Hamilton suggests that the moderation of the advance in wine prices during the second half of the sixteenth century is attributable either to the development of colonial wine production or to the conversion of Spanish wheat lands into vineyards, a conversion of land which may account for the 1650-1700 advance in Spanish wheat prices.[106] He suggests that the decline in the fruit-nut prices after 1580, particularly 1610-1650, was probably a result of the sluggish, downward adjustment by fruit-nut growers to the decreased demand of a Spanish "depopulation."[107] Grape production, as well, must have failed to respond immediately to the downward price pressures of the declining population, for bearing grape vines, similar to fruit and nut trees in their extreme longevity, were not readily withdrawn from

---

[106]Hamilton. American Treasure..., op. cit., pp. 299-300, footnote 2.

[107]Ibid., pp. 236-237. Dr. Hamilton attributes depopulation to the economic decline in Spain during the seventeenth century.

production. A surplus of wine should have resulted, weakening wine prices during the 1610-1650 period. That wine prices advanced more rapidly than the general price level during the portion of the seventeenth century prior to the run-away inflation of 1663-1680 is largely attributable to a divergence between wages and prices which offset the downward price effects of the declining population. Wages during nearly all of the 1600-1650 period advanced more rapidly than prices.[108] The average wage earner, therefore, enjoyed a period of relative plenty during which his expenditures for wine appear to have increased both relatively and absolutely.

Another factor influencing the advance of wine prices during the second and third quarters of the seventeenth century was the popularity of Spanish wines. They were in demand not only in the Spanish colonies but in Europe as well. A 1787 writer[109] discussing England in the era of Charles I gives the following account of British wine tastes:

> ...the best French wines in those times sold at a much lower price than the best Spanish wines did; and this difference held pretty near the

---

[108]Ibid., pp. 272, 273.

[109][Adam Anderson.] An Historical..., (787 1271180), p. 351.

> same in the reign of his son King Charles II and (such is the humour of the world) until the high duty laid on wines from France brought them into high esteem: ever since which period, French wines have been in much greater esteem than Spanish or Portugal wines.

After the price collapse of 1680, New Castile wine prices fluctuated over a wider range than the general price level but, on the whole, remained in line with it until 1760. Wine prices, however, remained markedly behind the general price level when it advanced rapidly toward its apex in 1797. According to Earl Hamilton,

> "new Castilian wine prices, based on small purchases at retail, advanced very little; and brandy, or distilled wine, moved horizontally throughout the eighteenth century. In the other three regions, [109] wine prices, based on wholesale transactions, oscillated violently from year to year; but the trend was not clearly upward before the 1780's. The great increase in vineyards and possible improvements in the art of wine-making apparently neutralized the upward pressure upon prices resulting from monetary depreciation and from increased consumption at home and abroad."[110]

According to Commodity Mercantilism theory, a distinct turnabout in Spanish royal policy concerning the enactment or enforcement of colonial wine regulations should occur around 1760. Such a reversal does, in fact, occur. It reflects the declining relative price of wine after 1760.

---

[110]Hamilton. War and Prices..., op. cit., pp. 180-181.

New Castile is the only region for which wine price data are available for the 1650-1800 period. The above quotation is the total amount of information on Andalusia, Old Castile-Leon, and Valencia wine prices 1650-1800. Ibid., pp. 100, 101.

From 1680 to 1760 the researcher finds a paucity of regulations unfavorable to colonial wine interests; royal edicts, such as the 1718 legalization of Peruvian wine exports,[111] even appear to favor the colonial American wine industries. The one notable exception--the 1737 prohibition issued by Viceroy Bizarron on the manufacture of liquors in Mexico that could hurt the consumption of the "Caldos de Castilla" [wine of Castile]--[112]reinforces the Commodity Mercantilism thesis. It came directly after a short slump in the price of Castilian wine.[113]

From 1760 until at least 1814 wine prices advanced less than the general price level in Spain, thus paralleling the enactment of prohibitions thwarting colonial viticultural and wine production ventures. Enforcement of these prohibitions was lax as colonial officials sought more the welfare of their own regions than the implementation of royal policy. The intendant of Guanajuato, for example, was promoting the cultivation of vineyards throughout this period. The royal decree was never read at Celaya.[114]

---

[111]Supra, Vol. 1, pp. 91-92.

[112]Ibid., Vol. 1, p. 90.

[113]Alaman. Historia de Mejico, op. cit., Vol. 1, Adiciones, 74.

[114]Fisher. The Background..., op. cit., p. 144.
Alaman. Historia de Mejico, op. cit., Vol. 1, Adiciones, 75-76.

In 1761, Viceroy Cruillas issued an order prohibiting the planting of vineyards in New Spain.[115] The ineffectiveness of this order is indicated by a suggestion of Ortia de Landazuri in 1771 that the prohibition of grape cultivation in Mexico be renewed, and that violators pay a six percent tax.[116] In 1774, instructions were sent to Viceroy Amat of Peru to republish earlier prohibitions against Peruvian viticulture and to enforce them.[117]

The opening of direct trade between Spain and Buenos Aires in 1781 was at least a significant means of creating a new market for Spanish wine at the expense of the colonial product. Mendoza, the supplier of wine to the port city of Buenos Aires, found her product undersold: sea transport costs from Spain were lower than the cost of hauling wine overland from Mendoza. The Bishop of Mendoza petitioned the Crown to prohibit the exportation of Spanish wines to Buenos Aires; Charles III, however, turned down his request.[118]

Mexican viticultural prohibitions were repeatedly ordered by the ministers between 1802 and 1814. These

---

[115] Fisher. The Background..., op. cit., p. 145.

[116] Ibid.
Jose M. Perez. "La publicacion del reglamento de comercio libre a Indias," Annuario de Estudios Americanos IV (1947), p. 647.

[117] Romero. Historia..., op. cit., p. 126.

[118] Pedro S. Martinez. Historia economica de Mendoza durante el virreinato, Madrid: 1961, p. 293.

orders, like many other executive orders designed to curtail the colonial vintage were never enforced.[119]

This discussion has concentrated upon provisionment's balance-of-trade aspect--that aspect on which the Crown primarily focused from 1550 to at least 1814. It has emphasized, as well, that measures designed to achieve immediate revenue for Spain's colonial governments at times directly countered Crown provisionment policy.

The Spanish shift between the objectives of provisionment and fiscalism, as between the availability and balance-of trade aspects of provisionment itself, distinguishes Spanish colonial viticultural policy from that of the other European states. The economic objectives of these other states demanded a more consistent application of a single policy approach. Thus, the Dutch did not at any time encourage colonial attempts at wine production, for they had a supply of wine through entrepot trade. Similarly, the French sought to discourage colonial viticulture to assure a market for home production. The English, in contrast, continually strove to promote colonial viticulture both to thwart colonial balance-of-trade losses and, hopefully, to develop a source of wine supply. Spanish competition in economic, military and political spheres strongly influenced the policies of the Dutch, French and English until the early seventeenth century. Spain's role, thereafter, was

---

[119]Supra, Vol. 1, pp. 90 to 93.

imited to a market for the exports of these European states nd as a source for their raw materials, wines, oils and ruits. Accordingly, the policies of these countries volved independently of any major Spanish influence.

CHAPTER IV

The Dutch and the French Experiences

The Netherlands was at once a trade hub, a warehouse, and a processing center for wine and virtually all other commodities. As Daniel Defoe aptly remarked,

> The Dutch must be understood as they really are, the _Carryers of the World_, the middle Persons, in Trade, the Factors and Brokers of Europe: that, as is said above, they _buy_ to _sell_ again, _take_ in to _send_ out: and the Greatest Part of their vast Commerce consists in being supply'd from all Parts of the World, that they may supply all the world again.[1]

"All kinde of staples, of corne, of wine...not to feed home-bred consumption, but to maintain trade..."[2] entered Dutch ports. Antwerp and then Amsterdam were the primary wine ports.

In 1491, Antwerp, instead of Bruges, was chosen as the Flemish staple town for wines.[3] Its importance grew

---

[1]Daniel Defoe. _A Plan of English Commerce_, London: 1728, p. 192.

[2]Edward Misselden. _The Circle of Commerce_..., (623 1271257), p. 135.

[3]Andre Simon. _The History of the Wine Trade in England_, London: The Holland Press, 1964. [1906 edition reprint], Vol. 2, p. 202.
Hans Hartmeyer. _Der Weinhandel_..., (905 1270535), pp. 17 to 27.

so rapidly that, at the close of the following century, Antwerp had become the largest wine mart of the world. A great abundance and variety of wines were exported from there to England and other countries.[4]

When the importance of Antwerp as a commercial center declined in the late sixteenth century,[5] that of Amsterdam began its ascent.[6] Tobias Gentleman complained in 1614 of the usurpation of the English Bordeaux fleet: "this last yeare, now, the Hollanders themselues haue also gotten that [wine] trade..."[7] By 1700, Amsterdam was "the staple market about which international trade and finance revolved."[8] It also was a major wine port and wine entrepot center, for, especially in times of war or trade restriction, European states satisfied their demand for French, Spanish and German

---

[4]Andreas Bacci. De Naturali Vinorvm Historia, Rome: Nicola Muzio, 1596, p. 350 cited in Simon. The History..., op. cit., Vol. 2, p. 202, footnote 4.

[5]Herbert Heaton. Economic History of Europe, (1948$1271238), pp. 273-274.
R. W. K. Hinton. "The Mercantile System...," (1955$1280893), p. 287.
Shepard B. Clough. The Economic Development..., (1959$1271239), pp. 187 to 189.

[6]Adam Smith. An Inquiry...Wealth of Nations..., (1776 1270256), pp. 446, 447, 454-455.
Heaton. Economic History..., op. cit., pp. 274, 281.
Charles Andrews. The Colonial Period..., (938 1270950), Vol. 4, p. 30.

[7]Tobias Gentleman. England's VVay to VVin..., (1614 1261098), p. 35.

[8]Charles Wilson. Anglo-Dutch Commerce and Finance in the Eighteenth Century, Cambridge: University Press, 1941, p. 4.

wines through trade with Amsterdam and other Dutch staple trade centers. The Anglo-Dutch wine trade amply illustrates the importance of the Netherlands in the industry.

When, in 1626, "The Privy Council...promulgated a regulation which prohibits the importation of every description of French goods...,"[9] English merchants went on importing French and other wines largely through Flemish or Dutch agents. Strict enforcement of the 1626 prohibition was impossible: the English merchant marine was not sufficiently large to cope with the entire import trade; and, the English, accustomed to French wines, were loath to forego this preference. Hence, evolved the frequent application for "permissions" sanctioning the import of wine to England in foreign vessels[10] and the establishment, by 1628, of English factors in Holland who imported wines from France and re-exported them to England.[11]

---

[9] Salvetti Correspondence quoted in Simon. The History..., op. cit., Vol. 3, p. 26.
Calendar of State Papers: Domestic..., (547 1221117), Vol. 1, p. 511, item 131 [Dec.?] 1626; p. 523, item 31 [1626?].

[10] Calendar of State Papers: Domestic..., (547 1221117), Vol. 2: p. 1, item 1 [1 Jan. 1627]; p. 3, item 20 [3 Jan. 1627]; p. 8, item 60 [7 Jan. 1627]; p. 40, item 40 [[Jan.] 1627]; p. 63, item 64 [2 Feb. 1627]; p. 264, item 54 [20 July 1627]; Vol. 3: p. 33, item 16 [22 March 1628]; p. 217, item 26 [18 July 1628]; p. 237, item 31 [29 July 1628].
Simon. The History..., op. cit., Vol. 3, pp. 27 to 37.

[11] Ibid. [Simon]. Vol. 3, pp. 32-33; p. 33, footnote *

An attempt to enforce the Navigation Act in 1651 again revealed the extensive English dependence upon the Dutch for wines. The 1651 Act, aimed at thwarting Dutch maritime supremacy by restricting English imports to commodities solely grown and manufactured by the shipper's territorial state,[12] drastically curtailed England's wine supply. It precipitated the first Dutch war (1652-1654) which severely limited the direct shipment of French, Spanish or German wines to England in Dutch vessels, or the indirect shipment via Dutch ports.[13] English wine prices broke upward sharply with curtailment of Dutch shipments--shipments which were the mainstay of the English wine trade.[14]

The approval of many applications for the direct import of French and Spanish wines somewhat alleviated the wine dearth. An extra duty of 40s., a tun (252 gallons) on these

---

[12] Smith. An Inquiry...Wealth of Nations..., op. cit., pp. 429 to 431.
Andrews. The Colonial Period..., op. cit., pp. 35 to 39, 41 to 44.
Violet Barbour. "Dutch and English...," (930 1280872), pp. 267-268.

[13] Simon. The History..., op. cit., Vol. 3, pp. 35 to 39, 41 to 44. Mr. Simon errs in underestimating the extent of Dutch wine entrepot. See Infra, Vol. 1, pp. 118 to 126.

[14] James E. Thorold Rogers. A History of Agriculture and Prices..., (882 1270184), Vol. 5, pp. 472, 474; Vol. 6, p. 419.
William Beveridge. Prices and Wages..., (939 1270716), pp. 88, 148.
Simon. The History..., op. cit., Vol. 3, pp. 66-67, 414-415.
The dearth and high price of wine was eased after February 28, 1654, when Parliament restored the English wine trade.

direct imports was designed to foster fiscal rather than restrictive ends.[15] Fiscalism was also a primary argument in a petition to Parliament requesting permission to import French wines in ships of any nationality. This petition, however, was not affirmed,[16] and a subsequent request also failed.[17]

The English Navigation Acts of 1660 and 1663 reiterated England's desire to deal a heavy blow to Dutch trade.[18] Yet,

---

[15]Not all Englishmen favored a system of wine imports based upon privilege:

> ...for they procure (upon some pretext or other) particular licences for many prohibited commodities contrary to that act, as namely French wines...so as either directly or indirectly they have the whole trade for themselves.
>
> [1651 or 1652 (ambiguous reference to "a writer already quoted") in Andrews. The Colonial Period..., op. cit., pp. 42-43.]

[16]Calendar of State Papers: Domestic..., (649 1221118), Vol. 4, p. 280 [9 January 1653].

[17]Ibid., Vol. 5, pp. 91, 136, [31 January 1653] cited in Simon. The History..., op. cit., Vol. 3, p. 67.

The State Papers do not spell out the grounds upon which the petitions were rejected. Judging from the general autonomy of trade during wars between the colonial powers [Jacob Viner. The Long View..., (958 1270954), pp. 297-298; p. 298, footnote 53.], it is probable that fiscalism, not a reluctance to trade with the Dutch enemy, accounted for the petition's failure, viz., a greater royal revenue was available to the Crown from the extra duties than could have been collected by levying normal duties on an unrestricted trade.

[18]Barbour. "Dutch and English...," op. cit., pp. 266-267.

Andrews. The Colonial Period..., op. cit., pp. 43, 44, 110 to 113.

Consult also the sources cited Supra, Vol. 1, pp. 51-52, footnote 87.

the Navigation Acts failed to stem the wine trade primarily because of exemptions in the Acts and because of close ties existing between certain Dutch and English exporting firms. These ties made it possible for Dutch firms to transfer vessels to their English branch houses.[19]

The depradation of wine-laden merchant ships by warships and privateers following the 1665 declaration of war by Charles II on Holland and France further documents the extent of the Anglo-Dutch wine trade. The <u>State Papers</u>[20] record the seizure of these prizes by the belligerents, and substantiate the failure of the Navigation Acts to stem Anglo-Dutch wine trade.

Despite the risks of the new war, England's wine trade remained active. Even the prohibition of Canary wine imports in 1666--a fair portion of the wines consumed in England came from the Canaries--,[21] and the prohibition of French wines in 1667 failed to cower the trade. Permits to import French and Canary wines on payment of additional

---

[19]Simon. <u>The History</u>..., <u>op</u>. <u>cit</u>., pp. 83 to 88. Wilson. <u>Anglo-Dutch</u>..., <u>op</u>. <u>cit</u>., pp. 6-7.

[20]Simon. <u>The History</u>..., <u>op</u>. <u>cit</u>., Vol. 3, p. 93, footnote * cites many <u>Calendar of State Papers</u>: <u>Domestic</u> entries.

[21]<u>Ibid</u>., Vol. 3, p. 94. The English preference for sweet wines, existing years before the Methuen Treaty (1703), is discussed <u>Infra</u>, Vol. 1, pp. 220 to 222; pp. 221-222, footnote 90.

duties prevailed;[22] petitions for repeal of the prohibitions were denied.[23]

By 1670, three years after the Treaty of Breda, an unrestricted English wine trade again flourished.[24] In May 1672, when England declared war against Holland, Dutch ships in English ports once again were seized. The large quantity of Madeira and Canary wines taken in these seizures and sold by the Commissioner of Prizes[25] witnessed the continued involvement of the Dutch in the English wine trade.

The Low Countries' involvement in the Spanish, French and German wine trade centered around wine entrepot, that is, the racking of wines, the manufacture of Brantywein[26] (brandy), and, not incidentally, wine adulteration.

---

[22] In two days alone, February 5 and 6, 1667, Parliament issued warrants allowing ninety-five ships to land cargos of French wines, brandies, and other goods. Mr. Simon lists the warrant recipients and the cargo of their ships *Ibid*., Vol. 3, pp. 95-96.

[23] *Ibid*., Vol. 3, pp. 94-95.

For a possible explanation of this refusal see *Supra*, Vol. 1, p.116, footnote 17.

[24] [Adam Anderson.] *An Historical and Chronological*..., (787 1271180), Vol. 2, pp. 496, 497.
Simon. *The History*..., *op*. *cit*., Vol. 3, pp. 106 to 109.

[25] *Ibid*., Vol. 3, p. 110; p. 110, footnote *.

[26] The manufacture of *Brantywein* evolved from the Dutch wine trade with the port of La Rochelle on the Charente River in France. A Dutch shipmaster conceived the idea of concentrating the wine and transporting the spirit of the wine to Holland where it could be reconstituted with the addition of water. The aim was to reduce the costs of transporting the wine and the peril of its spoilage during the transport. When the merchant arrived in Holland, the concentrated wine

The racking of wine consisted of its storage through a single winter. During this storage, the wine would purify itself by precipitating foreign elements and improve in quality through aging. The Dutch profited handsomely, as the costs of wine storage were far less than the price differential between rack and vintage (wine consumed shortly after the autumn grape harvest).

What improvement the Dutch bestowed upon wines by racking, they, at best, nullified by adulteration.[27] Such practices spoiled wine quality, diminished wine popularity and influenced wine producers to falsify, sophisticate and adulterate[28] their wines in order to compete with the cheaper

---

was well-received without reconstitution. The Dutch called the new product Brantywein, as fire, or heat, was used in its preparation. This term was later Anglicized to the present-day word brandy. [Harold Grossman. Grossman's Guide, (955$1270157), p. 197.]

Soldiers who returned from campaigns in the Low Countries were instrumental in cultivating the taste for brandy in Elizabethan England. [Simon. The History..., op. cit., Vol. 3, p. 391.]

[27]Cole. Colbert..., op. cit., Vol. 1, pp. 216-217, 351, 413-414.

Hartmeyer. Der Weinhandel..., op. cit., p. 350.

Etienne Laspeyres. Geschichte der Volkswirthschaftlichen..., (863 1270274), pp. 140, 141.

[28]The adulteration or "cutting" [coupement] of wine generally consisted of mixing poorer with better wines, or simply wine with water or other liquid agents. Sophistication implied the addition of substances designed to improve an initially disappointing wine. Falsification denoted wine produced from substances other than grapes.

The method of adulteration and sophistication is obvious. These techniques, under more glamorous names, are yet employed in the manufacture of fortified wines, wines

Dutch entrepot wines. Colbert, who in 1670 was certain that the goodness of French wine would secure its market despite its higher prices,[29] in 1683 sympathized with the continued "cutting" of French wines in order that they might compete with the corrupted Dutch wines.[30]

As a result of these practices, wine served at English tables was notoriously impure.[31] It suffered corruption not only at initial production and at the hands of Dutch

---

such as Madeira to which spirits or high proof wine is added.

Artificial wines and the methods of their manufacture are described in detail in many books on distillation and gardening. Consult, for example, John French. The Art of Distillation..., (667 1270221), pp. 140. 141, where recipes are given for artificial Mallago and Claret Wine made of raisons, and for artificial Malmsey produced of "two gallons of English Honey."

[29]Cole. Colbert..., op. cit., Vol. 1, p. 413.

[30]Ibid., Vol. 1, p. 351; p. 351, footnote 114; pp. 413-414. [Colbert. Letter to de Ris, January 18, 1683].

[31][Hugh Platt]. The Jewell House..., (594$1271061), third book, p. 16.

John Glauber. A Description of New Philosophical Furnaces..., (651 1270196), pp. 341 to 355.

Kenelm Digby. The Closet..., (669 1271057), pp. 112, 113, 127, 128, 175.

The Mysterie of Vinters..., (669 1270227), pp. 142 ff.

J. S. Elsholt. The Curious Distillatory..., (667 1270233), pp. 47, 48.

W. Y-Worth. A New Art of Making Wines..., (691 1270232), pp. 10 to 13, 65 to 71, postscript.

entrepot, but Dutch merchants in England,[32] and English traders, too,[33] engaged in deleterious practices. Promoters

---

[32] Certificate from the Lord Mayor to the Lords of the Council, that the wines of Peter Van Payne had been racked in his presence. In eight of the pipes had been found bundles of weeds, in four others some quantities of sulphur, in another a piece of match, and in all of them a kind of gravel mixture sticking to the casks...

[Analytical Index...Remembrancia, (878 1250176), p. 529, item VII. 148, 10 July 1635.]

Peter Van Payne, described as a "Merchant Stranger," [Ibid., p. 529, item VII. 146], only a month earlier was ordered to trial for the sophistication and falsification of French wines [Ibid., p. 529, item VIII, 161, 3 June 1635].

The involvement of other Dutch merchants in the English wine trade is recorded Ibid., pp. 529 ff.

[33] ...and in our immoderate drinking of them [wines], we more than ordinarily dispose our bodies to the Stangury, Fevers, Gout, and Stone, when they are pure: and to so many more Diseases as when they are so many ways sophisticated and adulterated by vintners...

[Roger Coke. A Discourse of Trade..., (670 1271253), Pt. 1, p. 38.]

As to the Frauds in the Wine Trade, they are so publickly known that no Body wants to be inform'd of 'em.

[A Dialogue Between Sir Andrew Freeport and Timothy Squat, Esquire, On the Subject of Excises. London: 1733. p. 35. Consult also pp. 36, 37; similarly, Sir Robert Walpole. "A Letter...," (733 1260309), pp. 16, 29.

Now, Wine-Traders, stand clear, and hear this Charge upon you: Why you truly sell a poisonous Composition of unknown Materials, and this is an undeniable Truth;

[Letter from a merchant of London..., (733 1270114), p. 20.]

Simon. A History..., op. cit., Vol. 3, pp. 382 to 389.

of English agriculture advised Englishmen seeking wholesome wines to turn to the cultivation of their own vineyards,[34] or to turn to colonial wine production.[35] Thus, in a circuitous fashion, wine adulteration markedly stimulated English colonial viticulture in the second half of the seventeenth century and thereafter.

The sizable involvement of the Dutch in wine entrepot is reflected in a 1646 appraisal of the yearly trade

---

[34]William Hughes. The Compleat Vineyard..., (665 1270197), folio A_2, [A_3], [A_4], chapter XI.

John Rose. The English Vineyard..., (675$1271046), folio A_3 verso, A_4, pp. 39ff.

J. Mortimer. The Whole Art of Husbandry..., (721 1270986), Vol. 2, pp. 313-314.

Edward Hyams. Vineyards in England..., (953 1270218), pp. 35, 36.

________. The Grape Vine in England..., (949$1270715), pp. 45 to 51.

George Ordish. Wine Growing in England, (953$1270901), pp. 22, 120.

[35]Production of colonial wines was urged "as these Wines are more pure, so much more wholsom than [those that are the product of] the Brewing Trade of Sophisticating and Adulterating of Wines, as in England, Holland (especially) and in some other places..."

[Gabriel Thomas. An Account..., (698 1260351), p. 322.]

> So little foreign wine is sold in our country in its pure state, that a friend of the author...remarked, that the only certain way to obtain it unadulterated, was to press out the juice and make the wine yourself, bung it tight, and then get astride the cask and ride it all the way home.
>
> [R. H. Phelps. The Vine..., (855 1270244), p. 6.]

balances between France and the Netherlands,[36] in the estimates of the relative importance of wine to other items of trade in Dutch markets,[37] and in a 1669 estimate by Colbert, that yearly

> The Dutch went to the Garonne and the Charents Rivers in France, with 3,000 or 4,000 ships, to get wine. They took it to Holland, landed it, and paid import duties. Of the wine, one-third was consumed in Holland, and two-thirds was sent the next spring to Germany and the countries of northern Europe. The ships which took the wine north brought back naval stores and other goods.[38]

With such sizable quantities of wine entering and leaving their ports, the Netherlands became a wine-drinking nation within a short span of time. In 1614, the Dutch are

---

[36] Of the 15,701,466 *livres* of goods taken out of France by the Dutch each year, wines, brandy and vinegar (etc.) were valued at 6,192,632 *livres*.

Jean Eon [Mathias de Saint-Jean]. *Le Commerce honorable*, [Nantes, 1646], quoted in Cole. *Colbert*..., *op. cit.*, Vol. 1, pp. 212, 213.

[37] To establish a 1634 price index, Professor N. W. Posthumus, [N. W. Posthumus. *Inquiry into the History of Prices in Holland*, Leiden: E. J. Brill, 1946, Vol. 1.], examined 359 commodities' prices of which 10 were Spanish wines, 11 French wines [*Ibid*., p. xxxvi]. In his investigation of 1734 prices, of 590 commodities studied, 12 were Spanish wines, 27 French wines. [*Ibid*.] Wine prices received a 4 percent weight in establishing the wholesale price index for Amsterdam [*Ibid*., p. lxxxvi]. Weight percentages of French wine expressed first as a percent of harvest articles, then as a percent of harvest and non-harvest articles were *1620-1699*: 57/567; 57/1000. *1700-1759*: 86/696; 86/1000. [*Ibid*., p. xcv.]

[38] Colbert. *Lettres* II[2], 462-464 quoted in Charles Cole. *Colbert*..., *op. cit.*, Vol. 1, pp. 440-441.

described as importing "their Mault, Barley and best double drinke from England,"[39] Thomas Mun, writing about 1628, lauds Dutch sobriety and valor.[40] Yet, by 1633, the Dutch of New Amsterdam were proudly described as knowing "well how to get at the bottom of a cask of wine, being a beverage just fitted to their taste."[41] By 1669, as Colbert noted, the Dutch were consuming yearly more than a thousand shiploads of wine.

Dutch involvement in Anglo-French wine trade diminished after 1678 when the English resorted to restrictive excises to stem a pernicious and disadvantageous French trade.[42] In the following year, the importation of French wines was entirely prohibited.[43] This prohibition, lasting until

---

[39]Gentleman. England's VVay..., op. cit., p. 6. Wine was in use, though not popular, in Holland at the time--it is listed as a therapeutic agent in The Pharmacopocia of Amsterdam (1616). [Salvatore P. Lucia. A History of Wine as Therapy, (963$1270185), p. 220.]

[40]Thomas Mun. England's Treasure..., (664 1271261), pp. 179-180.

[41]David de Vries. "Extracts from the Voyages...," (633 1260940), p. 255.

[42]An Account of the French Usurpation upon the Trade of England and what great damage the English do yearly sustain by their Commerce, London: 1679, passim.
Andrews. The Colonial Period..., op. cit., Vol. 4, p. 355; p. 355, footnote 2.
H. Warner Allen. A History of Wine..., (961$1270231), pp. 194-195.
Simon. The History..., op. cit., Vol. 3, pp. 110, 125.

[43]Andrews. The Colonial Period..., op. cit., Vol. 4, pp. 356-357; p. 356, footnote 1 [a good sampling of authors arguing against the French wine trade].

.685, proved more harmful to the English royal purse than ;o the French growers who found new markets for their vines.[44]

With the repeal of the prohibitions against French goods in 1685 there "ensued an inundation of French commodities...whereby all the evils formerly complained of were renewed so that the nation would have been soon beggared, had it not been for the happy Revolution in 1688 [the Act: 1689] when all commerce with France was actually barred."[45] Duties on all wines continually were increased beyond the 1696 expiration date. They reached their peak in 1698 when the duty on French wines was set at L51 2s. 0d. per tun, or an advance of L49 2s. 0d. per tun in less than a century.[46] As a consequence of the prohibitive duties, requests for permissions to import French wines were fewer, the Dutch role in French-English wine trade diminished and a dearth of French wines intensified yearly during the last decade

---

[44]Simon. The History..., op. cit., Vol. 3, p. 110, 125 to 127.

[45][Anderson.] An Historical and Chronological..., op. cit., Vol. 2, p. 571.

[46]Simon. The History..., op. cit., Vol. 3, p. 127.

of the seventeenth century.[47] Spirits became more popular among the masses and the majority of wine drinkers learned to resign themselves to Spanish and especially to Portuguese wines.[48] The Dutch supplied English claret and burgundy drinkers by clandestine shipments of French wine. Adam Smith remarks about this trade:

> One of the most important branches of the Dutch trade, at present, consists in the carriage of French goods to other European countries. Some part even of the French wine drank in Great Britain is clandestinely imported from Holland and Zealand.[49]

Dutch trade, however, was not limited to European ports. The Netherlanders were, as well, important suppliers of their

---

[47] Les Anglais viennent peu à Bordeauz; on y voit quelques Ecossois, le fort du commerce s'y fait avec la Hollande.

["Memoir of the Intendant of Guyenne" (1699) quoted in Simon. _The History_..., _op. cit._, Vol. 3, p. 253.]

[Richard Ames]. _The Search After Claret; or a Visitation of the Vintners_, London: Hawkins, 1691, passim; Advertisement.

________. _The Bacchanalian Sessions: or The Contention of Liquors. With a Farewell to Wine_, London: Hawkins, 1693, passim.

Smith. _An Inquiry...Wealth of Nations_..., _op. cit._, pp. 440 to 443.

Simon. _The History_..., _op. cit._, Vol. 3, pp. 126 to 139.

[48] A discussion of English drinking habits follows _Infra_, Vol. 1, pp. 220 to 222.

[49] Smith. _An Inquiry...Wealth of Nations_..., _op. cit._, p. 442.

colonies and of the Spanish, French and English colonies in the West Indies and the Americas.[50]

In the charter of the Dutch West India Company, which founded New Netherland, the words "navigation and trade," "Trade," "traffic," and "commerce" are everywhere repeated. Thus, while one purpose of the Company was "the peopling of those fruitful and unsettled parts," the Dutch had no national immigrations comparable to those of the English colonies.[51] The aim of the Dutch was the creation of

---

[50]Clarence H. Haring. The Spanish Empire in America, New York: Oxford University Press, 1947, pp. 331, 332, 339.

John Parker. Van Meteren's Virginia..., (961$1270480), pp. 8 to 35, 37.

Cole. Colbert..., op. cit., Vol. 2, pp. 26 to 28.

Ferdinando Gorges. A Briefe Narration..., (658 1261105), p. 51.

Frances Davenport. (ed.). European Treaties..., (929 1221131), pp. 53 to 57. [Treaty of Amnity and Commerce between Virginia and New Netherland (1660)].

The Records of New Amsterdam from 1653 to 1674..., (647 1241020), Vol. 4, p. 153 [28 October 1662]; Vol. 5, p. 20 [11 February 1664].

> ...but indeed our liberty to do good onely to our selves, is the main obstacle of our progress to staple-commodities in our Plantations...
>
> Had the Dutch Virginia, they would make it the Fortresse; Mart and Magazin of all the West Indies...
>
> [William Berkeley. A Discourse and View..., (663$1261169), p. 4.]

George L. Beer. The Old Colonial..., (912$1271261), Vol. 1, pp. 160-161; Vol. 2, pp. 272-273.

________. The Origins..., (922$1271268), pp. 228-229.

[51]Christopher Ward. The Dutch & Swedes on the Delaware 1609-64, Philadelphia: University of Pennsylvania Press, 1930, p. 376.

foreign investment centers rather than "plantations."[52] Both commercial and political interests in the mother country supported such enterprises.[53]

From their earliest trade ventures, the Dutch noted the fertility of New Netherland and the abundance of vines growing there.[54] One early settler remarked that,

> Almost the whole country, as well the forests as the maize lands and flats, is full of vines, but principally--as if they had been planted there--around and along the banks of the brooks, streams and rivers which course and flow in abundance very conveniently and agreeably all through the land. The grapes are of many varieties; some white, some blue, some very fleshy and fit only to make raisins of; some again are juicy, some

---

[52]Harold C. Syrett. "Private Enterprise in New Amsterdam," (956$1280866), pp. 538-539.
L. J. Pierre M. Bonnassieux. Les Grand compagnies de commerce, Paris: E. Peon, Nourrit et Cie, 1892, p. 33.
John S. Barry. The History of Massachusetts..., (855$1270769), pp. 19-20.
Clough. The Economic Development..., op. cit., pp. 227-228.

[53]Bonnassieux. Les Grand compagnies..., op. cit., pp. 33, 69 to 79.

[54]Johan de Laet. "The New World...," (609$1260355), p. 48, 49.
Emanuel Van Meteren. "On Hudson's Voyage...," (610$1260354), p. 7.
Cornelis Hendricksen. "Captain Hendricksen's...," (616 1260375), Vol. 1, p. 14.
Lyman Carrier. The Beginnings of Agriculture..., (923$1270209), p. 31. [Dr. Carrier quotes a Dutch writer who, in 1644 described "each Grape as big as the end of one's Finger or a middle sized Plumb."]
"Broad Advice...," (649 1281244), p. 248.
"Representation of New Netherland...," (650$1260360), pp. 295-296.
De Vries. "Short Historical and Journal-Notes...," (655 1260359), p. 219.
Daniel Denton. A Brief Description of New York..., (670 1260632), p. 3.

> very large, others on the contrary small; their juice is pleasant and some of it white, like French or Rhenish Wine; that of others again, a very deep red, like Tent; some even paler; the vines run far up the trees and are shaded by their leaves, so that the grapes are slow in ripening and a little sour, but were cultivation and knowledge applied here, doubtless as fine Wines would then be made as in any other wine growing countries.[55]

The potentiality of a wine industry excited their imagination,[56] particularly in view of the success that the

---

[55]"Remonstrance of New Netherland...," (649 1260377), Vol. 1, p. 277.

[56]Several early accounts illustrate their enthusiasm:

> Grapes are of very good flavor, but will be henceforward better cultivated by our people...
>
> Vines grow wild there; were there wine growers who understood the pressing, good wine could be brought hither in great quantity, and even as must, the voyage thence being often made in thirty days.
> [Wassenaer. "Historisch Verhael...," (624$1260356), pp. 77, 71.]
>
> Wild grape vines are abundant... if properly attended to, [they] seem to promise a rich supply of wine.
> [Johan de Laet.] Novus Orbis, [1633] quoted in J. Franklin Jameson. Narratives of New Netherland, New York: Charles Scribner's Sons, 1909, pp. 54, 56.
>
> If people would cultivate the vines they might have as good wine here as they have in Germany or France. I had myself last harvest a boatload of grapes and pressed them. As long as the wine was new it tasted better than any French or Rhenish Must...
> [Johannes Megapolensis. "A Short Account...," (644$1260359), p. 169. Consult also p. 168.]

Swedes enjoyed with their oenological attempts.[57] Adriaen Van der Donck commented,

> That the wild vines, with proper care and management, will produce as good grapes and as good wine as is made in Germany and France, is clear and undeniable. Proofs and examples of this fact are seen at the South river, where the Swedes reside, who have laid down vines from which others have sprung, which they name suckers, from which they make delightful wine year after year.[58]

---

[57]Johan Printz [Relation to the Noble West India Company..., (644 1260341), pp. 95 to 100] in his detailed description of New Sweden fails to mention viticultural attempts. It appears, therefore, that in 1644 he had not yet acted upon the 1642 instructions directed to him, as governor of New Sweden, by the Swedish Royal Council:

> ...as almost everywhere in the forests wild grapevines and grapes are found, and the climate seems to be favorable to the production of wine, so shall the Governor also direct his thoughts to the timely introduction of this culture, and what might herein be devided and effected.
>
> ["Instructions to Lieut. Col. John [Johan] Printz," [1642], quoted in Carl Raymond Woodward. The Development of Agriculture..., (927$1270484), p. 6.]

In Plantagenet's 1648 description of New Albion [Delaware] a marked change is reported, for by that year, there "may be gathered and made two hundred tun in the Vintage Moneth..."

> [Beauchamp Plantagenet. New Albion. quoted in L. H. Bailey. Sketch of the Evolution of our Native Fruits, (906 1270200), pp. 4-5.]

[58]Adriaen Van der Donck. A Description of the New Netherlands..., (656 1260941), p. 154.

In 1657, Jacob Alrich, vice-director of the Swedish colony on the Delaware, secured low beer and wine prices for the Swedish colonists avowing that "working people must sometimes take a drink of beer or wine to comfort their heart." [Jacob Alrich. "Letter of August 13, 1657," quoted in Edward

The Dutch colonists, however, were neither self-reliant nor accustomed to viticultural pursuits,[59] as Van der Donck observed:

> Our Netherlanders are unaccustomed to the management of vineyards, and have not given much attention to the cultivation of the vine. Some of them have occasionally planted vines, but they have never treated them properly, and for this reason they have derived very little profit from their labour. I have, however, frequently drank good and well tasted domestic wine, and remark, that the fault is in the people, not in the grapes. Within the last few years, the lovers of the vineyard have paid more attention to the cultivation of the vine, and have informed themselves on the subject. They have also introduced men to come over from Heidelberg who are vine dressers, for the purpose of attending to the vineyards; and to remedy every defect in the management of the grape, men are also coming over, who posses the most perfect skill in the planting and management of vineyards.
>
> At this time, they have commenced the planting in good earnest, and with proper care. Several persons already have vineyards and wine hills under cultivation, and Providence blesses their labours with success, by affording fruit according to the most favourable expectation. Hereafter, from year to year, the cultivation of the vine will increase; for every one takes hold of the business--one man learns from another--and as the population increases rapidly, it is expected that in a few years there will be wine in abundance in the New-Netherlands.[60]

R. Emerson. The Story of the Vine, (902$1270387), p. 184.] It is little wonder the Dutch colonists envied their Swedish compatriots for fiscalism and high beer and wine prices prevailed in the Dutch colonies. [Infra, Vol. 1, pp. 134 to 137.]

[59] Ward. The Dutch & Swedes..., op. cit., pp. 374, 375.

[60] Van der Donck. A Description..., op. cit., pp. 154-155.

An Abundance of wine did not materialize. Jasper Danckaerts explained that,

> Although they have several times attempted to plant vineyards, and have not immediately succeeded, they, nevertheless, have not abandoned the hope of doing so by and by, for there is always some encouragement, although they have not, as yet discovered the cause of the failure.[61]

The colonists, therefore, relied upon their motherland for the supply of wines.

The New Netherlands colony was plentifully supplied with imported wine. So abundant was the supply in 1638 that an ordinance "occasioned by immoderate Drinking" forbade all persons to sell wine in their houses and limited sales to the

---

[61] J. Franklin Jameson and B. B. James.(eds.). Journal of Jasper Danckaerts..., (679 1260335), p. 59.

Also, Jasper Dankers and Peter Sluyter, Journal of a Voyage to New York in 1679-80, p. 130, quoted in U. P. Hedrick The Grapes of New York, (908$1270201), p. 11. [Dr. Hedrick, considered an authority, states that "There are no detailed accounts of grape-growing by the Dutch of New York... ." He cites only the work of Jasper Dankers and Peter Sluyter.]

Contrasting the oenological failures of New Netherlands was the Swedish colonial success at wine production. Swedish colonists utilized four varieties of native grapes to make "eight sorts of excellent wine" [Plantagenet. New Albion..., quoted in Bailey. Sketches..., op. cit., p. 5]. For additional commentary consult: Adolph B. Benson and Naboth Hedin. (eds.). Swedes in America, (938 1270495), pp. 25, 76 to 78, and Amandus Johnson. The Swedish Settlements..., (911 1270882), Vol. 1, p. 355; p. 355, footnotes 48, 49.

ompany's store where "wine can be procured at a fair price nd where it will be issued in moderate quantity."[62]

The abundance of wine occasioned ordinances regulating runkenness,[63] behavior in inns,[64] tapping on the Sabbath,[65]

---

[62] Laws and Ordinances of New Netherland 1638-1674. 638$1241023), p. 12 [17 May 1638].

Professor Syrett ["Private Enterprise in New Amsterdam," op. cit., pp. 539-540] rightly asserts that of the umerous laws adopted to regulate the trade in beer and wine 'some were clearly revenue measures..." while others "were esigned to standardize the practices of a business that 'urnished the inhabitants of New Amsterdam with one of the staples of their diet." He presents a very good listing of he latter regulations.

[63] The Records of New Amsterdam from 1653 to 1674..., op. cit., Vol. 1, pp. 1, 2 [31 May 1647]; pp. 6, 7 [10 March 1648].

Drunkenness in and of itself was not a felony. The Court of New Amsterdam even considered a case wherein the plaintiff sued to dismiss a contract agreed to when he "was n drink." [Ibid., Vol. 6, pp. 350, 351 [20 December 1671]]. Most cases brought against drunkards were for damages:

assault: Ibid., Vol. 1, p. 167 [19 February 1654]; pp. 238, 239 [7 September 1654]; p. 356 [6 September 1655];

personal abuse: Ibid., Vol. 3, p. 76 [18 November 1659]; p. 134 [24 February 1660].

The immoderate drinking prevalent in the colony is decried Ibid., Vol. 1, pp. 1, 2 [31 May 1647]; pp. 18-19 [31 December 1655]; p. 420 [31 December 1655]; Vol. 3, pp. 148, 149 [23 February 1660]; Vol. 6, pp. 403 to 405 [28 August 1673]; Laws...New Netherland..., op. cit., p. 12 [17 May 1638]; pp. 93, 94 [10 March 1648].

[64] The Records of New Amsterdam..., op. cit., Vol. 1, pp. 1, 2 [31 May 1647]; pp. 6, 7 [10 March 1648]; p. 34 [3 December 1657]; pp. 255-256 [19 October 1654]; Vol. 3, p. 223 [28 September 1660].

Laws...New Netherland..., op. cit., pp. 94, 95 [10 March 1648]; p. 259 [26 October 1656].

[65] The Records of New Amsterdam..., op. cit., Vol. 1, pp. 1, 2 [31 May 1647]; pp. 6, 7 [10 March 1648]; p. 24

and prohibiting the sale of liquor to Indians.[66] These laws often were not obeyed; hence their frequent reinstatement. Notwithstanding, many colonists resorted to "Tavern-keeping, so that nearly the just fourth of the city New Amsterdam consists of Brandy shops, Tobacco or Beer houses..."[67]

When wars with the Indians required an extraordinary number of soldiers "who must necessarily be paid," the directors and council of New Netherland "with the advice of the Eight Men chosen by the Commonalty" decided

> to impose some Duties on those articles from which the good inhabitants will experience least inconvenience, as the scarcity of money is sufficiently general.
>
> Therefore We have enacted and Ordained, and do hereby enact and Ordain, that there shall be paid on each half barrel of Beer tapt by the Tavern Keeper, two Guilders, one-half payable by the Brewer and one-half by the Tapster; the Burgher who does not retail it, to pay half as much; on each quart of Spanish Wine and Brandy, four Stivers; French Wine, two Stivers, to be paid by the Tapsters; on each

---

[26 October 1656]; Vol. 2, p. 204 [26 October 1656]; Vol. 4, pp. 45-46 [7 March 1662].

Laws...New Netherland..., op. cit., pp. 60, 61 [27 September 1646]; pp. 98, 99 [20 April 1648]; pp. 258-259 [26 October 1656]; pp. 310 to 312 [12 June 1657].

[66] The Records of New Amsterdam..., op. cit., Vol. 1, pp. 1, 2 [31 May 1647]; pp. 6, 7 [10 March 1648]; p. 24 [26 October 1656]; p. 206 [1 June 1654]; p. 241 [7 September 1654]; Vol. 2, pp. 51, 52 [3 March 1656]; p. 145 [25 July 1656]; p. 205 [26 October 1656]; Vol. 5, p. 85 [8 July 1664].

Laws...New Netherland..., op. cit., p. 34 [18 June 1643]; p. 52 [21 November 1645]; p. 64 [1 July 1647]; p. 160 [13 May 1648]; p. 182 [28 August 1654]; pp. 446, 447 [19 July 1663]; p. 451 [31 December 1663].

[67] Laws...New Netherland..., op. cit., p. 93 [10 March 1648].

> merchantable Beaver, purchased within our limits, and brought here to the Fort, one guilder; the three-quarters and halves in proportion.[68]

Again, in 1653, the "low state of the Treasury" ccasioned deliberation into

> what supplementary means may be devised the least burthensome and onerous to the Inhabitants, have found no better, fitter nor easier expedient than the imposition of some tax on the Wine, Brandy and Spirits which can best be spared yet are most consumed in this country, at a great advance both by buyers and sellers by the large and small measure.[69]

Much litigation surrounded these excises. Suits were rought to enforce the privileges of tax farmers[70] -- those ho for a stipulated sum purchased from municipal authorities he right to collect the excise -- to prevent fraud and

---

[68] *Ibid.*, pp. 38-39 [21 June 1644].

[69] *Ibid.*, p. 142 [26 March 1653].

[70] The excise for wine and beer was first farmed to Paulus on der Beeck. His privileges as the tax farmer were pub-ished and affixed on the City Hall so that "nobody may plead gnorance." [*The Records of New Amsterdam*..., *op. cit.*, ol. 1, p. 28 [6 December 1656]].

Other references to the privileges of the tax farmers re contained in *Ibid.*, Vol. 2, pp. 239-240 [6 December 1656]; . 313 [25 January 1658]; Vol. 3, p. 68 [31 October 1659]; ol. 5, p. 154 [8 November 1664]; p. 159 [22 November 1664].

smuggling,[71] and to settle excise debts.[72] The Directors and Council of New Netherland took keen interest in the excise as "in the present time [1654] there is no other revenue than beer and wine excise."[73]

The excise on wine, brandy, and spirits continued as the mainstay of New Netherland's revenue, although attempts were made to broaden the tax base by introducing other charges. The issue was voted in 1671 and resolved in favor of continuing the wine, brandy and spirits excise and against adopting the general tax on all towns.[74]

Adjunctive excise regulations were issued to afford additional revenue to the municipality. These measures, designed to implement and extend colonial fiscalism in New Netherland, included a system of licensing for taverns and

---

[71] The Records of New Amsterdam..., op. cit., Vol. 1, p. 25 [26 October 1656]; pp. 193 to 195 [4 May 1654]; p. 92 [2 August 1653]; p. 128 [19 November 1653]; p. 129 [25 November 1653]; Vol. 2, pp. 239, 240 [6 December 1656]. Laws...New Netherland..., op. cit., pp. 70, 71 [4 July 1647]; pp. 184, 185 [18 November 1654]; pp. 220, 221 [27 April 1656]; p. 231 [7 June 1656]; p. 296 [23 January 1657].

[72] The Records of New Amsterdam..., op. cit., Vol. 1, p. 202 [1 June 1654]; p. 225 [10 August 1654]; Vol. 3, p. 28 [19 August 1659]; p. 103 [20 January 1660]; p. 150 [13 April 1660]; Vol. 4, p. 258 [27 September 1670].

[73] The Records of New Amsterdam..., op. cit., Vol. 1, p. 150 [12 January 1654].

[74] The Records of New Amsterdam..., op. cit., Vol. 6, p. 311 [16 July 1761].

retailers,[75] a gauge "marking" requirement for casks[76] and an extension of the excise to include new beverages developed in the colonies during wine or grain shortages.[77] Given this colonial dependence upon wine imports for revenue, and given the emphasis of the Dutch upon trade rather than colonization, the efforts of the New Netherland government to develop and maintain the wine and spirits trade, and their failure to sustain or encourage colonial viticultural attempts are readily understood.

New Netherland as a trading center was the envy of the American colonies just as Holland was the envy of the European states.[78] Jealousies, based on a static conception of national strength and value,[79] were manifest in vituperative attacks upon Dutch domination of the carrying trades in general, and specifically of the spice trade (Portugal), the fisheries (Spain, England, France), and the wine trade (France). For the French, the anti-Dutch sentiment extended

---

75 _Ibid._, Vol. 1, p. 7 [10 March 1648]; p. 328 [28 June 1655].
Laws..., _New Netherland..._, _op. cit._, pp. 296, 297 [23 January 1657]; p. 367 [10 December 1659]; p. 384 [21 July 1660].

76 _The Records of New Amsterdam..._, _op. cit._, Vol. 1, p. 328 [28 June 1655]; Vol. 2, p. 15 [17 January 1656]; Vol. 4, p. 265 [26 June 1663].

77 _The Records of New Amsterdam..._, _op. cit._, Vol. 6, p. 403 [28 August 1673]; pp. 55-56 [29 January 1666].

78 _Supra_, Vol. 1, p.127, footnote 50; pp. 29-30, footnote 35.

79 _Supra_, Vol. 1, pp. 2 to 5.

beyond issues of trade. The Dutch had not only introduced the wholesale adulteration of French wines[80] but had, earlier, weakened the French economy by stimulating overproduction of wine and underproduction of wheat and other staples necessary for French national survival.[81]

French wine overproduction had its origin, however, long before the Dutch influence. In the sixteenth century, France assumed the role of an essentially agricultural nation, largely dependent upon foreigners for manufactures.[82] Viticulture, experiencing a general resurgence, developed rapidly throughout the century.[83] Agricultural specialization which limited viticulture to areas of suitable terrain and climate supplanted regional self-sufficiency.[84] This restriction of the viticultural domain--its abandonment in the marginal growing areas of Normandy, Picardy and

---

[80] Supra, Vol. 1, pp. 119-120.

[81] Eon. Le Commerce honorable [1646] quoted in Cole. Colbert and a Century of French Mercantilism, New York: Columbia University Press, 1939, Vol. 1, pp. 216, 217.

[82] A. Dubois. Précis de l'histoire..., (903 1270611), p. 102.
Cole. French Mercantilist..., (931$1270952), pp. 20 to 24.
________. Colbert..., op. cit., Vol. 1, pp. 8 to 12.

[83] Le Vicompte Georges D'Avenel. Histoire économique de la propriété, des salaries, des denrées...jusqu' en l'an 1800. Paris: Nationale, 1894, Vol. 3, pp. 266, 320.

[84] Ibid., Vol. 1, pp. 348 to 351; Vol. 3, pp. 321 to 325.
Gustav Fagniez. L'Economie sociale de la France sous Henri IV 1589-1610. Paris: Librarie Hachette et Cie, 1897, pp. 66-67.

Brittany--resulted in increased vintage yields and in the decline of wine prices.[85] Wine was so inexpensive that the author of _Discours sure les causes de l'extrème cherté_ [1586] said everyone was drinking it.[86]

Low wine prices in France consistently signaled economic dislocations. The abundant vintage of 1544 which collapsed wine prices, correspondingly raised the prices of food staples.[87] To sustain the price of wine in export markets and to maintain royal revenue, the monarchy--attributing the dearness of staples to disorderly markets--restricted the exportation of wine, placed an excise on wine exports, and tightened its control over the wine markets by limiting the number of intermediaries in the wine trade.[88]

In contrast to the 1544 measures, an edict in 1557 gave permission to all persons to direct or conduct ventures in all foodstuffs, wares, wine and other commodities with the

---

[85] D'Avenel. _Histoire économique..., op. cit._, Vol. 1, pp. 350,351, 365 to 367, 384-385; Vol. 4, pp. 205 to 213.
Paul Degrully. _Essai historique...le marché des vins_, (910 1270442), p. 137. The arithmetic averaging of wine prices is also employed in Professor Degrully's table, "Average Wine Prices of all Qualities 1157 to 1789" [_Ibid._, pp. 142-143]. The results of such non-weighted averaging are spurious, at best.

[86] _Discours sure les causes de l'extrème cherté_ cited in Fagniez. _L'Economie sociale..., op. cit._, p. 67. Fagniez doubts the validity of this statement.

[87] Degrully. _Essai historique..., op. cit._, p. 31.

[88] _Ibid._, pp. 31, 57.

exception of grains and munitions of war.[89] In 1558, wheat shipments were allowed for a period of six months because of an abundance of "all grains, wines, and other fruits necessary for sustenance."[90] In 1559, however, Henry II established a regulatory bureau in Paris to control the export of wheat and wine.[91]

When Charles IX ascended the throne of France in 1561, he prescribed a wine impost in hopes of settling the debts of his predecessor.[92] The impost, initially enacted for six years only, received scant notice on its revival in 1568.[93] Of greater importance was a 1567 statute[94] which regulated

---

[89] Code dv roy Henry III. Roy de France et de Pologne. Paris: 1587, pp. 301-302.
Les Edicts et ordonnances des roys de France..., Paris: Iaques de Puys, 1580, Vol. 1, p. 692 [VI Henry II, (14 February 1557)].

[90] Ibid., Vol. 1, p. 693. [VII Henry II, (1558)].

[91] Ibid., Vol. 1, p. 694. [VIII Henry II, (1559)].
Recueil général des anciennes lois francaises, Paris: H. Fournier, 1830, Vol. 14, p. 16, item 17 [20 December, 1559].
Degrully. Essai historique..., op. cit., p. 31.

[92] Les Edicts et ordonnances..., op. cit., Vol. 2, p. 1536 [I Charles IX, (22 September 1561)].
Degrully. Essai historique..., op. cit., p. 109.

[93] Les Edicts et ordonnances..., op. cit., Vol. 2, p. 1540 [VIII Charles IX (1568)].

[94] Code dv roy Henry III..., op. cit., pp. 154-155 [VII Charles IX, (February 1567)].
Les Edicts et ordonnances..., op. cit., Vol. 1, p. 562 [VII Charles IX, (February 1567)].
D'Avenel. Histoire économique de la propriété..., op. cit., Vol. 3, p. 320.

Arsene T. de Berneaud [The Vine-Dresser's Theoretical

the use of wine and forbade the excess planting of vines. This edict stipulated that two-thirds of all land be kept for grain and that land suitable for prairie be given over to vines. Nevertheless, it was adamently condemned in 1568 by Jean Bodin:

> As for the opinion of some, who wish that we tear up the vines to plant everything in wheat, or at the least that it be prohibited to plant vines in the future;
>
> ...God by his grace has taken care that all is not either in vine or wheat. For the best land for the vine is worth nothing for the wheat, inasmuch as the ones like the strong and fat plain, the other demands the rocky slopes.
>
> Moreover, the vine is not able to grow beyond the 49th degree on account of the cold, so that all the people of the north have almost no other wines than those from France and the Rhine; and yet they are so fond of these that they burst drinking them.
>
> Therefore by tearing up the vines we would tear up the greatest of the riches of France.[95]

---

and Practical Manual..., (829 1270917), p. 11] and Alden Spooner [The Cultivation of American Grape Vines..., (846 1270637), p. 8], who plagiarized de Berneaud, both mention but do not cite a 1556 French statute ordering the uprooting of vineyards in France. A search of Recueil général des anciennes lois francaises..., [op. cit., Vol. 10 to 22], La Conférence des ordonnances royavx..., [Paris: Iean Petit-Pas, 1620, Vol. 1, pp. 28ff], Code dv roy Henry III..., [op. cit., passim], and Les Edicts et ordonnances..., [op. cit., Vol. 1, 2, passim] failed to uncover such a statute or any mention thereof. Similarly no trace could be found of the spurious 1556 statute's supposed 1567 repeal.

95 Jean Bodin. The Response of Jean Bodin...,

The 1567 statute was renewed ten years later.[96] Although no expiration date was set, the statute apparently was not enforced during the seventeenth and early eighteenth centuries:[97]

> Touching the opinion of those that would have the vines taken vp and corne sowed in the place; or at the least to commaund that no vines should be planted hereafter; the

(568 1271242), p. 54.

Bodin viewed the uprooting of vineyards as a destruction of "natural wealth." He did not conceive of a possible increase in the total French wealth by decreasing the amount of "natural wealth" available to the market in periods of overproduction.

[96] La Conférence des ordonnances royavx..., op. cit., Vol. 2, p. 1585 [IV Henry III, November 1577].

Code dv roy Henry III..., op. cit., pp. 154-155 [IV Henry III, November 1577].

[97] Professor D'Avenel [Histoire économique..., op. cit., Vol. 3, p. 320.] suggests that "des mesures administratives [1567, 1577] furent prises dans ce sens jusqu'au milieu du règne de Louis XV; défense, par arrêt du conseil, de planter des vignes nouvelles." He offers no evidence affirming his contention of the continued enforcement of the 1567, 1577 statute prior to its reenactment in 1731. He apparently was unaware of Gerrard de Malynes' writing [England's Vievv, in the Vnmasking of Two Paradoxes..., (603 1271254), pp. 44-45, 88-89] describing non-enforcement of the edict and of the urging of tax farmers in 1685 to 1687,

> that the wines and brandies of Touraine, Anjou, Orleanais, and Blesois be favored as against those of Brittany...[that] either the vines of Brittany should be pulled up, or the exports of its wines and brandies should be taxed.
>
> [Cole. French Mercantilism..., op. cit., p. 221.]

> husbandman doth with reason laugh this to scorn. For God himselfe did so direct and dispose the nature of the ground, that all should not be for corne, or all wine; seeing the one hath need of a fat, and the other of a stonie ground. And if the vines were pulled vp, wee should (saith hee) [Bodin] deprive Fraunce of one of the greatest riches of the land.[98]

In 1731, however, the statute was revived.[99] The planting of vines again was prohibited in France. Adam Smith outlined the circumstance of this prohibition:

> In France the anxiety of the proprietors of the old vineyards to prevent the planting of any new ones...In 1731, they obtained an order of council prohibiting both the planting of new vineyards, and the renewal of those old ones...The pretence of this order was the scarcity of corn and pasture, and the super-abundance of wine. But had this super-abundance been real, it would, without any order of council, have effectually prevented the plantation of new vineyards, by reducing the profits of this species of cultivation below their natural proportion to those of corn and pasture.[100]

The prohibitions on the planting of new vineyards did protect the proprietors of the old vineyards. Their main objectives, however, were to further French national

---

[98] Ibid., [Malynes], pp. 44-45.

[99] Recueil général des anciennes lois francaises..., op. cit., Vol. 21, p. 361, item 422 [16 January 1751]. D'Avenel. Histoire économique..., op. cit., Vol. 3, p. 320; p. 320, footnote 4.

[100] Smith. An Inquiry...Wealth of Nations..., op. cit., pp. 154-155.

self-sufficiency,[101] to lessen overproduction of wine[102] and to assure (grain) provisionment in the interest of national

---

[101]Cole. French Mercantilist..., op. cit., pp. 20 to 24.

________. Colbert..., op. cit., Vol. 1, pp. 8-9, 81, 87 to 89, 338, 348.

Seeking their own economic advantage, the Dutch [Supra, Vol. 1, p. 138; p. 138, footnote 81] and English discouraged French self-sufficiency:

> For those countries where the vines do grow, are vnapt for corne, and must haue their prouision from the countries adjacent, and many times out of England:
> [Malynes. England's Vievv..., op. cit., pp. 89-90.]

> A celebrated author reckons it bad policy in the English to obstruct the use of French wines: and would encourage the French to turn their labor to the making more wines by the free use of them in England; because each new acre of vineyard planted in France, in order to supply England with wine, would make it requisite for the French to take the produce of an English acre sown in wheat, in order to subsist themselves: 'and it is evident that we have thereby got the command of the better commodity.'
> [John. B. Bordley. Necessaries; Best Product of Land; Best Staple of Commerce, Philadelphia: James Humphreys, 1776, p. 8.]

[102]Sources contemporary to the 1567 and 1577 edicts reveal that "France dispath[ed]...wheat, wine, salt..." and was "never hungry...it...[having] wealth to feed its people however bad the year, provided that the foreigner does not empty...[her] granaries" [Bodin. The Response..., op. cit., p. 50, 32. Consult also the 1557, 1572 and 1583 writings quoted in Cole. Colbert..., op. cit., Vol. 1, pp. 8-9.] Thus, the viticultural prohibitions of the sixteenth century primarily sought to limit wine overproduction and only secondarily to promote wheat culture, whereas the prohibition of 1731 emphasized both the grain shortage and wine overproduction problems. [Consult footnote 103, below.]

lefense.[103] These goals were interwoven with French balance-of-trade resolves. France sought to stem excessive imports by regulating consumption of luxury items[104] and by fostering the home-production of imported foodstuffs and manufactured goods.[105] Like England and Spain, she, too, enforced restrictive colonial policies. These measures were designed to assure commodity availability, to bolster royal (public) finance and to enhance trade balances. These practices molded the economic environment of the French colonies.

The economic success of French colonization, however, hinged little upon these practices. It rather depended upon the French colonists' role as a clearer-of-land, a cultivator and a trapper. Although the colonists, with their experience in cultivation, emulated the agrarian economy of the mother country, they did not develop agricultural exports. As late as the last two decades of the seventeenth century

---

[103]After the battle of Blenheim (1704), "France, in the midst of almost uninterrupted victories and conquests, whilst her labor and attention were much engaged by wine and silk, was compelled to make peace, and relinquish all her fine prospects merely from a great scarcity of corn in that kingdom. Ever since that sore-felt scarcity, it has been her policy to encourage the making of corn [wheat] preferable to all other produce; seeing the feeling as we may suppose, that however great or flourishing they may be in other respects bread being wanting submission must follow." Bordley. *Necessaries...*, *op. cit.*, pp. 7-8; p. 8, footnote ≁.]

[104]Gabriel Hanotaux. *La France vivante en Amerique du Nord*, Paris: Libraire Hachette, et Cie, 1913, p. 104.

[105]Cole. *French Mercantilism 1683-1770*. New York: Columbia University Press, 1943, p. 66f.

"the Canadian economy was still poised squarely on the flat back of the beaver."[106] This circumstance prevailed despite repeated attempts of the mother country to foster the availability of timber, naval stores, and marine staples and to increase colonial self-sufficiency in mineral and manufactured products.[107] Indeed, during the seventeenth century, the economic dependence of the French colonists and the mother country upon furs paralleled the dependence of the English colonists and England upon tobacco.[108] In both cases, the trade was virtually the sole support of the colony and its sole source of revenue for the purchase of imports from the mother country. For both realms, the trade was of paramount importance as a source of royal (public) finance.[109] In both instances the mother country sought to discourage a single staple economy and to encourage colonial production of those commodities whose availability would most benefit her. Thus, while England encouraged colonial viticulture

---

[106] Ibid., p. 66; pp. 66 to 77.

[107] Ibid., pp. 64 to 66.
Cole. Colbert..., op. cit., Vol. 2, pp. 77 to 82.

[108] The dependence of the English upon tobacco is detailed Infra, Vol. 1, pp. 225 to 233; Appendix II.

[109] French fiscal solvency was twice-tied to the fur trade. First, the Crown taxed the fur imports of the West India Company and later, after that company's dissolution in 1675, it collected tax revenue by farming the fur taxes. Second, after 1672, the realm levied import duties on wine and brandy, important media of exchange in the fur trade. [Cole. Colbert..., op. cit., Vol. 2, p. 68.
________. French Mercantilism..., op. cit., p. 67.]

and wine production for availability and balance of trade reasons, France discouraged these pursuits in her colonies, fearing that they would lessen the demand for imposted French wine and brandy imports.

Brandy, particularly, was an important medium of exchange in the colonists' fur trade with the Indians. Directly, through imposts, and indirectly, through facilitation of the fur trade, it was a significant source of royal revenue. Thus, attempts by the Bishop backed by the Jesuits, to curtail the liquor traffic met strong opposition from governmental officials. The dispute attained "unequalled animosity" when Colbert, lending his support to the fur traders, sanctioned the sale of liquor to the Indians as a necessity of commerce.[110] The conflict's resolution, while appeasing the Church, sustained wine and brandy imports;[111] it acknowledged the importance of the fur, and the wine and brandy trades to French fiscalism.

The increasing fiscal importance of wine and brandy imports, _per se_, and the increasing reliance of the French upon liquor in fur trading paralleled a shift in the French attitude toward colonial viticulture and wine production. Tracts of early explorers and those of the French colonizers

---

[110] Cole. _Colbert..._, _op_. _cit_., Vol. 2, p. 67.

[111] The resolution allowed the sale of liquor to Indians who came to the French settlements but prohibited its sale to Indians in their own villages [_Ibid_., pp. 69-70].

describe this shift. The early tracts portrayed the bounty of the vine: Laudonnier attributed to it alone the possibility of French colonization;[112] Lescarbot regarded it as a "most beautiful mine."[113] The narrations of the French settlers, in contrast, cited colonial viticultural restrictions and lamented the high cost of grain imports that called forth grain rather than wine production.

Verrazano, cartier, Ribault, De Lery, and other early explorers for the French[114] described luxuriant vines growing

---

[112] The trees were environed rounde about with Vines bearing grapes in such quantitie, that the number would suffice to make the place habitable.
[Rene de Laudonniere. "A Notable Historie...," (564 1260457), Vol. 9, p. 11.]

[113] Les demandes ordinaires que l'on nous fait sont: Y a-t-il des trésors? Ya-t-il des mines d'or et d'argent?...Quant aux mines, il y en a vraiment, mais il les faut fouiller avec industrie, labeur et patience. La plus belle mine que je sâche, c'est du blé ou du vin, avec la nourriture du bétail. Qui a de ceci, il a de l'argent. Et de mêne, nous n'en vivons point quant à leur substance.
[Marc Lescarbot quoted in Hanotaux. _La France vivante_..., _op_. _cit_., p. 97.]

[114] De Laudonnierre. "Note of Such Commodities...," (562 1260030), p. 116.

Jacques Le Moyne. "The Narrative of...," (564 1260444), pp. 41, 45, 47. [Le Moyne accompanied the French expedition to Florida in 1564; although his narrative does not discuss grapes or vines, his engravings clearly depict vines laden with free-standing grape clusters. The leaves on the vine are three-lobed, characteristic of the native grape _Vitis labrusca_.]

Nicolas Le Challeux. "Narratives of Captain...," (565 1260445), p. 96.

De Laudonnierre. "A Notable Historie...,"

on the East Coast from the Cape Breton Islands to Florida, and in Brazil.

> Also we saw many goodly Vines, a thing not before of us seene in those countries, and therefore we named it Bacchus Iland [Isle of Orleans].[115]

> this wood [beyond Canada and the Port of Saincte Croix]...is all covered with Vines, which we found laden with grapes as blacke as Mulberies, but they be not so Kind as those of France because the Vines bee not tilled, and because they grow of their owne accord.[116]

> ...the fayrest vines in all the world, with grapes according, which without natural art and without mans helpe or trimming will grow to toppes of Okes and other trees that be of wonderfull greatnesse and height [The River May, Florida].[117]

(587 1260456), Vol. 8, p. 451.

Marc Lescarbot. The History..., (609$1260721), pp. 186, 187.

Ruben Thwaites. (ed.). The Jesuit Relations..., (959$1260673), Vol. 9, p. 155, [New France, 1636]; Vol. 13, p. 85 [New France, 1637], Vol. 51, p. 121 [44th parallel latitude, 1666-1668].

[115]H. P. Biggar ["The Exploration of New England by the French" in The Landmark, Vol. 13, No. 4, (1931), p. 233], claims that Champlain named an island The Island of Bacchus on July 8, 1605. At that date, too, the French describe the luxuriant growth of vines on Bacchus Island.

Jacques Cartier. "Cartier's Second Voyage," (535$1260127), p. 48.

[116]________. "Cartier's Third Voyage," (541$1260131), pp. 97, 98.

[117]John Ribault. "The True and Last...," (562 1260097), p. 101. Consult also pp. 113, 140. The same account, except for minor spelling variations, appears in Jean Ribault. The Whole and True..., (563 1261167), p. 72. Consult also p. 95.

Sir John Hawkins ["The Voyage...," (565 1260458), p. 56.] asserts that "in the time that the Frenchmen were there [Florida], they made 20 hogsheads of wine."

"Vray est que pour l'esgard du fruict, i'ay opinion que si les Francois & autres que demeurèrent en ce pays là après nous, continuèrent à faconner nostre vigne, qu'es ans suyvans ils en eurent de beaux & bons raisins. [Brazil][118]

These early accounts motivated the explorations of later French voyagers. Marc Lescarbot's 1609 narrative,[119] for example, repeated almost verbatim Verrazano's 1529 description of Indian viticulture on the Virginia coast.[120] Thus, the fertility and abundance of vines on the shores of the Americas were well-known to early French settlers and, through their literary exposition, to the French, English, and Dutch as well.[121]

In New France, attempts to cultivate both domestic and French vines were successful. The vines were well adapted

---

[118] Jean De Lery. _Histoire d'un voyage faict en la terre du Bresil_ [1578]. Editor, Paul Gaffarel, Paris: Alphonse Lemerre, 1876, Vol. 1, ch. 9, p. 146. Consult also _Ibid_., Vol. 2, ch. 13, p. 27.

[119] Lescarbot. _The History_..., _op_. _cit_., p. 57. Lescarbot, prior to his own narrative, reviewed the findings of earlier French explorers.

[120] _Supra_, Vol. 1, p. 82 , footnote 28.

[121] The importance of this knowledge in stimulating English trade ventures is discussed _Infra_, Vol. 1, pp.243 to 246.

to the rigors of the northern climate.[122] Samuel de Champlain remarked,

> ...I had some native vines planted, which came on very finely. But after I had left the settlement, to come to France, they were all spoiled from neglect, which was a great grief to me on my return.
> ...wild Vines...in mine opinion, if they were dressed, they would be as good as ours.[123]

> There are also plenty of wild vines that bear grapes. The grapes are not so large as those on our vines in France, nor are the bunches so full of them; but I think if they were cultivated they would not differ from them in any respect...
> Some persons have planted in their gardens grape vines brought from France, which have borne very fine and good grapes.[124]

Success at colonial viticulture, however, was inopportune, for the French discouraged or outlawed it, "fearing it might prove prejudicial to the wine trade of France."[125]

---

[122] A possible explanation for the survival of the vine was suggested in <u>The Jesuit Relations</u> [Thwaites. (ed.). <u>op. cit</u>., Vol. 9, p. 155 (1636)].

> ...and when I urged against this the rigor of the cold, they replied that the vine-stock will be safe all Winter under the snow, and that in the Spring it need not be feared that the wines will freeze as they do in France, because they will not sprout so early. All this seems probable.

[123] Samuel de Champlain. "The Voyages and Explorations...," (604$1260496), Vol. 1, p. 181; Vol. 2, pp. 180 to 183. Consult also <u>Ibid</u>., Vol. 1, p. 8.

[124] Pierre Boucher. <u>Histoire véritable natvrelle des moevis et prodvctions du pays de la Novvelle-France</u> (1664), [p. 59] translated in Edward L. Montizambert's <u>Canada in the Seventeenth Century</u>, Montreal: George E. Desbarats & Co., 1883, p. 35.

[125] <u>Calendar of State Papers: Colonial</u>..., (574$1221125), Vol. 18, p. 674 [1706].

> The land is sandy, but is nevertheless good. I also had the Vine planted there, which succeeded admirably. But two years later D'Aunay dispossessed me of it by virtue of a Decree of the Council, although I had a concession from the Company, in consideration of which he made an arrangement with the one who commanded there for me.[126]

> I remember Major de la Valliere told me they had begun to plant vineyards and make wine about Montreal in Canada...and that it was a good table wine, but that the Court of France, fearing it might prove prejudicial to the wine trade of France, forbad their making any more wine in Canada, so that they were forc'd to bury their vines before they could destroy them.[127]

These restrictions notwithstanding, the colonists of New France explained their failure to plant vineyards in economic terms. They stressed the relative scarcity and higher cost of imported grain, compared to wine imports. Pierre Boucher, Nicolas Denys and M. Chambon delineate this position:

---

[126] Nicolas Denys. The Description and Natural History..., (672 1260722), p. 203.

Dr. William Ganong, transistor and editor of Denys' work, states [Ibid., p. 203, footnote 2], "The concession from the Company is unknown; it was most probably from Razilly...Nor is the Decree of Council to D'Aulnay known; I suspect this was simply his commission as Governor of Acadia, which he obtained from the King of France in that year." This author, in seeking to verify Denys' statement, also was unable to find any record of the concession from the Company, or the Decree from the Council. The supposed date of these edicts was circa 1647.

[127] Earl of Bellomont. "Earl of Bellomont to Lords of Trade," (700$1260381), Vol. 4, p. 788.

The enforcement of the French colonial viticultural restrictions in 1700 may well have related to the abundant French vintage in that year. The French were unable to consume the wines of that year. [Cole. French Mercantilism..., op. cit., p. 250.] Under such circumstances of overproduction, French restrictions on colonial viticulture were assuredly enforced.

I will begin with a very frequent... [question] which was whether vines grow well here. I have said already that there are plenty of wild vines and that some from France have been tried and have done pretty well. But why do you not plant vineyards? To this I answer that eating is more necessary than drinking, and therefore the raising of wheat has to be attended to, before the planting of vineyards; one can do better without wine than without bread. It has been as much as we could do to clear land and raise wheat, without doing any thing else.

Is wine dear?...ten sous a quart...

Is wheat dear?...one hundred sous [per] sixty pounds...sometimes it is worth six francs.

...men's daily wages...[are] thirty sous if fed during summer.[128]

If vines have not yet been planted there [New France], it is because the necessary plants have always first place, and these do not require so much time to obtain as wine, for which six or seven years are requisite before a vine can come into bearing, that which it bears before that time being of small worth. For one, two, three, or four hogsheads which one can obtain from the arpent are not of great account. This makes it very plain that it is much more needful to sow grain, and one can much more easily do without wine than without bread.[129]

Or quel pays plus interessé à tirer les vins de Provence que nos établissmens dans

---

[128]Boucher. Histoire véritable...[pp. 136-137], op. cit., p. 70.

Thirty-five years later (1699) Lahontan remarked, "In the taverns a bottle of wine costs six French sous..." ["Lahontan's Travels in Canada" in John Pinkerton. A General Collection of the Best and Most Interesting Voyages and Travels, London: Longman, Hurst, Rees, Orme and Brown, 1812, Vol. 13, p. 362.]

[129]Denys. The Description..., op. cit., pp. 253-254.

> les Isles de l'Amerique? La vigne ne croit point dans ces climats, & quand elle y croitoit, le vin y reviendroit plus cher que de le faire venir de Marseille.[130]

Their explanations indicated that the French problem of grain provisionment affected not only the policies and practices of the mother country but also those of her colonies. At home, France prohibited the planting of new vineyards to assure adequate grain acreage and to lessen overproduction of wine. She similarly prohibited colonial viticulture to assure an export market for her wine and to assure colonial self-sufficiency in grains. The short supply of French grain exports and the reliance of the French upon wine as a primary export thus directed French colonists away from viticulture and wine production.[131]

Explorers traversing the interior regions of North America[132] and traveling along the great rivers of Illinois

---

[130] M. Chambon. Traité général du commerce..., (783$1271228), Vol. 1, p. 55.

[131] The colonists' increasing penchant for beer and bouillon also may have curtailed their viticultural endeavors. Consult Boucher. Histoire véritable...[p. 137], op. cit., pp. 71-72.

Emile Salone. La Colonisation de la Nouvelle-France, Paris: E. Guilmoto, 1906, p. 200.

[132] Hanotaux. La France vivante..., op. cit., pp. 99-100.

Charles de la Ronciere. Histoire de la marine francaise, Paris: Plon-Nourrit et Cie, 1910, Vol. 4, pp. 307 to 337, 629 to 641.

Consult also other sources cited Supra, Vol. 1, pp. 38-39, footnote 58.

and Wisconsin, also noted the abundance of vines. They, too, attempted wine production:

> ...Our Men were immediately sent to view the Country round about that Place, and found a great quantity of ripe Grapes, each Grain of which was as big as a Damascen [a small black plum]: We fell'd several Tree to gather them, and made pretty good Wine...All the Trees in that Country are loaded with Vines, which, if cultivated, would make as good Wine as any in Europe.[133]

> It is true some of these Grapes, for want of Culture, tho' large as Damsons, have great Stones, and a tough Skin; yet they might be easily meliorated by European Skill; tho' as they are, especially Two or Three Sorts of the smaller Kind, are as grateful to the Palate, as most we have in England; but the very worst, duly managed, produces Brandy...[134]

> In some Countries of North-America, the Grape is little, but very well tasted; but towards the Missisipi, 'tis long and thick, and so is the cluster. There has been some Wine press'd from the Grapes of that Country, which after long standing became as sweet as Canary, and as black as Ink.[135]

---

[133]Louis Hennepin. A New Discovery..., (698 1260204), Vol. 1, pp. 129-130. Consult also Ibid., Vol. 2, pp. 151, 213, 224, 309, 405, 622, 642-643, 663.

[134]Daniel Coxe. A Description of La Louisiane, (741 1261176), p. 75.

[135]Baron de Lahontan. New Voyages to North-America, (703$1261199), Vol. 1, p. 368.

Attempts to cultivate the vine in Louisiana proved successful.[136] The cultivation, however, was not extensive. Thomas Hutchins observed that the climate of Louisiana was so favorable that,

> ...France, though she sent few or no emigrants into Louisiana but decayed soldiers, or persons in indigent circumstances, (and those very poorly supplied with the implements of husbandry) soon began to dread a rival in her colony particularly in the cultivation of vines, from which she prohibited the colonists under a very heavy penalty.[137]

Thus, in 1721, "the French government appeared to be smitten with absolute madness"[138] when it adopted an ordinance which prohibited the colonists of Louisiana from cultivating the vine.

Diron d'Artiguiette, Inspector General of Louisiana from 1722-1723, in a "Memorandum of the things which are necessary for the establishment of this colony and which are absolutely indispensable," attacked the 1721 prohibition:

---

[136] Le Page du Pratz, Histoire de la Louisiana, Vol. 2, pp. 15 to 18; and, W. Beer. "Early Census Tables of Louisiana" in Louisiana Historical Society Publications, Vol. 93. Both these sources are cited in Lewis C. Gray. History of Agriculture..., (941 1270207), Vol. 1, p. 75, footnote 147.

[137] Thomas Hutchins. An Historical Narrative...of Louisiana..., (784 1271097), pp. 29-30.
Consult also N. M. Miller Surrey. "The Commerce of Louisiana...," (916 1280634), p. 166.

[138] Robert Lowry and William H. McGardle. A History of Mississippi..., (891$1270758), p. 58.

> That the colony should not be permitted to lack for wine or brandy until the time when every one is permitted to plant vines and should be producing--a thing the company has forbidden.
>
> That the company should send into this colony Frenchmen who have a thorough knowledge of indigo, tobacco and silk, and also vine-dressers, wheelwrights...so that the concessionnaires and other inhabitants should have them at hand when they need them.[139]

Despite such protests, French restriction of colonial viticulture extended as late as 1796. During that year the French government continued to order that the Jesuit vineyard at "Kaskaskia on the borders of the Mississippi" remain untended, "for fear grapes should spread in America and hurt the wine trade of France."[140]

---

[139] Diron d'Artaguiette. "Journal of Diron d'Artaguiette...," (722 1260470), pp. 21-22.

[140] John J. Dufour. The American Vine-Dresser's Guide..., (826 1270248), p. 18.

George Husman [The Cultivation..., (868 1270214), p. 16] records that "in 1796 French settlers in Illinois made one hundred and ten hogshead of strong wine from native grapes." His plagiarism from John Phin [Open Air Grape Culture..., (862 1270215), p. 25] was subject to a typographical error: the correct date is 1769. [The 1769 date is mentioned again without reference to its origin, in James L. Denman. The Vine..., (864 1270219), p. 297].

French opposition to colonial viticulture in Louisiana is commented upon in:

United States Census on Agriculture..., (860$1230261), p. clix. [The 1794 date (Para. 3) should read 1796].

Edward R. Emerson. The Story of the Vine, (902$1270387), pp. 204 to 206.

L. H. Bailey. Sketch of the Evolution..., (906$1270200), pp. 23 to 25.

France's desire to restrict colonial viticulture and wine production in North America extended beyond her own colonial domain. Arthur Hirsch believes that, "the French government intervened on behalf of what she held to be her monopoly on grape culture."[141] He proposes that France attempted to restrict her nationals' viticultural endeavors even within the domain of English colonization.[142]

David Wallace counters, "Charges of the French government's corrupting a British Minister shortly before the Revolution and secretly undermining South Carolina grape planting after the Revolution are too scandalous to be accepted on the 'evidence' offered."[143] Professor Wallace suggests that viticultural trials "based on the skill of the French immigrants for grape culture met...splendid success horticulturally [but were] unprofitable compared with staples financially."[144]

---

[141] Arthur H. Hirsch. "French Influence...," (930 1280799), p. 5.

[142] Ibid., pp. 5-6.
Hirsch. The Huguenots of Colonial South Carolina, (928$1270518), pp. 208 to 210.

[143] David Wallace. The History of South Carolina, (934$1270752), Vol. 1, pp. 387-388.

[144] Ibid., p. 387. Dr. Wallace, himself, does not document his assertion.
Evidence supporting his conclusion is presented Infra., Vol. 1, pp. 160 to 168.

Neither Dr. Hirsch nor Dr. Wallace properly assessed France's role in advancing and restricting the English vintage. Neither academician evaluated the importance of French viticultural technique and skilled labor in advancing English wine production. Neither scholar sufficiently investigated the French desire to restrict her nationals from aiding or abetting English viticultural attempts. The ensuing discussion will reveal that Dr. Hirsch erred in estimating that "economic laws operated against the success of silk... [but] not wine,"[145] and that Dr. Wallace dismissed Dr. Hirsch's contention without investigating other sources which support it.

In their quest for the knowledge necessary to attempt colonial diversification, the English turned to French writers and to French gardening literature. The Perfect Vse of Silk-Wormes was "Done out of the French originall of D'Oliuier de Serres.[146] Similarly, Sir Edwin Sandys "moved that some of the [Virginia] Comp[a]: would please to take the paines to translate...a ffrench book of Silkewormes...into English."[147]

---

[145]Hirsch. The Huguenots..., op. cit., p. 208.

[146]Oliuier de Serres. The Perfect Vse of Silk-Wormes..., (607 1261099), title page.

[147]Susan M. Kingsbury. (ed.). The Records...Virginia Company..., (906 1251144), Vol. 1, pp. 422, 432 (November 15, 1620, December 13, 1620).

In "commanding the present setting vp of silke works, and the planting of vines in Virginia," King James I relied upon a Treatise "By Iohn Bonoeil Frenchman, seruant" to set forth "the Art of making Silke" and "instructions on how to plant and dresse Vines."[148] This treatise was not well-received by the colonists[149] who were bent upon developing

---

[148] Iohn Bonoeil. His Maiesties Graciovs Letter..., (622 1261194), title page.

[149]

> As for ye rest [of the commodities suggested for development] they were had in a generall derision euen amongst themselues, and ye Pamphlets y^t had published there beinge sent thither by Hundreds wer laughed to scorne, and euery base fellow boldly gaue them ye Lye in diuers perticulers, Soe that Tobacco onely was ye buisines & for ought y^t I coulde here euery man madded vppon y^t and lyttle thought or looked for ~~else~~ anything else.
>
> ["The Vnmasked Face of Our Colony in Virginia...," 1622 , quoted in Kingsbury. (ed.). The Records..., op. cit., Vol. 2, pp. 383-384.]

This statement was emphatically denied by the Virginia Company ["The Answers of Diuers Planters...vnto...The Vnmasked Face..." quoted in Kingsbury. (ed.). The Records..., op. cit., Vol. 2, p. 384]. The Company attributed the failure of wine production and silk culture to the 1622 Indian massacre [Ibid., Vol. 2, p. 349 (April 12, 1623); Vol. 4, p. 142 (May, 1623)].

Other statements within The Records [Ibid., Vol. 4, p. 163 (May 2, 1623); p. 452-453 (January 30, 1623/1624)] suggest that wine production had not developed prior to the massacre. Despite an edict ordering viticulture [Ibid., Vol. 3, p. 166 (July 30-August 4, 1619)] and the subsequent mention of creditable vine planting [Ibid., Vol. 2, p. 349 (April 12, 1623)], vineyards apparently had not matured sufficiently at the time of the massacre to yield an extensive vintage.

the tobacco staple.[150] Nevertheless, other tracts followed detailing "the implanting of mulberry trees...the dressing and keeping of vines."[151] These works, also taken from French sources, were seldom heeded in the colonies.[152]

---

[150]The colonist's preference for tobacco culture is discussed _Infra_, Vol. 1, pp. 225 to 229; Appendix II.

[151]E[dward] W[illiams]. _Virginia's Discovery of Silke-VVormes_..., (650 1261193), title page. Quaritch [_General Catalogue_, Vol. 5, pp. 2991-2992] says that John Farrer (or Ferrar) who is refered to in the preface, supplied E. Williams with the material for this work. It appeared in 1650 under the above title and was incorporated within _Virginia: More Especially the South Part Thereof Richly and Truly Valued_ and _Virgo Triumphans_: or, _Virginia Richly and Truly Valued_...

[152]John Lawrence lamented England's reliance upon such tracts.

> Indeed it seems to me no small reproach to the _English_ Nation, that we suffer so many _French_ Books of Gardening to be obtruded upon us, containing Rules calculated for another climate, and which tend to lead us into many Errors.
>
> [John Laurence [Lawrence]. _The Fruit-Garden Kalendar_..., (718 1270989), p. iij.]

Richard Bradley [_A General Treatise_..., (724 1270995), Vol. 2, p. 263] voices a similar complaint against the unsuitability of French tracts. The nonapplicability of these tracts was realized by Edward Williams [_Virginia's Discovery_..., _op. cit._, pp. 31 to 33, 36, 38, 41ff.], who, in adopting a translation of Conrad Heresbach [_Foure Bookes of Husbaudry_, (577$1270971)], inserted passages correcting the French materials for the climate and soil of Virginia. Unfortunately, he had little, if any, first hand knowledge of the viticultural milieu in Virginia. Thus, his statement, "I dare lay my life that if the Vine were but set on foot in VIRGINIA, the ground prepared for it as they doe their Tobacco there, by a right line, holes made instead of their Hillocks, but larger, deeper,..."[W[illiams] _Virginia's Discovery_..., _op. cit._, p. 32.] found little practical application. The colonists adapted the French _chapele_ viticulture technique, wherein the vine is wound on the ground and piled up in such a way as to form a closed bower whereunder it shaded its own ground and thereby retained necessary moisture. [Hirsch. _The Huguenots_...,

The Virginia Company, and later the Crown, preferred to enlist the French themselves to instruct the colonists. There were two major periods of such French settlement: the era of the Virginia Company (1606-1624)[153] and the episode of Huguenot emigration (1680-1732).[154] In the first period, the French government remained taciturn; in the second period, she vituperatively attacked the encroachment of the English upon her silk and viticultural skills.[155]

In the initial colonization of Virginia, the Virginia Company leaned heavily upon Frenchmen to cultivate wine, silk, olives and other English imports, and to instruct the English colonists in the ordering of these pursuits. The encouragement of wine production was of major importance in implementing English policies to promote availability and favorable trade balances.

---

op. cit., p. 206.] The merits and drawbacks of French pruning techniques are discussed by John Lawson ["A New Voyage...," (714 1260428), pp. 115-116.]

[153]John B. Stoudt. Nicolas Martiau..., (932 1270113), pp. 26-27.

[154]R. A. Brock. (ed.). Documents...Huguenot Emigration..., (886 1270112), passim.
"Huguenot Immigrants 1670...," (897$1280764), passim.
Hirsch. The Huguenots..., op. cit., pp. 3 to 43, especially pp. 10 to 14.

[155]Cole. French Mercantilism..., op. cit., pp. 6, 64, 68, 113 to 115, 251.

> ...of each of these [commodities] small quantities...and some wine of those countrie grapes for a triall...
> This happy proceeding caused...Sir Thomas Gates...[to] set saile...the first of June 1609.[156]

The 1610 proposal "to set a Frenchman heere a worke to plant Vines, which grew naturally in great plenty,"[157] was acted upon in that same year.[158] By 1612 vineyards were prevalent in Virginia.[159] Despite this promising

---

[156]"The New Life of Virginea," (612$1260896), p. 204.
J. Leander Bishop. [A History of American Manufactures..., (866$1270016), Vol. 1, p. 267] mistakenly reports that "a sample of wine from native grapes was sent home in 1612." Although he does not cite a source, it is likely that he confused the 1612 year of publication, for 1609, the date of the event. That wines were then produced (1609) in the Virginia Colony is known from Francis Maguel, who, when visiting the Colony in 1609, declared that wines from the grapes of Virginia reminded him of Spanish Alicante. [Philip A. Bruce. Economic History of Virginia..., (896 1270217), Vol. 1, pp. 243-244.]

[157]William Strachy. True Reportoire..., (610 1260512), p. 63.
Gilbert Chinard [Les Refugies Huguenots..., (925 1271224), p. 187] attributes this quote to Lord Delaware.

[158]
> ...especially since the Frenchmen (who are with the Lord Governor) do confidently promise, that within two yeares we may expect a plentifull Vintage.
> ["A Trve Declaration...," (610 1261102), p. 23.]

[159]
> What man or woman soever shall...robbe any vineyard, or gather vp the grapes ...shall be punished with death.
> [Strachey. "For the Colony...," (612 1261083), pp. 16-17 (Item 31).]

beginning under the tutelage of Lord Delaware, viticulture and wine production did not prosper. The colonists' attention was devoted to food staples and tobacco.[160]

The Virginia Company, however, did not let the inadequate returns of prior colonial viticultural experiments discourage their efforts to diversify the colonial economy and to establish wine and silk production as important colonial staples. In 1619 and 1620, "skillfull Vignerons... [sent], wth store allso from hence of Vine plants of ye best Sorte."[161] In 1621 and 1622, "Contract [was] made wth the ffrenchmen procured from Languedock, and sent to Virginia."[162] Vignerons from Spain[163] and the Rhineland[164]

---

[160]The interdependence of these crops is discussed by P. A. Bruce in Economic History of Virginia, [op. cit., Vol. 1, pp. 238-239].

[161]Kingsbury. (ed.). The Records..., op. cit., Vol. 1, p. 353 (May 17, 1620). Consult also Vol. 1, p. 392 (July 7, 1620); Vol. 3, p. 116 (?); Vol. 3, p. 258 (January 16, 1619/1620); Vol. 3, p. 279 (May 17, 1620).

[162]Ibid., Vol. 1, p. 466 (May 2, 1621); Vol. 1, p. 627 (April 10, 1622).
Calendar of State Papers: Colonial..., op. cit., Vol. 1, pp. 498-499, [1621? Addenda].
"Virginias Verger," (625 1260516), p. 246.
Robert Beverley. The History..., (705$1260701), pp. 135-136.

[163]Kingsbury. (ed.). The Records..., op. cit., Vol. 3, p. 258 (January 16, 1619/1620).

[164]"A Declaration...," (620 1261174), p. 15.

also were sought. These vignerons were to implement the Virginia Company edict of 1619,

> ...that every householder doe yearly plant and maintaine ten vines untill they have attained to the art and experience of dressing a Vineyard either by their owne industry or by the Instruction of some Vigneron.[165]

In 1621, further encouragement was offered to silk and wine production.[166] The Virginia Company offered to receive these commodities in exchange for newly-imported servants, and to allow the cultivators first choice of the servants.[167] For a time, the viticultural outlook was hopeful. Vineyards were established, some containing 10,000 vines.[168] A sample of wine sent to England in 1622, however, spoiled

---

[165] Kingsbury. (ed.). The Records..., op. cit., Vol. 3, p. 166 (July 30-August 4, 1619), The edict also required the planting of mulberry trees. Consult Ibid., Vol. 3, p. 581 (January 1621/1622).

[166] Alexander Brown. The First Republic..., (898$1270090), p. 458.

[167] Brock. (ed.). Abstract of Proceedings..., (888 1270100), Vol. 1, p. 92.

No rate of exchange, however, was advanced for colonial wine. The rates established for silk were low and had doubled by 1650 from the original 1621 offer price without a major production response from the colonists. A 1621 valuation of the Commodities growing in Virginia is set forth by W[illiams]. Virginia..., op. cit., pp. 51 to 53.

[168] Kingsbury. (ed.). The Records..., op. cit., Vol. 2, p. 349 (April 12, 1623).

en route, "so that it hath been rather of scandall than creditt unto us."[169]

The Indian massacre later that year more pointedly discouraged the Company's wine producing schemes:

> The vignerouns that haue beene sent are some of them dead, & vnder those that remayne very fewe or noe servants are put, soe can Wee hope for little of that Comoditie from Virginia in manie Yeares: last yeare Wee had a taste of Wyne, this Yeare nothinge, (the Massacre...[170]

Attempts, however, were made to overcome this reversal. Additional French vignerons were requested.[171] An enactment of the Assembly in 1623 required, "that for every four men in the Colony a garden should be laid off to be planted in part in vines."[172] These measures, however, were to littl avail, as greater economic incentives existed for producing other staples, particularly silk, tobacco and rice.[173] Thus,

---

[169] Neill. Virginia Company of London, p. 303 quoted in Lewis C. Gray. History of Agriculture..., op. cit., Vol. 1, p. 23.

[170] Kingsbury. (ed.). The Records..., op. cit., Vol. 4, p. 142 (May, 1623). Consult also Ibid., Vol. 2, p. 349 (April 12, 1623).

[171] Ibid., Vol. 4, p. 68 (March 28, 1623).

[172] Bruce. Economic History of Virginia..., op. cit., Vol. 1, p. 246; p. 246, footnote 1.

[173] Ibid., Vol. 1, pp. 239 to 247.
Gray. History of Agriculture..., op. cit., Vol. 1, pp. 22 to 30.

the Company employed Frenchmen in endeavors that yielded a more immediate return:

> The vignerouns are placed together at Elizabeth City and altogether employed about Silk Worms that they may send home silk next year...[174]

Later colonists, too, remarked about the relative economies of production that discouraged early viticultural endeavors:

> Vines in abundance and variety, do grow naturally over all the land...but some men of worth and estate must give in these things example to the inferiour inhabitants and ordinary sort of men, to shew them the gain and commodity by it, which they will not believe but by experience before their faces: and in tobacco they can make 20 £ sterling a man, at 3d. a pound per annum; and this they find and know, and the present gain is that, that puts out all endeavours from the attempting of others more staple, and

---

[174] "George Sandys to George Ferrar," [1623] in Virginia Magazine of History and Biography, Vol. 6, No. 3, (January 1899), p. 241.

The company also sought to minimize the expense of viticulture:

> A Motion being made that for so much as private planters received by the Frenchman's skill and instructing of others in the art of setting and planting of vines, and in the mystery of making wine, that they be ordered to bear part of the charge thereby to ease the Company, which motion was well approved.
>
> [Brock. (ed.). Abstract of the Proceedings..., op. cit., Vol. 1, p. 170 (April 3, 1622).]
>
> Kingsbury. (ed.). The Records..., op. cit., Vol. 1, pp. 627-628 (April 10, 1622).]

> solid, and rich commodities, out of the heads and hands of the common people...[175]

Notwithstanding, English colonists advocating colonial wine production sought to disguise the comparative economic disadvantage of wine production by shifting the blame for viticultural failure from economic factors to the French vignerons. Edward Williams claims that because the vine-dressers had been "compelled to labour in the quality of slaves" they "could not but express their resentment of it ...[by] conceale[ing] their knowledge." He concludes the

> ...contract made with those vignerons [that] ...the non-performance of this hath beene the originall cause why Virginia at this day doeth not abound with that excellent commodity.[176]

His conclusion echoes that voiced by other activists for viticulture two decades earlier.

> ...with respect to the planting of vines, they have great hope, that it will prove a beneficial commodity; but the vignerors sent here either did not understand the business, or concealed their skill; for they spent their time to little purpose.[177]

---

[175]"A Perfect Description of Virginia...," (649 1260898), pp. 109-110.

[176]W[illiams]. Virginia..., (650 1261196), p. 17.
John Lawson. ["A New Voyage to Carolina...," (714 1260428), p. 117] further details the plight of "these French Refuges [who] have had small Encouragement in Virginia."

[177]The Statutes at Large...Virginia..., (619 1241034), Vol. 1, pp. 135-136 (March 26, 1628).

Such arguments against the French, however, did not dissuade the English from seeking to encourage Huguenot emigration to the colonies. England's second major attempt to encourage the colonial cultivation of wine, silk, olives and other commodities that she purchased abroad, occurred during the episode of Huguenot emigration and, more particularly, during the years proximate to the Revocation of the Edict of Nantes (1685).

Numerous tracts appeared encouraging the French to emigrate to the New World, not only from France but from intermediate locations in Plymouth, Bristol and, above all, London.[178] To the third (1681) edition of _Histoire naturelle et morale des Isles Antillies de L'Amerique_[179] Charles de Rochefort added a forty-three page addendum outlining the fertility and promise of Virginia, Maryland, Carolina, New York, Pennsylvania and New England.[180] This latter tract

---

[178] Gilbert Chinard. _Les Refugies Huguenots..._, _op. cit._, pp. xvii-xviii; p. xvii, footnote 1; pp. 58 to 70
Beer. _The Old Colonial..._, _op. cit._, Vol. 2, p. 188-189; p. 188, footnote 1, 2; p. 189, footnote 1.
Durand Echeverria. _Mirage in the West..._, (957 1270493), pp. 15, 16.

[179] Charles de Rochefort. _Histoire naturelle..._, (665 1261165), [second edition; first edition 1658], passim. Pages 71-72 relate to viticulture.

[180] De Rochefort. _Recit de l'estat présent..._, (681 1261166), passim. Pages 6, 7, 12, 144 relate to viticulture and wine production.

and others, appearing almost contemporaniously, urged persons "to transplant themselves and families to any of the English plantations in America."[181] They related among other inducements the presence of abundant wild vines. They suggested the possibility of viticulture and wine production.[182]

A bill of lading hence describes among the worldly goods of a Huguenot family emigrating to Massachusetts in 1686, a "bundle of wrought yron," and "two chests of vine plants."[183] Analogously, Narraganset County, Rhode Island, developed as a viticultural center until 1692 when resentful English colonizers from Warwick, Rhode Island, pillaged the French crops and tore up young vines hoping to drive out the foreigners.[184] Lord Bellomont indicated the promise of this Rhode Island settlement in 1700, saying,

> there would have been by this time above 500 French families, had they not been most barbarously persecuted and driven away by the people of Rhode Island. The French found the climate and soil in the Naraganset country proper for vineyards, and that dispos'd them to settle there; and I was

---

181 Plantation Work, the Work of This Generation..., [London: 1682], title page. quoted in Chinard. Les Refugies Huguenots..., op. cit., p. 62.

182 Ibid., [Chinard] pp. 62 to 67.

183 Charles W. Baird. History of the Huguenot Emigration..., (885$1270479), Vol. 2, p. 171.

184 Alice B. Lockwood. (ed.). Gardens..., (931$1270869), Vol. 1, p. 184.
Baird. History of Huguenot..., op. cit., Vol. 2, pp. 297 to 302.

> told by some people at Boston that tasted of some wine that grew in that country, that they thought it as good as Bordeaux claret.[185]

Pennsylvania[186] and Carolina,[187] particularly, encouraged French colonists, promising them favorable conditions. They encouraged emigration of specialists in various branches of agriculture, hoping that as immigrants, the French would develop viticulture and other staples.[188] The English Crown also actively encouraged Huguenot emigration to the

---

185 *Calendar of State Papers: Colonial*..., *op. cit.*, Vol. 18, p. 674 [1700].
"Lord Bellomont...," (700$1260381), pp. 787-788 [November 28, 1700].

186 *Lettre de Monsieur Pen...contenant une description générale de la province*, Philadelphia: 1683.
Eclaircissemens de Monsieur Furly sur plusieurs articles touchant l'etablissement de la Pensylvanie, Rotterdam: 1684.
William Penn. *Brief recit de la Province de Pensylvanie*, La Haye: 1684.

187 Samuel Wilson. *Account of the Province of Carolina*..., London: 1682.
Thomas Ash[e]. "Carolina, or a Description...," (682 1260367), passim.
Plan pour former un établissement en Caroline, La Haye: 1686.

188 Chinard. *Les Refugies Huguenots*..., *op. cit.*, p. 62, 65. Other sagas exposing the inaccuracy of the promotional tracts at times countered colonization propaganda, warning the would-be settlers of misgovernment and exaggeration of economic opportunities in the colony. Consult, for example, the "Summary of Remarques...," (686 1260765), pp. 88-89.

plantations of Carolina:[189]

> His Majesty, to support so fine a design, gave to these Frenchmen, whom we transported thither, a free passage for themselves, their wives, children, property and domestics, because many of them are very skilful in the cultivation of the vine and the olive--and also to try if a silk manufactory could succeed in that country.[190]

The results of such immigration were soon noticed in Virginia and also in Carolina:

> ...wine can be made in Virginia in large quantities, & very good...
>
> I know Frenchmen like wine better than either beer or cider, & there are six times more grapevines in these two provinces [Rappahannock and Estafort, Virginia] than elsewhere.[191]

> ...some of the wine [from Carolina] has been transported for England, which by the best palates was well approved of, and more is daily expected...Some of the proprietors and planters had already sent them the best vines of Europe, the Rhenish, Claret, Muscadel, Canary &C. His Majesty, to improve so hopeful a design, gave those French we carried over, their passage free...

---

[189] Richard B. Morris. Government and Labor in Early America, (946$1270718), pp. 22 to 26; p. 24, footnote 15. "Huguenot Immigration...," op. cit., pp. 9 to 11. Hirsch. The Huguenots..., op. cit., pp. 10 to 13. Infra, Vol. 1, p. 275 , footnote 91.

[190] Ash[e]. "Carolina, or a Description...," op. cit., quoted in M. Charles Weiss. History of the French Protestant..., (854 1270533), Vol. 1, p. 348.

[191] Francois Durand. "Voyages...," (687 1260435), pp. 173, 175.

> they being most of them well experienced in the nature of the Vine.[192]

ware of these colonial successes, the French attempted to estrict the exodus of vinedressers and others who ossessed viticultural skills.[193]

The French, however, were unnecessarily concerned bout their nationals in English colonial viticulture, for hese colonists generally did not decide in favor of such ursuits. Madeira, Canary and wines of the Azores increasngly replaced imported French dry wines, reflecting the

---

[192] "Description of Carolina, 1682," quoted in Abiel olmes. (ed.). The Annals..., (829 1270212), p. 433, footote 2.

The Huguenot immigrants, too, predicted favorable intages ahead:

> ...inasmuch that the French Protestants who are there [in Carolina] and skilled in wines do no way doubt of producing great quantities and very good.
>
> [Samuel Wilson. "Account of the Province of Carolina...1682," quoted in "Huguenot Immigrants...," (897$1280764), p. 11.]

[193] Cole. French Mercantilism..., op. cit., pp. 6, 64, 8, 113 to 115, 251.

The overproduction of wine in 1700 heightened such ttempts, for it paralleled in time the near-prohibitive xcises (1698) of the English upon French wines and the ethuen Treaty (1703) which placed French wines at an conomic disadvantage to those of Portugal. All these vents deepened France's concern for the sanctity of her ine market, especially in the face of the dissipation of er virtual skills monopoly. She thus renewed her colonial iticultural restrictions in 1700 and continued to enforce ich restrictive measures throughout the eighteenth century Supra, Vol. 1, pp. 151f.]. The evidence adduced by Dr. Hirsch Supra, Vol. 1, pp.158-159] suggesting the restriction of renchmen's viticultural endeavors even within the domain of nglish colonization is, therefore, but a single element of larger, more uniformly, applied French policy. Dr. Hirsch nd Dr. Wallace fail to identify this policy.

changing colonial and mother country tastes.[194] These changing tastes made other commodities such as silk, rice and indigo promise a better market and consequently higher and more immediate returns on labor and capital investment.

> The dearness of labour, and the cheapness of foreign vines [wines] in America, have both contributed to prevent the planting of vineyards more frequently. The French refuges planted some in South Carolina, and I have drank a red wine of the growth of that province little inferior to Burgundy.
>
> ...it will, probably, not be owing to any defect either in soil or climate, but to the dearness of labour, or negligence of the inhabitants, if wine is not produced hereafter in some plenty upon this continent.[195]

---

[194]The availability and popularity of these sweet wines is discussed in:

Robert Beverly. The History..., (705$1260701), p. 293.

William Byrd. William Byrd's Natural History..., (737 1260772), pp. 89-90.

"A Description of South Carolina," (761$1260397), p. 231.

Hinton. "A Short Description...," (763 1260398), p. 497.

[195]William Stork. (ed.). A Description...by John Bartram..., (769 1261107), p. 29.

Not all colonists, and particularly not Robert Beverly, a staunch advocate of colonial wine production, [Bruce. Economic History.. , op. cit., Vol. 1, pp. 470 to 472], were willing to admit the economic failure of viticulture in Virginia and Carolina.

> But here I find an Objection...that Vineyards have been attempted both in Virginia and Carolina; and that several French Men went over to Carolina, on purpose to make wine; and yet they could not succeed in it, but miscarried in all their Attempts. This I readily own: But I'll tell you what Progress they made,

In stark contrast to the curtailment of colonial viticulture and to the attempted protection of French viticultural skills and wine markets were the feeble efforts of the French to develop and maintain a wine trade.[196] In this respect, French wine trade policy diverged sharply from that of the Netherlands. Both countries, however, similarly failed to encourage colonial grape culture, the Dutch having a copious supply of wine through entrepot trade, the

---

> and why at last it came to nothing.
> The Pine-Tree and Fir are naturally very noxious to the Vine...
> [Beverley. _The History_..., _op_. _cit_., pp. 133-134.]

[196] Roger Dion. _Histoire de la vigne_..., (959$1270166), pp. 30 to 32.

M. L. Bachelier. _Histoire du commerce de Bordeaux_..., (862 1270612), pp. 70, 71 to 89, 104-105, 205-206.

Guillaume Geraud-Parracha. _Le Commerce de vins et des eaux-de-vie en Languedoc sous l'ancien regime_, Montpellier: Universite de Montpellier, 1955, pp. 10-11.

Emile Coornaert. _Les Francais et le commerce international à Anvers_..., (961 1270740), pp. 98 to 103, 111; 305 to 315 [a fine bibliography].

Cole. _Colbert_..., _op_. _cit_., Vol. 1, pp. 443 to 450.

> From the particular _Trade_ of the Cities of _France_, let us view the trade in generall of this _Kingdome_, and we shall not finde it of any great consequence, for heere it is found that the Gentlemen doe not meddle with Traffique, because they thinke such Traffique ignoble and base, and so unfit for them.
> [Lewes Roberts. _The Merchants Mappe_..., (637$1271191), Bk. 2, pp. 48. Consult also _Ibid_., pp. 49-50.

Simon. _The History_..., _op_. _cit_., Vol. 3, pp. 253 to 271; 272 to 298.

Consult also _Supra_, Vol. 1, pp. 120, 124-125.

French, hoping to assure a market for home production. In contrast, the English strove to promote colonial viticulture both as a means of thwarting colonial balance of trade losses and, hopefully, as a means of developing a source of wine supply. The origins of this English notion for commodity availability from colonization and particularly for the availability of wine from colonial vineyards appear in earliest Elizabethen times. They stem not only from economic considerations but, as well, from causes as remote as paradisical images of the vine.

CHAPTER 5

The English Experience

Colonization was too abstract a design to suit the Elizabethan. Englishmen of that era contemplated gains through trade, the fortunes of piracy, and the reap and carry of gold, silver and pearls.

Yet, the idea of colonization was soon to take hold. It evolved from the English need to augment their imports of raw materials and their exports of finished goods in order to accomodate the increased production of staples, and to strengthen their defense forces. It became more acceptable when trade, piracy, plunder, warfare and restrictive maritime policies no longer could meet the expanding commercial and military demands of the state. In these circumstances, England encouraged colonization ventures to promote royal (public) revenue, commodity availability and favorable trade balances.[1]

---

[1]These motives of English colonization parallel those of other European states. They are discussed Supra, Vol. 1, pp. 68 to 72; Infra, Vol. 1, pp. 300 to 302.

In presenting an "economic theory of colonization,"[2] Professor George Beer concluded that, "This desire to free England from the necessity of purchasing from foreigners formed the underlying basis of English commercial and colonial expansion."[3] He detailed the importance of colonial expansion in freeing England from dependence on European rivals. England accomplished this by obtaining direct access to the Far East, by expanding the English fishing industry and by developing new supply sources in America.[4]

Dr. Beer and others who support commodity availability as the germ motive of English territorial expansion[5] have

---

[2]George Beer. The Origins..., (922$1271268), pp. 53 to 77.

________. "The Early English...[Pt. 2]," (908$1280786), pp. 245 to 253.

[3]Beer. The Origins..., op. cit., p. 57.

Dr. Beer demonstrated that "the predominance of this idea was a direct consequence of the prevailing economic theories and of the conditions existing in England's foreign trade." [Ibid., pp. 70-71.]

In "The Early English...[Pt. 1]," (908$1280785), pp. 75-78, Professor Beer discussed England's expansion within a broader framework.

[4]Beer. The Origins..., op. cit., p. 59 to 65.

[5]Susan Kingsbury. "A Comparison of the Virginia Company...," (908 1280046), pp. 161 to 164.

Louis B. Wright. The Colonial Search..., (953$1270463), pp. 7, 23 to 32.

________. The Dream of Prosperity..., (964$1270464), pp. 22 to 39.

A. L. Rowse. The Expansion of Elizabethan England, (955$1271230), pp. 160 to 162.

E. G. R. Taylor. Late Tudor and Early Stuart..., (934 1270654), pp. 159-160, 163 to 167.

Wallace Notestein. The English People..., (954 1270700), pp. 250-256.

William R. Scott. The Constitution..., (910 1270946),

cited England's dependence on "supplies, such as copper, iron, steel, shiptimber, masts, cordage, and soap ashes, otherwise obtainable only 'at the curtesie of other Princes, under the burthen of great Custons, and heavy impositions.'" They have emphasized that initially it was the erection of trading posts, and not the establishment of new communities in America, that entertained the Elizabethan.[7] The search for gold, silver, pearls, naval stores, drugs, spices, silk and fishing grounds dominate in their writings and in statements depicting early colonization attempts. England's efforts to promote domestic and colonial viticulture and wine production receive scant attention.

This chapter, however, demonstrates the importance of wine in English mercantile practice. In supporting the Commodity Mercantilism thesis, it argues that domestic and colonial oenological endeavors were advanced to thwart balance of trade losses and to develop sources of wine supply. It shows that the popularity of wine in England propelled these efforts as well as measures to stem the foreign wine trade and to curb wine prices.

Vol. 2, passim.

[6]"A True and Sincere Declaration...," [1609] quoted in Beer. The Origins..., op. cit., p. 67.

[7]Beer. "The Early English...[Pt. 2]," op. cit., pp. 250-251.

__________. The Origins..., op. cit., pp. 55,56.

Kingsbury. "A comparison of the Virginia Company...," op. cit., p. 162 to 167.

Eli Heckscher. Mercantilism, (935$1270922), Vol. 1,

The sum of these tendencies, however, was periodic English interest in the wine trade. While the promotion of English shipping, the augmentation of royal (public) revenue, and the satisfaction of the royal palate all advanced the wine trade, the desire for still greater revenue averted English interest from wine to tobacco production, silk culture, and gin manufacture. Viticulture was promoted only when it manifested comparative advantages in production.

The traditional policy of encouraging the wine trade[8] was discarded under Edward VI, because the navy had dwindled so during his reign that it could not serve the merchants properly.[9] In 1558, Elizabeth partially restored the old rule; a statute was passed imposing discriminatory duties on the cargo of foreign ships.[10] Another statute superceded it in 1563, reviving the traditional policy of

---

p. 340.

[8] The Statutes of the Realm, (377$1221136), Vol. 2, p. 535 [4 Henry VII. c. 10]; Vol. 3, p. 177 [7 Henry VIII. c. 2]; Vol. 3, p. 374 [23 Henry VIII. c. 7].

[9] Ibid., Vol. 4, pt. 1, p. 154 [5 & 6 Edward VI. c. 18].

[10] Ibid., I Elizabeth c. 13 discussed in:

W. Cunningham. The Growth of English Industry and Commerce in Modern Times, Cambridge: The University Press, 1903, p. 70; p. 73, footnote 2.
George L. Craik. The History of British Commerce..., (844 1270746), pp. 239-240.

limiting foreign wine imports to "Ships of [English] Subjects."[11]

In a paper entitled "The Inconveniences of enlargyng any power to bryng any more wyne into the realme," William Cecil attacked this policy. He hypothesized the consequences of the excesses and losses implicit in the development of the wine trade.[12] He demonstrated that encouraging the fisheries would have none of these disadvantages.[13] William Cecil asserted:

> It is manifest, that nothyng robbeth ye realme of England, but what moore marchandises is brought into ye realme than is carryed forth... because the balance must be payd with mony...the remedy hereof is by all pollyces to abridg ye use of such forrayn commoditiees as be not necessary for us. Whereof sit ye excess of silks is one, of wyne and spyce is another. And thereor wyttyngly to make a law to increas any of theis is to consent to ye robbery of ye realme.[14]

---

[11] The Statutes of the Realm, op. cit., Vol. 4, pt. 1, pp. 423 to 427 [5 Elizabeth c. 5 § 8]. This act was repealed by 3 George IV. c. 41 § 2.

[12] William Cecil's paper is discussed in:

E. Lipson. The Economic History..., (961 1271271), Vol. 3, p. 99.
Cunningham. The Growth of English Industry..., op. cit., pp. 70 to 73.
John R. Jones. London's Import Trade..., (942 1210188), pp. 225 to 227.

[13] Encouragements offered to the fishing trade under his authority are discussed Supra, Vol. 1, p. 54; pp. 54-55, footnote 98.

[14] Calendar of State Papers: Domestic..., (547 1221116), Vol. 1, p. 277; item XLI. 58 [1566?].

Regarding these excesses, William Cecil maintained "that none is more hurtfull to the realme than wyne." He advanced four points supporting this contention. First, the wine trade "enrycheth France whose power England ought not to increase." Second, the wines from Bordeaux and Rouen must be paid for in money, "for in Burdeaux they have an ordonance forbyddyng barteryng with Englishmen for wynes," so that the gold brought home by merchants from "Spain or the Low Countries...is conveyed into France" instead of enriching England.[15] Third, the increasing number of taverns in England would encourage domestic disorder, by promoting the drunkenness of "vulgar people who...[would] wast ther small substance which they gett by ther hand labor." Fourth, "the excessyve drynkyng of wyne deminisheth the use of ale and beare, and consequently decayeth tillage for grayne which of all labors in the realme wold be favored, and cheriched and preferred before such an unnecessary forrayn commoditee as wyne is."[16]

---

[15]The annual export of fine gold to France at this time was estimated at £100,000 [Lipson. The Economic History..., op. cit., Vol. 3, p. 99; p. 99, footnote 3]. Excesses in the imports of foreign commodites, including wine, were lamented. ["The Reasons Why...," (558$1260617), p. 419, item 3]. Hitchcock in A Politique Platt, [London: 1580], maintained that French wares, "beside the wines," amounted to six times the value of English exports to France.

[16]Calendar of States Papers: Domestic..., (547 1221116), op. cit., Vol. 1, p. 277; item XLI. 58 [1566?].

Lord Burghley (William Cecil) also feared rising wine prices. He reasoned that the increasing popularity of French wines in England would advance wine prices rapidly if they were not checked by statutory restrictions. To further this end, in 1572, he became one of a committee of six which regulated wine prices.[17]

Lord Burghley was instrumental, as well, in blocking the incorporation of the "Mere merchants trading to France" who sought a monopoly of the French trade. This group cogently argued that a monopoly could fix the purchase season for French wines (assuring thereby the quality and readiness of the wines shipped to England), and could lessen competition for French wine among English merchants and retailers. The merchants held this competition responsible for the high retail price of French wines in England.[18] The Privy Council, fearing that these merchants would facilitate the French trade and beggar England, repeatedly refused the incorporation.[19]

---

[17]Jones. London's Import Trade..., op. cit., pp. 227-228.

[18]The merchants argued "that some of theis retaylers now beginne, and the rest will follow to sue for higher [wine] price...the profitt whereof will runne to Fraunce where yt will staye." [Calendar of State Papers: Domestic..., (547 1221116), op. cit., p. 504, item 47 [September ? 1575].]

[19]The French Company was finally incorporated in 1611 under the name "Governor and Company of Merchants of London trading into France and the Dominions thereof." [Lipson. The Economic History..., (961 1271270), p. 363.] The delay emphasizes English awareness of the deleterious nature of

Despite these endeavors, both the satisfaction of the royal palate and the promotion of royal revenue favored availability over balance of trade considerations. The refusal of William Cecil to promote the carrying and re-export of wine and his alternative encouragement of the English fishing trades, thus, handicapped his later schemes to control English wine imports and wine prices. With foreign states dominating the English wine trade, attempts to mitigate trade losses by controlling the trade itself were futile. Wine imports mounted,[20] particularly those of

---

the French trade.

The incorporation of the Spanish Company in 1577 and of the Eastland Company in 1578 attests to the beneficial nature of these trades [Ibid., p. 364; R. H. Tawney. Studies in Economic History..., (958 1270953), pp. 183 to 194; and, F. J. Fisher. "Commercial Trends...," (940 1281233), pp. 170 171.] It served as a poignant contrast to the "mere merchants trading to France" whose most intense efforts for incorporation occurred between 1574 and 1579. [Jones. London's Import Trade..., op. cit., pp. 228 to 231; p. 231, footnote 1.]

20

> The quantity of wine that pours into England and the Low Countries from France might seem incredible, yet it is a fact. I have no better evidence of this than the fact that in 1578 one Lauda, a merchant of Cambrai, was responsible for exporting 33,000 modii [268 liters per muid barrel] of wine [from France]... overland...
>
> [Jean Bodin. The Six Bookes..., (606$1271243), p. A158, item 662 K_2.]

> And as all estate doo exceed herin, I meane for strangenesse and number of costlie dishes, so these forget not to vse the like excesse in wine, in somuch... [as we import] yearelie to the proportion of 20000 or 30000 tun and vpwards,...

France;[21] wine prizes (statutory price ceilings) more than

> Neither doo I meane this of small wines onlie, as Claret, White, Red, French, &c: which amount to about fiftie six sorts...but also of the thirtie kinds of Italian, Grecian, Spanish, Canarian, &c: whereof Veruage, Cate pument, Raspis, Muscadell, Romnie, Bastard Tire, Ossie, Caprike, Clareie & Malmeseie are not least of all accompted of, bicause of their strength and valure.
> [Raphael Holinshed. Holinshed's Chronicles..., (586 1270038), Vol. 1, p. 281.]

"Journal de l'ambassade d'Hurault de Maisse en 1597-1598," folio 293 quoted in Gustav Fagniez. L'Economie sociale de la France sous Henri IV 1589-1610. Paris: Librarie Hachette et c^{ie}, 1897, p. 260.

"A Special Direction...," (590$1280183), pp. 429 to 437.

Edward Ieninges [Jenings]. A Briefe Discouery..., (590 1261052), folio B_3 verso.

21 FRENCH WINE IMPORTS TO LONDON

YEAR	QUANTITY (TUNS)	MARKET PRICE PER TUN	ESTIMATED VALUE ▯
1558-1559	958*	L5 6s. #	L5,077 8s. 0d.
1561-1562	2,457*	L10 0s. 0d.#	L24,570 0s. 0d.
1564-1565	2,002*	L7 6s.8d. #	L14,674 13s. 4d.
1565-1566	1,119*	[L7 0s. 6d.]@	L7,860 19s. 6d.
1566-1567	3,062 2/3**	L6 8s. 6d. #	L19,667 12s. 0d.
1594-1595	4,062 1/6**	L22 10s. 0d. #	L91,398 10s. 0d.
1596-1597	7,374 1/4**	[L20 0s. 0d.]@	L147,530 0s. 0d.
1599-1600	8,535 2/3**	L16 0s. 0d.#	L136,565 6s. 8d.

▯ Values are calculated by multiplication of columns two and three. The wide divergence between these estimates for 1558 to 1566 and those of Dr. Jones [London's Import Trade..., op. cit., p. 216] is a result of my use of market prices. Dr. Jones' values are based on "The Port Book" rates which purportedly remained constant for the entire period [Ibid., p. 81]. He does not estimate any values for French wine imports between 1566 and 1600.

* Jones. London's Import Trade..., op. cit., p. 216.

doubled between 1564 and 1591.[22] The market price of wine

\# Andre Simon. The History of the Wine Trade in England, London: The Holland Press, 1964, [facsimile reprint of the 1906 edition], Vol. 2, pp. 282 to 291. "Gascony [Bordeaux]" wine prices are listed for dates when "French" prices are unavailable. The wine prizes of these wines were identical between 1564 and 1591. [Consult footnote 22, below.]

** Jones. London's Import Trade..., op. cit., p. 217. Dr. Jones gathered import figures (1558 to 1600, as above) from "The Port Book" of London [Ibid., pp. 1-2]. These figures do not include any allowance for smuggling which, for all goods, Dr. Jones estimates "conservatively [at] fifty per cent" [Ibid., p. 30].

@ Values are estimated are from Simon. The History..., op. cit., Vol. 2, pp. 282-291.

22 WINE PRIZES 1564-1591

DATE	"BEST FRENCH" AND "BEST GASCONY" PER TUN	PAGE*	ITEM*
Dec. 22, 1564	L6 6s. 8d.	64	603
Dec. 20, 1565	L7 6s. 8d.	65	615
Dec. 22, 1572	L8 6s. 8d.	73	678
Nov. 24, 1578	L11 13s. 4d.	78	730
Nov. 24, 1579	L12 0s. 0d.	79	741
Nov. 11, 1581	L13 0s. 0d.	81	761
Nov. 6, 1583	L12 0s. 0d.	83	771
Nov. 13, 1584	L11 0s. 0d.	83	776
Nov. 26, 1588	L15 0s. 0d.	88	808
Dec. 1, 1590	L15 0s. 0d.	91	828
Dec. 17, 1591	L16 0s. 0d.	93	841

*Page and Item numbers refer to pages and items in James L. Crawford (ed.), Tudor and Stuart..., (910 1271130).

increased almost fourfold during Elizabeth's reign,[23] thereby advancing the price of wine farms and generally promoting fiscalism.[24]

---

[23] Supra, Vol. 1, pp. 185-186, footnote 21.
Simon. The History..., op. cit., Vol. 2, pp. 173-175.
William Beveridge. Prices and Wages in England..., (939 1270716), Vol. 1, pp. 87, 88, 114.
James E. Thorold Rogers. A History of Agriculture and Prices..., (882 1270184), Vol. 4, pp. 688, 690; Vol. 5, pp. 470, 472, 476.

[24] The privilege of collecting the excises on imported wines was sold, or "farmed," to tax collectors who for a stipulated sum purchased from the Crown the right of collection. The purchase prices, or bids and offers for these wine farms are listed below (1568 to 1619) and Infra, Vol. 1, pp. 212 to 214, footnote 75 (1611 to 1701).

WINE FARM DATA: ENGLAND, 1568-1619

DATE	FARM PRICE	COMMENT	SOURCE
1568	L7,000 13s. 4d.	-	Frederick Dietz. English Public Finance 1558-1641, (932$1270729), p. 314.
1571	L7,000 13s. 4d.	Impositions on French wines.	Ibid., p. 315.
1574	-	Wine farm allowed to lapse; wine impositions, customs and subsidies collected directly in Queen's name.	Ibid., p. 316.
1593	L12,000 plus 240 tuns wine	French wine farm reinstated.	Ibid., p. 74, 316.

The extent to which royal prerogative influenced the inundation of French wines and demoralized efforts to stem balance of trade losses is delineated in the *Calendar of State Papers: Domestic*.[25] Two cases suggest the nature of these entries:

1595 24 March	L10,000 plus 200 tuns wine	-	*Calendar of State Papers: Domestic*... (547 1221116), *op. cit.*, Vol. 4, p. 19, item 64.
1599 20 July	L11,385 12s. 11d.	Collected by tax farmer in 1598. Suggested offer price for 1599 L14,000 plus 200 tuns good wine.	*Ibid.*, Vol. 5, p. 248, item 99.
1599	L15,000 plus 200 tuns wine	L10,000 paid in hand; L4,000 at Lady Day.	Dietz. *English Public Finance*..., *op. cit.*, p. 91.
1603	L14,000	-	*Ibid.*, p. 346.
1611	L22,000 plus L6,000 fine	Swinnerton bids for wine farm charging fraud on part of present farmers "by which the King lost L70,000 yearly."	*Ibid.*, p. 154.
1619 1 July	L50,000	-	*Ibid.*, p. 177.

[25]Hubert Hall. "The Imperial Policy...," (886 1280267), p. 208ff.

10 January 1564
"Proclamation prohibiting the import of French wines by reason of the enmity between England and France."[26]

22 June 1564
The Queen to Winchester: "To permit subjects of the French king to import wines and woad in their own vessels, notwithstanding the statutes to the contrary."[27]

September ? 1575
Wine prices were restrained to L10 the tun.[28]

15 July 1576
Council to Lord Mayor of London: Remove price-fixing on wine "until wines may be procured at a lower rate than L10 per tun."[29]

Elizabeth I demanded, and was accustomed to, the finest wines.

> Having found that her Majesty, some time ago, was pleased with their wine, they are sending her some barrels of Neustadt and Bacharach. Although this, the best there is in their country, will seem poor to her, accustomed as they are in England to the best wines, they pray her majesty not to disdain to accept it with a kind heart and cheerful countenance.[30]

Her example influenced the Court and the lesser nobility, who increasingly turned from the treacle and medicinal uses

---

[26] Calendar of State Papers: Domestic..., (547 1221116), op. cit., Vol. 1, p. 234, item 3 [10 January 1564].

[27] Ibid., Vol. 1, p. 241, item 30 [22 June 1564].

[28] Ibid., Vol. 1, p. 504, item 47 [September ? 1575].

[29] Ibid., Vol. 1, p. 525, item 58 [15 July 1576].

[30] Calendar of State Papers: Foreign..., (558 1221124), Vol. 19, p. 160 [Heidelberg 19 November 1584].
Consult also Ibid., Vol. 11, p. 361, item 880 [20 August 1576]; Vol. 18, p. 272, item 314 [16 December 1584]; Vol. 20, p. 381 [16 February 1586].

of wine[31] to wine as a beverage. John Stow noted that,

---

[31]Wines were mixed with herbs to serve as treacles in the administration of medicines. * They, too, served as the carrying agents in the distillation of medicinal compounds.** With oil, they were used to cleanse wounds.*** Wine by itself was recommended as a therapeutic adjunct to the diet.# These uses followed the humoral doctrine which assigned to all things, including wine, complexions based upon their "quality."##

> White Muskadell, and Candie wine, and Greeke,
> Do make men's wits and bodies grosse and fat;
> Red Wine doth make the voyce oft-time to seeke
> And hath a binding qualitie to that;
> Canarie, and Madera, both are like
> To make one leane indeed; (but wot you what)
> Who say they make one leane, would make one laffe
> They meane, they make one leane vpon a staffe.
> Wine, women, Baths, by Art or Nature warme,
> Vs'd or abus'd do men much good or harme.###

The "humors" of dry wines differed markedly from those of sweet wines. Dry wines were thought to lack nutritional value and to be unsuitable for "them who either have or are in danger of the stone, the rheum, and divers other diseases."▯ Thus, sugar and honey were added often to the dry French wines.▯▯

* R. Banckes. An Herball..., (525 1270966), folio I iii-iv, II ii, F iv.
Floridus Macer. Macers Herbal..., (530 1270956), folio B1, B3, C3ff.
Thomas Moulton. This is the Myrrour..., (540 1271056), passim.
William Turner. A Book of Wines, (586$1260180), pp. 1, 3, passim ("annexed book").
John Gerarde. The Herball..., (633 1270959), pp. 75D, 1046D, 1130B, 1564F.
________. The Herball..., (636 1270960), pp. 75D, 1046D, 1130B, 1564F.
Robert Lovell. Enchiridon Botanicum..., (665 1270956), pp. 376, 468, 472.
John Smith. England's Improvement Revived..., (670 1271198), p. 206.

** [Conrad Gesner]. A New Booke of Destillatyon..., (565 1271053), pp. 124, 148, 152ff.
________. A Newe Iewell of Health..., (576 1271054), p. 74 recto.

*** Levinus Lemnius. An Herbal..., (587 1270967),

---

pp. 35, 134.

\# Arnaldus de Villanova. _The Earliest Printed Book on Wine_, (478$1270194), p. 24ff.
Francis Packard. (ed.). _The School of Salerum_..., (554 1271080), pp. 80 to 83.
Gerarde. _The Herball_..., _op_. _cit_., p. 881, items C., N.; p. 884, items C. to H.
T[obias] Venner. _Via Recta ad vitam longam_..., (628 1271059), pp. 21 to 28.
Lovell. _Enchiridon Botanicum_..., _op_. _cit_., pp. 452 to 454.
Jonathan Pereira. _The Elements of Materia Medica_..., (839 1270392), pp. 1225-1226.

\#\# Andrewe Boord. _Here Followeth_..., (576 1271060), folio C4 verso to D2 recto.
Thomas Cogan. _The Haven of Health_..., (596 1261062), pp. 202-203, 206-207.
Venner. _Via Recta ad vitam longam_..., _op_. _cit_., pp. 20 to 25.
Thomas Short. _Discourses on Tea_..., (750 1271190), pp. 308 to 310.
J. C. Drummond and Anne Wilbraham. _The Englishman's Food_, (940$1271070), pp. 72 to 75.
Paul R. Weidner. _An Elizabethan Wine List_..., (956$1211087), pp. 9, 10.

\#\#\# Packard. (ed.). _The School of Salerum_..., _op_. _cit_., p. 82.

▯ Turner. _A Book of Wines_, _op_. _cit_., pp. 1, 3ff. Dr. Turner offered "a confutation of an error of some men who hold that Rhenish and other small white wines ought not to be drunken." The peculiarities of Dr. Turner's approach are discussed by Philip M. Wagner. "An Oenological Note," (941$1270181), pp. xiii-xiv, passim.

▯▯
> In summer the ladies and some gentlemen put sugar in their wine, with the result that there are great goings on in the place [England].
>
> [_Calendar of Letters...Spain_, (554 1221126), Vol. 13, p. 30, item 37 [17 August 1554].]

George Gascoyne [B. Garter]. _A Delicate Diet_..., (576$1261050), folio C4 recto, C4 verso.
Thomas Milbourn. _The Vintners' Company_..., (888 1270013), p. 20.
F. W. Hackwood. _Good Cheer_..., (911$1271075), p. 125.
Weidner. _An Elizabethan Wine List_..., _op_. _cit_., pp. 5-6.

> no sacks were sold but Rumney, and
> that for medicine more than for
> drink, [1547], but now [1597]many kinds
> of sacks are known and used.32

The increasing popularity of wine at their tables is attested to in many Elizabethan narratives.[33] For example, George Wither wrote:

> Of Perry, cider, mead, metheglin, ale,
> Of Beer they have Abundant, but then
> This does not serve the richer sort of men;
> They with all sorts of foreign are sped,
> Their cellars are all fraught with white and red,
> Be it Italian, French, Spanish, if they crave it,
> Nay, Grecian or Canarian, they may have it,
> Cete, Pument, Vervage, if they so desire,
> Or Romney, Bastard, Capricks, Osey, Tire
> Muscadell, Malmsey, Clarey--what they will,[34]

---

[32]John Stow. Survey of London..., (598$1260175), p. 90, col. 2.

[33]Gascoyne [Garter]. A Delicate Diet..., op. cit., C4 recto.
Holinshed. Holinshed's Chronicles..., op. cit., p. 281 [Quoted Supra, Vol. 1, pp. 184-185, footnote 20.]
Frederick, Duke of Wirtenberg. "Letter...," (598$1260024), p. 109.
Weidner. An Elizabethan Wine List..., op. cit., pp. 1 to 5.

[34]George Withers is quoted in Charles Cooper. The English Table..., (929$1271218), pp. 43-44.

A shift to dry French wines accompanied the increasing wine consumption.[35] "The Port Book" unfolds "eloquent support to the assertion that...[French] wine imports constituted a flood and not a mere trickle."[36] Lord Burghley's fears were confirmed: wine drunkenness prevailed;[37] wine

---

[35]Dietz. "English Government Finance," (920$1280714), p. 208.

________. "The Exchequer in Elizabeth's Reign," (923$1280599), pp. 68 to 71, 80 to 91.

Hall. A History of the Custon-Revenue..., (892 1270712), passim.

These "Receipts of the Exchequer" offer accounts of royal revenue derived from "sweet" and "French" wine farms. They indicate that after 1578, and especially after 1589, the sale value of the French wine farm rose markedly [Consult Supra, Vol. 1, pp. 187-188, footnote 24 ,while that of the sweet wine farm remained at L2,743 13s. 11d. Even under "De Collectoribus" when sweet wine customs were not farmed (1601; 1602), the customs revenue (L5,927 15s. 10d.; L6,883 19s. 8d.) was substantially below the French farm price (L11,424 15s. 8d.; L14,896 0s. 0d.).

[36]Jones. London's Import Trade..., op. cit., p. 215.

[37]Gascoyne. [Garter]. A Delicate Diet..., op. cit., C_4 verso.

Sp. You spake of drunkenes, what say you of yt?

Phi. I say it is a horrible vice, and too too much used in Ail. [England] Every Country, citie, towne, village or other, hath abundance of ale-houses, taverns, and innes, which are so fraughted with mault-wormes, night and day, that you would wunder to see them. You shall have them there sitting at the wine and good ale all the day long, yea, all the night too, peradventure a whole week...Then, with the spirit of the buttery they are then possessed a world it is to consider their gestures and demenour, how they stut and stammer, stagger reele to and fro like madmen: some vomiting, spewing, and disgorging their filthie stomacks; other some (honor sit aribus) pissing under the boord as they sit.

[Phillip Stubbes. The Anatomie of

disproportionately supplemented domestic brews;[38] wine prices

---

Abuse..., (583 1261065), pp. 107-108.]

[Hugh Platt]. The Jewell House..., (594$1271061), p. 62, item 69.

William Shakespeare. The Merchant of Venice, I, 2, 73-82.

__________. Hamlet, V, 1, 165 to 170.

__________. 1 Henry IV, II, 4, 168ff.

[38]At the outset of Elizabeth's reign, beer and ale enjoyed equal popularity. # In the century since its introduction to England from the Netherlands, beer became a common home-brew as well as a major manufacture.## Prodigious quantities of it and other home-brews were consumed.### As a beverage, wine was little used.*

> Item, for your wyne, we have good-ale, bere, metheghelen, sydre, and pirry, beyng more holsome beverages for us then your wynes, which maketh your people dronken, also prone and apte to all fylthy pleasures and lustes.**

In 1585, London breweries alone produced 648,960 barrels of beer, or 23,362,560 gallons.*** English wine imports [1586] amounted "to the proportion of 20000 or 30000 tun and vpwards," or to better than 7,560,000 gallons. @ Considering that the population of London was 123,034 in 1580 and 152,478 in 1593, @@ each Londoner in 1586 reputedly consumed about 150 gallons of beer and about 40 gallons of wine, per year. (It is assumed that three-fourths of recorded wine imports were consumed in London. A population of 140,000 in 1586 is also assumed.)

\# Lemnius. "Letter...," (560$1260023), p. 79.
Hentzner. "Letter...," op. cit., p. 109.
L. F. Salzman. England in Tudor Times, (926$1271074), p. 88.
__________. English Life..., (926$1271073), p. 98.

\## John U. Nef. "A Comparison of Industrial Growth...," (936 1280757), p. 648.
__________. "Prices and Industrial...," (937 1280755), pp. 168-169.

\### Hall. Society in the Elizabethan Age, (886$1271071), p. 76.
George R. Gayre. Wassail..., (948 1270685), pp. 89 to 91.
George Wither, quoted Supra, Vol. 1, p. 192.

* Consult Supra, Vol. 1, pp. 190 to 192, footnote 31.

** John Coke. A Debate between the Heralds of

soared; and, England's balance of trade losses to France mounted.[39]

To meet this increased demand for wines and to insure wine availability without recourse to foreign powers, the English pursued viticulture and wine production, first at home, and then in their colonies. Significant oenological attempts in England *circa* 1580[40] eclipsed the minor vintages

---

England and France, London: 1549 quoted in Drummond and Wilbraham. *The Englishman's Food...*, *op. cit.*, p. 44.

*** Lansdowne MSS (British Museum) 71, folio 53 quoted in Nef. "A Comparison...," *op. cit.*, p. 648.

@ Holinshed. *Holinshed's Chronicles...*, *op. cit.* p. 281.

@@ The rapid increase in population occurred despite two plagues (1577-1582, 1592-1593). F. P. Wilson. *The Plague in Shakespeare's London*, Oxford: Oxford University Press, 1927, pp. 209 to 215; Norman G. Brett-James. *The Growth of Stuart London*, London: Middlesex Archaeological Society, 1935, pp. 496-497; Charles Creighton. *History of Epidemics*, Cambridge: Cambridge University Press, 1891, Vol. 1, pp. 345, 351 to 355, 474 to 478.

[39]W. S. "A Compendium...," (581 1260601), pp. 111 to 113.
Ienings [Jenings]. *A Briefe Discovery...*, *op. cit.*, B3 verso.
Gerrard de Malynes. *A Treatise of the Canker...*, (601 1271255), pp. 2-3, 5-6, 12-13.
__________. *England's Vievv...*, (603 1271254), pp. 44 to 46, 86 to 89, 147 to 152.
M. Beer. *Early British Economics...*, (938 1271272), pp. 116-117.
Lipson. *The Economic History...*, *op. cit.*, Vol. 3, p. 99.

[40]Richard Hakluyt. "Inducements to the Liking...," (585 1270028), p. 111.
Conrad Heresbach. *Foure Bookes of Husbaudry*, (577$1270971), pp. 77 to 80 [79].
Edward Hyams. *The Grape Vine in England...*,

produced earlier in the century.[41] Raphael Holinshed wrote:

> ...I touch in this place one benefit which our nation wanteth, and that is wine; the fault whereof is not in our soile, but the negligence of our countriemen (especiallie of the south partes) who doo not inure the same to this commoditie, and which by reason of long discontinuance, is now become vnapt to beare anie grapes...Yet of late time some haue assaied to deale for wine...But sith that liquor when it commeth to the drinking hath bin found more hard, than that which is brought from beyond the sea, and the cost of planting and keeping thereof so chargeable, that they may buie it far better cheape from other countries: they haue giuen over their enterprises without anie consideration, that as in all other things, so neither the ground it selfe in the beginning, nor successe of their trauell can answer their expectation at the first, vntill such time as the soile be brought as it were into acquaintance with this commoditie...[42]

These English endeavors were truly short-lived.

Frederick, Duke of Wirtenberg [1592], and Paul Hentzner

(949 1270715), pp. 43 to 45. Dr. Hyams finds Heresbach's tome "disingenuous...evidence for the prosperity of the vine in England during this time." [Ibid., p. 45.] He is unaware of Holinshed's viticultural discourse [above], which may indicate that the Heresbach tract found application in England shortly after its 1577 English translation.

[41]Rogers. A History of Agriculture and Prices..., op. cit., Vol. 4, p. 636.

Hyams. The Grape Vine in England..., op. cit., pp. 39-40.

These vintages were quite limited, for in 1552, Dr. Andrew Boord noted that "in England...there is nothing to make wine of." [Borde [Boord]. Dyetary of Helthe, quoted in Cooper. The English Table..., op. cit., p. 100.]

[42]Holinshed. Holinshed's Chronicles..., op. cit., Vol. 1, p. 186.

1598] commented that "there is no winegrowing in this kingom"[43] for "though the soil is productive, it bears no vines ine."[44] Thomas Cogan concurred:

> But this our Countrie of England for the coldnesse of the Clime wherin it is situate, bringeth no vines to make wine of though in other things more necessary it far surmounteth all other Countires. So God hath deuided his blessings, that one Nation might haue neede of another one Countrie might haue entercourse with another.[45]

Notwithstanding, the notion of securing wine supply without incurring balance of trade losses found continued expression in schemes advocating English colonial viticulture. Richard Hakluyt advised that,

> ...the first seate be chosen on ye seaside... so may you by your Navie within, passe out to all partes of the worlde, and so may the shippes of Englande have accesse to you to supply all wantes, so may your commodities be carried away also.
> ...if the soyle and clymate bee such as may yeelde you the Grape as good as that at Burdeus...or that in the Ilands of the Canaries, then there resteth but a woorkeman

---

[43]Frederick, Duke of Wirtenberg. "Letter...," op. cit., p. 52.

[44]Hentzner. "Letter...," op. cit., p. 109.

[45]Cogan. The Haven of Health..., op. cit., p. 207. Thomas Cogan's espousement of Divine will parallels that of Jean Bodin [The Response..., (568 1271242), p. 54]. "And God by his grace has taken care that all is not either in vine or wheat." Gerrard Malynes [England's Vievv..., op. cit., p. 44] repeated the Bodin-Cogan assertion and suggested England's advantage in being a wheat rather than wine producer. [Ibid., p. 89.]

> to put in execution to make wines, and to dresse Resings of the sunne and other, &c.[46]

Thomas Hariot specified:

> I will divide my treatise on the commodities into three separate parts...In the first I will enumerate commodities already found there, or which could be raised...A surplus of these can be provided by experienced men for trade and exchange with our own nation of England...These commodities, I call marketable.
>
> CONCERNING MARKETABLE COMMODITIES...
> Wine. There are two kinds of grapes that grow wild there. One is sour and the size of the ordinary English grape; the other is lusciously sweet and much larger. When they are planted and husbanded as they should be, an important commodity in wines can be established.[47]

Proponents of colonial viticulture acknowledged that "commodities in this abundant manner, are not to be gathered from thence, without planting and settling there."[48] They maintained that the rewards of colonization--religious, political, military and economic-- were sufficient to warrant planting. Wine was repeatedly stressed within their arguments for commodity availability.

---

[46]Hakluyt. "Notes on Colonization...," (578 1260020), pp. 181, 183.

[47]Thomas Hariot. "A Briefe and True...," (588 1260448), pp. 232, 233, 236.

[48]George Peckham. "A True Report...," (583 1260789), p. 117.

> For this alreadie we find, that what commodities soeuer Spaine, France, Italy, or the East parts do yeeld vnto vs in wines of all sortes, in oiles...these parts do abound with ye growth of them all.[49]

> ...there is one seat fit for fortification, of great safety, wherein these commodities following, especially are to be had, that is to say, Grapes for wine, Whales for oyle, Hempe for cordage, and other necessary things, and fish of farre greater sise and plenty...and of all these so great store, as may suffice to serve our whole realme.[50]

> ...but to conquer a country or province in climate and soil of Italy, Spain, or the islands from whence we receive our wines and oils, and to man it, to plant it, and to keep it, and to continue the making of wines and oils able to serve England, were a matter or great importance both in respect of the saving at home of our great treasure now yearly going away, and in respect of the annoyance thereby growing to our enemies.[51]

> ...when it is asked what may be hoped from thence after some yeeres, it... shall be very apt to gather the commodities... [including] Wines with a small helpe, since the grapes doe growe there of themselves alreadie very faire and in great abundance.[52]

---

[49]Ralph Lane. "Letter to Master...," (585 1260118), p. 208-209.

[50]Peckham. "A True Report...," op. cit., p. 118.

[51]Hakluyt. "Inducements to the Liking...," op. cit., p. 110. Consult also Ibid., p. 104, item 6; p. 107, item 24; p. 108, item 81; pp. 111, 112.

[52]Christopher Carlile. "A Briefe and Summary...," (583 1260452), p. 139.

Yet, English explorers, merchants, and trade companies first were interested in the search for El Dorado, the North-west Passage and the Ultima Thule.[53] The harvest of gold, silver and pearls, or the prodigious returns of overseas trade, attracted them more than did the long-term tangible and intangible rewards of colonization.[54] Thus, while

---

[53]Robert R. Cawley. Unpathed Waters..., (940$1270001), pp. 3 to 33, especially pp. 31 to 33.
________. The Voyagers..., (938$1270003), pp. 275, 276, 282ff.
Gustav Blanke. Amerika..., (962 1270468), pp. 13ff.

[54]The restrained enthusiasm of English adventurers for colonization (Richard Hakluyt notably excluded) was expressed by Sir George Peckham,

> And forasmuch as the use of trade and traffique (be it never so profitable) ought not to be preferred before the planting of Christian faith: I will therefore somewhat intreate of planting...
> [Peckham. "A True Report...," op. cit., p. 98. Consult also Ibid., pp. 96, 97.]

The Crown's reluctance to sanction openly the coloniza-tion of avowedly Spanish lands [A. W. Ward. Shakespeare and the Makers of Virginia, (919$1270004), p. 18; p. 18, footnote 2]. also influenced the Englishmen to abandon such ventures

> The Englishmen...so lately finding that parte which lieth betweene Florida and Nova Frauncia, was not enhabited by any Christians, and was a land very fruitfull and fitte to plant in, they sent thither two severall times, two severall companies, as Colonies to enhabit ...Virginia. But this voyage being enterprised on the charge of private men: and not thorowly being followed by the state: the possession of this Virginia is nowe discontinued, and the country at present left to the old inhabitants.
> [[George Abbot]. A Briefe Description... (599 1271114), folio [D8 versò].]

reluctantly accepting their failure to locate the fabled riches of El Dorado, the English adopted the conviction that, in the form of Virginia, they had located Terrestrial Paradise.[55] They anticipated that commodities available from the Virginia paradise would augment the "wealthe and force" of England.[56]

---

[55]Wright. The Colonial Search..., op. cit., pp. 7, 13 to 15, 21 to 23.

_________. The Dream of Prosperity..., op. cit., pp. 12 to 18, 21 to 25, 33ff.

Cawley. Unpathed Waters..., op. cit., p. 23; p. 23, footnote 5; p. 27, footnote 13, 14.

When Bartholomew Gosnold ["The Relation...," 602 1260507), pp. 302 to 309] returned to England in 1602, he announced that he had found a short, direct northern route to America, which avoided the diseases and delay of the West Indies route. This kindled new excitement over the possibility of yet discovering precious metals and pearls in Virginia. Martson's play, Eastward Ho, written in 1605, reflects this fervor:

> Seagull: Come, drawer, pierce your neatest hogshead, and let's have cheare...
> Spendal: More wine, Slave!...
> Seagull: Come boyes, Virginia longs till we share the rest of her maidenhead.
> Spendal: Why, is she inhabitated alreadie with any English?
> Seagull: A whole countrie of English is there, man, bread of those that were left there in '79...
> Scapethrift: But is there, such treasure there Captaine as I have heard?
> Seagull: I tell thee, golde is more plentifull there then copper is with us...Why, man, all their dripping pans and chamber-potts are pure gould...and for rubies and diamonds they goe forth in holydayes and gather 'hem by the sea-shore, to hang on their childrens coates...
>
> [Marston. Eastward Ho. Act III, Scene 2, quoted in Edward D. Neill. History of the Virginia Company..., (869$1270106), pp. vi-vii.]

Spanish, French and Italian accounts extolling the abundance and fertility of the eastern shore influenced the English to advance Virginia as the Terrestrial Paradise.[57]

In 1609, Richard Hakluyt ["The Epistle Dedicatorie...," (609$1270036), pp. 1 to 4], as well, revived the hope of gold, silver and pearl caches in Virginia.

Similarly, attempts to locate El Dorado continued in the seventeenth and eighteenth centuries [Raleigh. The Discoverie..., op. cit., pp. xciv, xcv] despite English acknowledgement that wealth from the colonies would depend not upon exploitable resources, but upon the productive effort of the colonists and upon trade.

[56]Hakluyt. "Discourse on Western Planting," [1584] in Documentary History of the State of Maine, Cambridge: John Wilson and Son, 1877, Vol. 2, pp. 152, 157, 158.

________. "Inducements to the Liking...," op. cit. p. 109.

[57]The extent to which the English drew upon Spanish, French and Italian accounts is documented in:

Gilbert Chinard. L'Exotisme Americain..., (911 1270008), pp. 104 to 124, 133, 144-145, 148, 219 to 246.

________. L'Amerique..., (913 1270007), pp. v to viii.

Blanke. Amerika..., op. cit., passim.

Cawley. The Voyagers..., op. cit., pp. 278-280.

George W. Cole. "Elizabethan Americana," (924$1280708), pp. 163 to 169.

Sidney Lee. The French Renaissance..., (910$1270017), pp. 211 to 220.

John C. Lapp. "The New World...," (948 1280461), pp. 151 to 160, 164.

Stefan Lorant. The New World..., (946 1270443), pp. 279 to 282 and passim.

Geoffroy Atkinson. The Extraordinary Voyage..., (920 1270011), pp. ix-x, 1 to 4, 8, 12-13.

In their writings, and in prefatory dedications to translations of the herbals, cosmographies and literary works of the Continent, Englishmen espoused the benefits of expanded trade. They exhorted royal participation in overseas ventures, pointing to the abundance and fertility of the newly-discovered lands and to prior Spanish gains.[58] America's land masses, waterways, flora and fauna were lavishly described.[59]

---

[58] Richard Eden. "Treatyse of the Newe India...," (553 1260063), p. 7.

Richard VVilles. The History of Truayle..., (577 1260173), p. 188.

Dionyse Settle. A True Reporte..., (577 1261162), folio [A_1 verso], A_2 recto; p. 3.

[Lopez de Gomara]. The Pleasant Historie..., (578 1261161), folio A recto.

Hakluyt. "The Epistle Dedicatorie...," (609 1261101), pp. [3 to 9].

Michael Lok. "Preface to Peter Martyr...," (612 1270121), p. 717.

T. N. Marsh. "Anglo-American Relations...," (956$1280763), pp. 57 to 62.

Franklin T. McCann. English Discovery..., (952$1270068), pp. 98 to 107, 117 to 119, 138ff.

[59] Hakluyt. The Principle Navigations..., (589 1270449), Vol. 8 to 12, passim.

Cawley. The Voyagers..., op. cit., pp. 310 to 319.

James E. Gillespie. "The Influence of Oversea Expansion...," (920 1280433), pp. 41 to 54.

Content uniformity in observations of the New World was suggested by Albertus Meierus [Albrecht Meier] in his Certaine Briefe and Speciall Instructions for Gentlemen, Merchants, Students, Souldiers, Merriners [(589 1260974), passim]. Among the items that he urged overseas travelers to observe was "vines, vineyards, and sorts of wine, and drinks." [Ibid., p. 9, ▯6, item 15.]

Particularly repetitive were accounts of the bountiful vine.[60]

---

[60] In his Discourse on Western Planting [1584] Richard Hakluyt quoted "the leafe and page of the printed voyadges of those which personally with diligence searched and viewed these countries" [Ibid., pp. 19-20.] Virtually every explorer Hakluyt quoted lauded the bountiful vine. For example.

> John Ribault writeth...[of] the fairest vines in all the worlde, with grapes accordinge...* Verarsana [Verrazzano]...describeth...many vines growinge naturally, which springinge upp tooke holde of the trees as they doe in Lumbardye, which, if by husbandmen they were dressed in goodd order, withoute all doubte they woulde yelde excellent wynes...** [Similarly] Iacques Cartier...writeth...[of] greate store of vynes, all as full of grapes as could be, that if any of our fellowes wente on shoare, they came home laden with them.***
>
> * Ibid., p. 20, Consult also Ibid., p. 21.
> ** Ibid., pp. 22, 23.
> ***Ibid., p. 27.

Richard Hakluyt's magnum opus, The Principle Navigations..., [op. cit., Vol. 8 to 12] and Samuel Purchas' Hakluytus Posthumus [(906 1270503), Vol. 16, 18, 19] encompass these and numerous other tracts which extol the fruitfull vine. Arthur Barlowe offers the most lavish praise:

> the lande [of the Carolina Banks is] very sandie, and lowe towards the water side, but so full of grapes, as the very beating, and surge of the Sea ouerflowed them, of which we founde such plentie, as well there, as in all places else, both on the sande, and on the greene soile on the hils, as in the plaines, as well on euery little shrubbe, as also climing towardes the toppes of the high Cedars, that I thinke in all the world the like aboundance is not to be founde: and my selfe hauing seene those partes of Europe that most abound, finde such difference, as were incredible to be written.
> [Arthur Barlowe. "Arthur Barlowe's Discourse...," (584 1260117), pp. 94-95.]

Such accounts came to symbolize the abundance of the New World, and to convey its paradisical fertility.[61] Hence, they were often reiterated to entice Englishmen to colonize.[62]

61

... ...
Britans, you stay too long,
Quickly aboord bestow you,
And with a merry gale,
Swell your stretch'd sayle,
With vowes as strong
As the winds that blow you.
... ...

And cheerefully at sea,
Successe you still intice,
To get the pearle and gold
And ours to hold
VIRGINIA,
Earth's only Paradise,

Where nature hath in store
Fowle, venisons, and fish;
And the fruitfull'st soyle
Without your toyle,
Three harvests more,
All greater than you wish.

And the ambitious vine,
Crownes with his purple masse
The cedar reaching hie
To kisse the sky,
The cypresse, pine,
And usefull sassafras,

[Michael Drayton. "Ode to the Virginian Voyage," (620$12700350), p. ii.]

The ode, published 1619-1620, reputedly was written before 1605 [Isaac B. Choate. "America in Early English Literature," (892$1280635), p. 21]. Edmund Waller's "The Battel of the Summer-Islands" [quoted in Cawley. Unpathed Waters..., op. cit., pp. 24 to 26] and George Sandys' "Ovid" [Richard B. Davis. " America in George Sandy's Ovid," (947$1280723), pp. 297 to 304] also suggest the illusionary posture of the New World in Elizabethan and early Stuart England.

62 The importance of the vine and other paradisical symbols in the promotion of the colonies is suggested by:

Blanke. Amerika..., op. cit., pp. 98 to 115, 118 to 127, 333 to 336.

Howard M. Jones. "The Colonial Impulse...," (946 1280711), pp. 153 to 155.

Elfriede M. Ackerman. Das Schlaraffenland..., (943 1210005), pp. 1 to 3, 48 to 50, 56-57, 67-68, 79.

Cawley. Unpathed Waters..., op. cit., pp. 20 to 31.

The vine remained synonomous with paradisical fertility beyond the Elizabethan Age.[63] Increasing wine consumption and the association of wine drinking with prosperity heightened

---

[63]Only the site of Paradise remained at issue. Richard Hakluyt,* John Brereton,** J. Rosier,*** Alexander Whitaker# and Edward Bland## selected Virginia. W. Crashaw suggested Bermuda;### R. Harcourt chose Guayana.▯ Benjamin Jonson extolled "The Fortvnate Isles."▯▯ Then with increasing disillusionment over sites of early American colonization, Paradise shifted.▯▯▯ Voyages to Africa, the Levant and the East Indies@ called forth new locations.@@ Throughout, the bountiful vine remained synonomous with paradisical fertility. John Gay suggests:

> Whether, at Lusitanian sultry Coasts,
> Or lofty Teneriff, Palms, Ferro
> Provence or at the Celtiberian Shores;
> With gazing Pleasure and Astonishment
> At Paradice, (Seat of our ancient sire,)
> He thinks himself arriv'd, the Purple Grape
> In largest Clusters Pendant, grace the Vines
> [[John Gay.] Wine a Poem, (709$1261051), p. 5.]

* Hakluyt. The Principle Navigations..., op. cit., Vol. 7, pp. 254-255; Vol. 8, pp. 297, 319, 347.

** John Brereton. A Briefe and True Relation..., (602 1260128), p. 10.

*** J. Rosier. A True Relation..., (605 1260168), p. 27.

\# Alexander Whitaker. Good News from Virginia..., (613$1261104), pp. 21, 33.

\## Edward Bland. The Discovery of New Britain, (651$1260918), Introduction, folio A4 verso.

\### W. Crashaw. [A Sermon Preached in London..., (610 1261168),] is discussed in Wright. Religion and Empire..., (943 1271269), pp. 100-101.

▯ R. Harcourt. A Relation of a Voyage to Guiana, London: 1613, folio B3 verso.

▯▯ [Benjamin Jonson.] The Fortvnate Isles..., (624$1261113), folio C_2 recto to D verso, passim.

▯▯▯ Wright, The Colonial Search..., op. cit., pp. 41 to 62.

________. The Dream of Prosperity..., op. cit., pp. 63 to 90.

Blanke. Amerika..., op. cit., pp. 5-6, 125 to 127, 335-336.

@ R. W. Frantz. "The English Traveler...,"

its symbolic importance.[64] Wine drinking evolved to national popularity, converting major segments of the English population

---

(934 1280874), pp. 9-10.

@@ Thomas Herbert. A Relation of Some Yeares..., (626 1261163), p. 141.

________. Some Yeares Travels..., (638$1261164), pp. 221-222, 266.

S. Baring-Gould. Curious Myths..., (872$1270006), pp. 264-265.

[64]These factors, as well, suggested the vine as a vehicle for satirizing English colonization attempts.

> There Milk from Springs, like Rivers, flows,
> And Honey upon hawthoren grows...
> There twice a year all sorts of Grain
> Doth down from heaven like hailstones rain:
> You never need to sow nor plough.
> There's plenty of all things enough:
> Wine sweet and wholsome drops from trees...
> [Laurence Price. "...Summons to Newe England...," (638$1260476), p. 28.]
>
> The Captain says, in every Town
>   hot roasted pigs will meet ye,
> They in the streets run up and down,
>   still crying out, come eat me:
> Likewise he says, at every feast
>   the very fowls and fishes,
> Nay, from the biggest to the least,
>   comes tumbling to the dishes.
>
> The rivers run with claret fine,
>   the brooks with rich Canary,
> The ponds with other sorts of wine,
>   to make your hearts full merry:
> Nay, more than this, you may behold
>   the fountains flow with Brandy,
> The rocks are like refined gold,
>   the hills are sugar candy.
> ["An Invitation to Lubberland," [1684], quoted in John Ashton. Humour, Wit & Satire..., (883$1271072), p. 36.]

The origin of these satirical verses may have been Gov. Edward Winslow's reply to the disgruntled colonists of New England who arrived totally unprovided [Edward Winslow. "Good News from New England," (624$1260069), p. 528],

from their home brews.[65] Huldricke Van Speagle observed that,

> But wisely they made hay whilst Sunne did shine,
> But now our Land is overflowne with wine:

---

expecting plentitude:

> And can any be so simple, as to conceive that the fountains should stream forth wine or beer; or the woods and rivers be like butchers' shops, and fishmongers' stalls, where they might have things taken to their hands?
> [*Ibid*., p. 598.]

[65]In estimating the effect on wage workers of the price revolution between the period 1571-82 and the decade 1633-42, Dr. John U. Nef asserted:

> that bread, and after bread, ale or beer, were the chief 'stay' of the poor*...[and that] if bread was rising in price appreciably less rapidly than wheat, and drink [beer and ale] hardly as rapidly as the wages of masons and carpenters, it is misleading to work out costs of living mainly or even partly on the basis of grain prices...[Thus] all authorities since Rogers' time have exaggerated the rise in the price of subsistence during the sixteenth and early seventeenth centuries. **...It follows that they [the workmen] were probably able to spend a more than negligible portion of the money wages they received on Commodities other than food. ***
>
> * Nef. "Prices and Industrial Capitalism...," *op. cit*., p. 165. ________. "A Comparison of Industrial Growth...," *op. cit*., p. 648.
>
> ** ________. "Prices and Industrial Capitalism...," *op. cit*., p. 169.
>
> *** *Ibid*., p. 171.

Dr. Nef did not observe that in the late Elizabethan and in the Stuart eras wage workers began to consume significant amounts of wine. Thus, because of rapidly rising money wages, which generated an "income effect," Elizabethans shifted from home brews to wine imports despite rising wine prices. They, therefore, devoted an increasing proportion of their money wages to wine. This suggests that the cost of living did not markedly decline.

Only the prohibitive wine excises (Wine Act, 1688)

With such a Deluge, or an Inundation
As hath besorted and halfe drown'd our Nation.
Some that are scarce worth 40 pence a yeare
Will hardly make a meale with Ale or Beere:
And will discourse, that wine doth make good blood,
Concocts his meat, and make digestion good,
And after to drinke Beere, nor will, nor can.[66]

By 1618, London had become "so pestered with taverns, that latterly the better sort of houses were taken up by vintners...and converted into taverns, to the maintenance of riot and disorder."[67] The "Methodicall drunkard, that drinkes by the houre...first so much Ale, then such a quantitie of Beere, then of Sacke, then of Rhenish, them back againe from Wine to Ale, from Ale to Beere."[68] studied his "art" in drinking academies, taverns and tap-houses.[69] Drunkenness

---

again stimulated beer and ale consumption by the lower and middle classes. [Drummond and Wilbraham. The Englishman's Food..., op. cit., p. 136; G. N. Clark. Guide to English... [Appendix] (697$1260619), p. 108.] Excises on ale, beer, cider and perry may have stimulated wine production. From their enactment in 1643, until beyond the re-establishment of the monarchy, they modestly augmented royal revenue. [George Dodd. The Food of London, (856$1271078), pp. 81-82; Hackwood. Inns, Ales..., (909$1270834), pp. 125-126.]

[66] Huldricke Van Speagle. Drinke and Welcome..., (673 1261048), folio C_2 verso.

[67] Analytical Index...Remembrancia..., (878 1250176), p. 544, item V. 27 [25 September 1618].

[68] Harris. The Drvnkards Cvp, (630$1261068), p. 12, passim.

[69] R. Younge. The Blemish of Government..., (655 1261067), pp. 7 to 9, passim.
Thomas Randolph. The Drinking Academy..., (628 1270462), pp. 22-23, lines 690 to 695, 715 to 725.

became "shrowded, (nay countenanced, iustified, and applauded,) vnder the popular, and louely Titles of Hospitalitie, Good-fellowship...Iouialitie, Mirth...Friendship, Loue, Kindnesse... and the like."[70] Numerous tracts lamented and documented the extensive wine drunkenness of the Stuart Era.[71]

The multiplicity of Statutes restricting the scope of the wine trade and controlling its trade flows suggest its economic importance in seventeenth century England.[72] Many

---

[70]William Prynne. Healthes Sicknesse..., (628 1261055), folio B recto. Consult also Ibid., B5 recto, p. 52.

[71]For examples, consult:
The Statutes of the Realm..., op. cit., 1 Jac. I. c. 9; 4 Jac. I. c. 5 [ ] 1; 21 Jac. I. c. 7.
Thomas Young. Englands Bane..., (617 1260192), pp. 36-37, passim.
[Gallobelgicus]. VVine, Beere, Ale..., (630$1260193), C_1 verso ("The Song"), passim.
[Richard Braithwaite]. Drunken Barnaby's..., (638 1261047), passim.
R. Iunius. The Drunkard's Character..., (638 1261079), pp. 44-45.
Packard. (ed.). Guy Patin..., (925 1270437), p. 51.
Ashton. Humor, Wit & Satire..., op. cit., pp. 27, 189-190, 276, passim.
Simon. The History..., op. cit., Vol. 3, pp. 390 to 400.
Wright. Middle-Class Culture..., (935$1270467), pp. 193 to 196, 291-292.

[72]Simon. The History..., op. cit., Vol. 3, pp. 1 to 139.
John Raithby and William Elliot. (eds.). The Chronological Index..., (828$1201135), pp. 902 to 904.
Crawford. Tudor and Stuart Proclamations..., op. cit., pp. 138ff.

The great deficiency in Andre Simon's investigation of the English wine trade is the lack of foreign source materials and, therefore, the segregation of the English experience from that of other European states. Specifically, Mr. Simon gives no account of the interrelationships between domestic and colonial policy. He, similarly, fails to suggest a common

tracts discussing England's commerce, and particularly those investigating her balance of trade losses, ruminate over the evils of excessive wine imports.[73] Vituperative attacks against wine farms, wine monopolies and wine excises punctuate

---

framework for the diverse practices of the European states. His account, however, is an adequate summary of the statutes.

[73]Critics of the wine trade included:

[Edward Miesselden]. Free Trade..., (622$1271259), pp. 12, 25, 27.
Malynes. The Maintenance of..., (622 1271256), p. 25.
Roger Coke. A Discourse of Trade..., (670 1271253), pt. 1, pp. 6, 38, to 40.
________. A Treatise..., (671 1271252), pp. 82-83.
Samuel Fortrey. "England's Interest and Improvement," (673$1260134), p. 233, item 13; pp. 234, 236-237.
"A Scheme of the Trade...," (674 1260603), pp. 249-250.
Thomas Manly. "A Discourse...Exportation of Wool...," (677 1260604), p. 278, item 25.
"Britannia Languens...," (680 1260136), pp. 415, 419, 424 to 426.

Among those who defended the trade were:

T[homas] M[un]. A Discovrse of..., (621 1271260), pp. 6-7, 57.
The author of "England's Great Happiness," (677$1260135), pp. 260-261.
Charles D'Avenant. "Discourses on the Public Revenues...," (698 1271246), pp. 347-348. Errors in D'Avenant's approach are discussed in: Margaret Priestly. "Anglo-French trade...," (951 1280889), p. 50; Ralph Davis. "English Foreign Trade, 1660-1700," (954$1280892), pp. 160-161.

the Stuart Era.[74] The fiscal importance of the wine trade,[75]

---

[74]Attacks on fraud and irregularities in wine farming are reviewed in Dietz. English Public Finance..., op. cit., pp. 154, 155, 195, 328ff.

Andre Simon [Bibliotheca Gastronomica..., (953$1200143), pp. 1 to 3] lists the full titles of twelve "more or less abusive anonymous pamphlets published in London in 1641 and 1642" concerning the Abel-Kilvert attempt to secure parliamentary approval for a "Project" giving the Vintners' Company new authority to control retail wine sales. The most enlightening of these tracts is [Henry Parker]. The Vintners Answer..., (642 1270119), passim. George Unwin [The Gilds and Companies..., (925$1270706), pp. 323 to 328], The Calendar of State Papers [Domestic..., (625 1221117), Vol. 17, pp. 289-290, item 63 [November? 1640]; Vol. 18, pp. 32-33, item 82 [June 1641]; Vol. 18, p. 226, item 31 [1641.]] and David MacPherson [Annals of Commerce..., (805 1270691), Vol. 1, p. 403] offer interesting sidelights on the proposed Abel-Kilvert "patent."

The issue of the Canary wine excise is discussed and documented by Charles Andrews. [The Colonial Period..., (938 1270950), Vol. 4, pp. 110 to 113.] The effectiveness of excises on curbing French wine imports was the subject of many terse exchanges. The disagreement between Samuel Fortrey ["England's Interest...," op. cit., passim] and the author of "Britannia Languens...," [op. cit., pp. 424 to 426] is one good example.

[75]Data available on fiscal returns during the Stuart Era are quite incomplete [Andrew Browning. (ed.). English Historical..., (953$1270301), p. 277]. The earliest of official wine import statistics are those of the Board of Trade. They commence in 1697. Even these figures [Simon. The History..., op. cit., Vol. 3, p. 131] are not reliable on account of extensive fraud and smuggling [G. N. Clark. Guide to English Commercial Statistics 1696-1782, London: Royal Historical Society, 1938]. Thus, the royal (public) revenue items listed below are merely suggestive of the fiscal importance of the wine trade.

ROYAL (PUBLIC) REVENUE ITEMS: ENGLAND, 1611-1701

DATE	REVENUE SOURCE	AMOUNT	SOURCE
1611	Wine Farm	L22,000 plus L6,000 fine	Dietz. English Public Finance..., op. cit., p. 54.
1613 13 January	Customs Collected	L33,700	Calendar of State Papers: Domestic..., (547 1221116), op.

			cit., Vol. 2, p. 166.
.619 . July	Wine Farm	L50,000	Dietz. English Public Finance..., op. cit., p. 177.
.622	Wine Farm: price demanded for its release	L56,654	Ibid., p. 195.
.614 to .628	Retail wine licenses	L16,833	Calendar of State Papers: Domestic..., (625 1221117), op. cit., Vol. 3, p. 436.
1632	Lord Treasurer stipulation for farm price	L44,005 to L60,000	Dietz. English Public Finance..., op. cit., p. 268.
1639	New impost on all wine in stock	L13,000	Ibid., p. 283.
1640 17 April	Wine Farm (value of farm L80,000 retail wine sales L232,000)	L30,000	Calendar of State Papers: Domestic..., (625 1221117), op. cit., Vol. 16, p. 47.
1663?	French wine imports: L600,000	-	Fortrey. "England's Interest...," op. cit., p. 210.
1663	Wine licenses	L20,000	Browning. English Historical..., op. cit., p. 331.
1663 and 1669 averaged	London wine and brandy imports: L144,000	-	Davis. "English Foreign Trade...," op. cit., p. 164.
1668 23 May	Impost Act expected revenue	L300,000	Calendar of State Papers: Domestic..., (660 1221119), Vol. 8, p. 406.
1680?	Canary wine imports: L20,000; French wine imports "a greater part of a million per annum"	-	"Britannia Languens..., op. cit., p. 419.
1668-1670 [dated	Excise on wines	L310,000	Calendar of State Papers: Domestic...,

the patriotic fervor of Englishmen promoting home-manufacture beverages,[76] and the comparative economic disadvantage of win manufacture discouraged attempts to promote domestic and colonial wine production.

1675?]			(660 1221119), op. cit., Vol. 17, pp. 99-100.
1699,1700 1701-- averaged	London wine and brandy imports: L467,000	-	Davis. "English Foreign Trade...," op. cit., p. 164.

[76][Miesselden]. Free Trade..., op. cit., p. 27 (margin commentary).

William Lawson. A New Orchard..., (638 1270977), p. 1

Richard Weston. Tracts on Practical Agriculture..., (769 1270992), pp. 205 to 207. [The production of fruit wine during the reign of Charles I is deduced.]

Walter Blith. The English Improver..., (653 1270978), pp. 269-270.

J. Worlidge. Vinetum Britannicum..., (676 1270195), folio B_3 recto-B_4 recto, pp. 20 to 26.

> Thus do we swallow and piss out inestimable Treasures [for French wine imports], and contemn our own excellent and more wholsom Drinks, which might be improved to a much greater Perfection, both for our Use at home, and Trade abroad...
> ["Britannia Languens...," op. cit., p. 419.]

William Y-Worth. A New Art of Making Wines..., (691 1270232), folio [B_5]; pp. 55 to 57; folio [J6?] (postscript opening); folio K_3 recto-K_3 verso.

A viticultural revival in England, however, did follow the early seventeenth century advent of market gardening. Domestic production increasingly met food demands, particularly those for fruits and vegetables.[77] The number of farming books dealing with animal husbandry, apiculture[78] and general farming multiplied.[79] Viticultural and horticultural material was included in the general farming tracts. Early Stuart viticultural prescriptions were, in general, either translations or plagiarisms of French sources.[80] Few English gardening books advocating domestic viticulture appeared until

---

[77]F. J. Fisher. "The London Food Market...," (935$1280867), pp. 46, 51 to 55.
Albert F. Schmidt. The Yeoman in Tudor and Stuart England, Washington, D. C.: Folger Shakespeare Libarary, 1961, pp. 14-15.
Drummond and Wilbraham. The Englishman's Food..., op. cit., pp. 117, 118.
Rogers. A History of Agriculture and Prices..., op. cit., Vol. 5, pp. 56 to 59.

[78]The English hoped to curb sugar imports by promoting honey production.

[79]George E. Fussell. The Old English Farming Books..., (947 1271093), pp. 21 to 68.
Schmidt. The Yeoman..., op. cit., pp. 12 to 14.

[80]Englishmen during the entire Stuart Era pirated French general farming tracts. These writings included extensive discussions of viticultural subjects. Thus, their translations served to disseminate French viticultural techniques.

Two early books whose translations were important in advancing English oenological knowledge were: Conrad Heresbach's Foure Bookes of Husbaudry and Charles Estienne's L'Agricvltvre et maison rvstiqve. The Heresbach tract was translated in 1577 by Barnaby Googe [Foure Bookes..., op. cit., pp. 77 to 85*]. It was reprinted in 1601 [(601$1270972), pp. 74 to 81*]; Gervase Markham "renewed, corrected, enlarged and adorned" it in 1631 [(631 1270973), pp. 149 to 164*]. All

the mid-century.[81] These tracts were complemented by others which either strongly advocated the domestic production of

---

three versions are virtually identical, despite Markham's claim to revision. (The asterisk indicates the pages discussing viticulture.) The Estienne book [(570$1270970), pp. 345, 550 to 602* ("Sixiesme Livre...La Vigne Le Proffit de la vigne bien cultiuee")] was translated by Richard Surphlet in 1616.

Later translations or adaptations of French texts relating to viticulture are presented by Fussell. The Old English Farming Books..., op. cit., pp. 66-67.

The importance and suitability of French gardening tracts to English colonial viticulture is discussed Supra, Vol. 1, p. 161, footnote 152.

[81]Hugh Plat. The Garden of Eden..., (655 1270985), p. 54, [item 32]. This tract is a reissue of Plat's Floraes Paradise, [(608$1270984).] Consult the Dictionary of National Biography, Vol. 15, p. 1295.

RA. Austin. A Treatise of Frvit-Trees..., (653 1270980), p. 58.

Blith. The English Improver..., op. cit., pp. 269 to 271.

John Beale. A Treatise of Fruit Trees showing their manner of Grafting, Pruning and Ordering, of Cyder and Perry, of Vineyards in England, Oxford: 1653.*

William Hughes. The Compleat Vineyard..., (665 1270197), folio A_3-[A_3]; pp. 1, 2.

John Rose. The English Vineyard Vindicated..., (675$1271046), folio A_3 verso to A_4 verso, The Preface, pp. 13 to 15.

John Rea. Flora..., (676 1270987), pp. 216, 218.

Anthony Lawrence. Nurseries, Orchards, Profitable Gardens and Vineyards Encouraged, London: 1677.*

Beale. Nurseries, Profitable Gardens and Vineyards Encouraged, London: 1677.*

Hughes. The Flower Garden and Compleat Vineyard, 3rd edition, London: 1683.*

(The asterisk denotes sources of which the author has been able to locate only bibliographic reviews.)

fruit wines,[82] or suggested the ornamental use of vines in gardens; they disparaged profitable English wine production.[83]

Viticultural trials in England during the Stuart Era [84] experienced limited success. Englishmen never progressed

---

[82] Worlidge. Vinetum Britannicum..., op. cit., pp. 17 to 20, 90 to 96, 160 to 186, 189 to 202.
T. Langford. Plain and Full Instructions..., (681 1270981), folio A_2 verso; passim.
John Chamberlayne. The Natural History..., (682 1270224), pp. [37 to 39].
Thomas Tryon. A New Art of Brewing..., (691 1270223), pp. 91 to 98.
Y-Worth. A New Art of Making Wines..., op. cit., folio [J6?] (postscript opening) folio K_3 recto - K_3 verso.
J. Lightbody. Every Man His Own Gauger..., (695 1270222), pp. 46 to 53.
R. Worthington. Invitation to the Inhabitants..., (812 1270937), pp. 8 to 10.
P. P. Carnell. A Treatise on Family Wine Making..., (814 1270296), pp. 45ff.

[83] Markham. The English Husbandman..., (613 1270982), p. 67.
________. The English Husbandman...Newlie Revised, (625 1270983), p. 153.
Nicolas De Bonnefons. The French Gardiner..., (675 1271045), p. 272.
Langford. Plain and Full Instructions..., op. cit., p. 116.

[84] OENOLOGICAL ENDEAVORS OF THE STUART ERA

DATE	ITEM	SOURCE
1603-1625?	Royal vineyards at Oatlands, in Surrey. Sir Robert Cecil vineyard at Hatfield	Hyams. The Grape Vine..., (949$1270715), p. 49.
1608	Vineyards and wine production described.	Plat. Floraes Paradise, op. cit., passim.
1621	Vineyards and wine production mentioned.	William Herbert. The History of the Twelve..., (836 1270628), Vol. 2, p. 638.

1629	"The grapes of the best sorts of Vines are pressed into wine by some in these dayes with vs... but the wine of late made hath beene but small, and not durable, like that which commeth from beyond Sea, whether our vnkindly yeares, or the want of skill, or a conuenient place for a Vineyard be the cause, I cannot well tell you." Grape varieties described.	John Parkinson. *Paradisi in Sole Paradisus*..., (629$1270696), p. 566; pp. 564-565.
1640	Grape varieties described.	Parkinson. *Theatrum Botanicum*..., (640 1270961), pp. 1555 to 1557.
1655	"...Colonel Blount... drunk of the wine of his vineyard, which was good for little."	John Evelyn. "Evelyn's Diary," quoted in George Ordish. *Wine Growing in England*, (953$1270901), p. 22.
1659	Samuel Hartlib mentions ingenious gentlemen in England making very good and long-lasting wine.	George Johnson and Robert Errington. *The Grape Vine*..., (847$1270105), p. 14
1665	Viticulture practiced in England 1632 to 1658. The manner of laying out a vineyard and making wine detailed.	Hughes. *The Compleat Vineyard*..., *op. cit.*, folio A2 verso; pp. 1-2, 3ff., passim.
1670	Viticultural techniques.	Thomas Hammer. *Garden Book*, [London: 1670], Eleanor S. Rohde. (ed.). re-issue, London: 1933, passim.
1670	"Grapes are vendible in Markets, and usefull in Housekeeping the profit being well known to those that make Wine of them."	Smith. *England's Improvement Revived*..., *op. cit.*, p. 205.
1675	Viticultural techniques. Grape varieties described. Vines offered gratis (1666).	Rose. *The English Vineyard Vindicated*, *op. cit.*, passim.
1676	Techniques of vine propagation.	Worlidge. *Vinetum Britannicum*..., *op. cit.*, pp. 74 to 84.
1676	Grape varieties described. Viticultural techniques.	Rea. *Flora*..., *op. cit.*, pp. 215 to 219.

beyond the ornamental use of the vine in gardens, or limited wine production. The realm, in contrast to its encouragement of colonial viticulture, did not promote forthrightly domestic wine production.[85] Despite the many tracts advancing oenological knowledge and the success of limited production ventures, commercial wine production in England did not take hold. Alternative land uses, or consumption of wine imports proved more feasible.[86]

1688	Grape varieties described.	Raio. Rea *Historia Plantarum*..., (688 1270969), Vol. 2, pp. 1613 to 1618.
1704	Grape varieties described.	*Dictionarium Rusticum*..., (704 1270968), folio VIN recto.
1705	"Where Phoebus shines too faint to raise a Vine, They serve for grapes, and make the northeren wine:" Cider and Perry replace wine.	Abraham Cowley. *The History of Plants*, (705$1270258), p. 146.
1705	"Grapes too and Plums their proper praise obtain, If props against a wall the trees sustain; Both the Muscat and the bright purple Vine Deserve a wall, and grace the fruitful line."	Rapin. "Discposition of Gardens," (705$1270258), p. 320.

[85]Edward Hyams [*The Grape Vine*..., *op. cit.*, p. 49] claims that "Under James I viticulture enjoyed Royal patronage." He offers no citation.

John Rose [*The English Vineyard Vindicated*, *op. cit.*, title page] was "Gardiner to his Majesty." His gratis offering of vines to Englishmen implies royal interest, but does not affirm it.

[86]Hyams. *The Grape Vine*..., *op. cit.*, pp. 50-51.

Decided changes in the Englishman's wine preference during the late Stuart Era also may have influenced the commercial failure of domestic viticultural attempts. French wine dominated the English market during the period from the accession of Charles I (1625) to that of William and Mary (1688).[87] Prohibitions (1678 to 1685)[88] and heavy excises

---

[87]"For the provision of sweet wines...a yearly assignment of L1,584 wherein considering your Majesty [Charles I] useth not those wines..."* This disdain for sweet wines represented an abrogation of parental taste. James I had favored Spanish sacks.**

By the reign of Charles II "the consumption of French wine was two-fifths that of the whole of England."*** "French wine before the first war [1678 to 1685] was the common draught of every tavern, and not only persons of condition but the lower sort of people drank almost no other wine."#

* The Manuscripts..., (626 1251141), [Coke MSS.], p. 293.

** Alexander Henderson. The History of Ancient and Modern Wines, (824$1270189), pp. 308-309. William Browne's confusion about the relative popularity of Claret and Canary in 1625 is understandable:

> Cheeke-swolne Lyoeus neere one pillar stoode,
> And from each hand a bunche, full with the blood
> Of the care-killing vyne, he crushed out,
> Like to an artifucial water spout;
> But of what kinde yt was, the writers vary:
> Some say 'twas clarett, others sweare canary.
> [William Browne. The Whole Works of William Browne..., (625$1260674), Vol. 2, p. 132.]

*** James E. Tennent. Wine, Its Use and Taxation, (855 1270252), p. 59. [Adam Anderson]. An Historical..., (787 1271180), Vol. 2, p. 351.

\# Clark. Guide to English..., op. cit., p. 108 [Appendix].

[88]Simon. The History..., op. cit., Vol. 3, pp. 125-126.

W. Bosville James. Wine Duties..., (855 1270253), p. 82.

1688, 1693, 1697, 1698)[89] on French wine imports during the quarter century culminating with the Methuen Treaty 1703),[90] and the Crown's encouragment of unrestricted gin

---

[89]The Statutes of the Realm..., op. cit., 1 W.&M. c. 34 [] 16;4 W. & M. c. 25; 7 & 8 W.&M. c. 20; 9 & 10 W. &M. c. 23.

[90]The Methuen Treaty provided that English woollen goods should be admitted into Portugal, and that the wines of Portugal should be admitted into Great Britain, at a third, or less, of the duty imposed on any French wines. Actually, the charge was much less, for the Treaty admitted Portuguese wines at L7 per tun, while French wines paid L55.* Notwithstanding this deterrent, French wines continued their popularity in England.** While before the Treaty the masses had abandoned French wine in favor of Portuguese vintages, when French wine prices soared, the "Gentlemen chuse to drink them [French wines] at twice the Cost of any other."*** Even ten years after the Treaty, when the Treaty of Commerce with France was argued, Daniel Defoe deemed it necessary to rebut his protagonists' argument that "' The Inclination of our People to French Wine is such, that if it be at the same price with the Portuguese Wine, none will Drink the latter.'"#

Despite the avowed English preference for French wine, the consumption of Portuguese wine, Port, in England was considerable even before the Methuen Treaty.## In 1697, an Englishman reported that, "the prohibition and high duties have turned our lesser gentry and common people at least to the use of Spanish and Portugal wines."### Thus, the Englishman readjusted his tastes from light, dry French wines to the heavier, more potent, fortified wines, before the turn of the century. Port was the transitional beverage@ between the delicate wines and crude eighteenth-century gin.

* Simon. History of the Champagne Trade..., (905$1270684), p. 35.

** Tennent. Wine, its Use and Taxation..., op. cit., pp. 59 to 62.
Cunningham. The Growth of English Industry..., op. cit., Vol. 2, pp. 459 to 463; p. 460, footnote 3.
Charles King. The British Merchant..., (721$1270225), Vol. 2, pp. 199-200.

*** The Consequences of a Law..., (713 1270234), p. 10.
[Daniel Defoe]. An Essay..., (713 1271245),

production, both acted to shift English beverage demands away from wine and toward domestic beverages or their distillation. Concerted efforts to develop domestic viticulture and wine production thus were discouraged.[91]

---

p. 31.

Both Charles Andrews [The Colonial Period..., op. cit., Vol. 4, p. 6] and R. Shannon [A Practical Treatise..., (805 1270773), p. 59] accepted and popularized John Croft's fallacious assertion that after the Methuen Treaty "we may date the general use of Port Wines in Great Britain."
[John Croft. A Treatise..., (788 1270534), p. 15.]
Charles Cole. French Mercantilism 1683-1700, New York: Columbia University Press, 1943, p. 251.
Lipson. The Economic History..., op. cit., Vol. 3, pp. 112-113.
H. Warner Allen. A History of Wine, (961$1270231), pp. 194 to 198. Mr. Allen further substantiates the heavy consumption of Port in England prior to the Methuen Treaty. His discussion is modeled after Simon. Bottlescrew Days, Boston: Small Maynard and Co., 1927, pp. 108-109.

Clark. Guide to English..., op. cit., p. 108. [Appendix].

@ Andre Simon. [Wine and the Wine Trade, (934$1270742), p. 11] aptly summarized the qualities of Port during the first half of the eighteenth century; It "had little to recommend it except its cheapness." But, their adulterated French wine was only a slight improvement at a much higher price. Cyrus Redding [A History and Description of Modern Wines, (851$1270529), pp. 401-402] gathers statistics for Portuguese wines imported into Great Britain from 1700 to 1849. Edward Barry. [Observations..., (775 1271181), pp. 435 to 441] also offers data.

[91]Not until the Hanoverian Era did attempts at domestic viticulture and wine production reoccur. The resurgence of endeavors to develop a domestic vintage are recounted

---

n:

John Lawrence. The Clergy-Man's Recreation..., (715 1270991), pp. 26 to 29.

Worlidge. A Compleat System of Husbandry..., (716$1270220), pp. 175 to 177, 218-219.

Lavrence [Lawrence]. The Gentlemen's Recreation..., (716 1270990), pp. 103-104.

Samuel Collins. Paradise Retrieved...Method of Managing and Improving Fruit Trees, London: 1717.

Laurence [Lawrence]. The Fruit-Garden Kalendar..., (718 1270989), pp. 11-12, 30-31.

J. Mortimer. The Whole Art..., (721 1270986), pp. 308 to 314.

Thomas Fairchild. The City Gardener, London: 1722.*

Richard Bradley. A General Treatise..., (724$1270995), Vol. 1, pp. 127, 227; Vol. 2, p. 263; Vol. 3, pp. 116 to 125.

Stephen Switzer. The Practical Fruit-Gardener, (724$1271042), pp. 159 to 164.

The Vineyard, a Treatise..., London: 1727.*

Batty Langley. Pomona: or, the Fruit-Garden Illustrated..., (729 1270997), pp. 110-111, 117ff.; plates 35 to 51.

Jethro Tull. The New Horse-Houghing Husbandry, or an Essay on the Principles of Tillage and Vegetation, Introducing a Sort of Vineyard Culture into the Corn-Field, London: 1731. The 1822 edition prefixed by William Cobbett, [(822 1270707), pp. 67-68, 88-89, 141-142] offers some usefull editorial comment. Extensive discussion of Tull's book is advanced by George E. Fussell. [More Old English Farming Books..., (950$1271094), pp. 3ff.]

D. Browne. The Vineyard...a Method of Planting Vines in England, 9th ed., London: 1733.*

William Graham. The Arte of Making Wine From Fruits, Flowers and Herbs, 8th ed., London: 1733.*

Philip Miller. The Gardeners Dictionary..., (741 1270988), [] VI. [pp. 12, 16, 17, 27].

Malachy Postlethwayt. The Universal Dictionary of Trade and Commerce, (774$1270725), p. WIS, remarks.

Barry. Observations...on the Wine of the Ancients, op. cit., pp. 470 to 478, 478-479.

Peter Le Brocq. A Description with Notes of Certain Methods of Planting, Training and Management of Fruit Trees, Vines, etc., London: 1786.*

F. X. Vispre. A Dissertation on the Growth of Wine in England, Bath: 1786.*

________. Le Vin du Pays, Londres: 1787.*

William Speechly. A Treatise on the Culture of the Vine..., (790 1270669), Book IV "On Vineyards."

Switzer. Ichonographia Rustica [1742] quoted in

The English, however, continued to promote viticulture in the American colonies. These trials were encouraged in conjunction with those to produce silk, although their importance, relative to the promotion of silk, markedly declined. Moreover, the sporadic nature of English viticultural encouragements in the colonies diverted settlers from wine production to the inexpensive Madeira imports or domestic brews.

During the seventeenth century, tobacco dominated English royal interest. Little was done to advance colonial staples as long as the tobacco market was firm. Only when tobacco prices fell precipitously in glut markets did demand for the colonial wine production become clamorous. Even then, however, attention centered upon the dire effects of the tobacco glut on the colonial economy and on the royal purse. At the end of each tobacco glut, therefore, the advantage of wine manufacture relative to other commodities had not improved.

The high price asked for tobacco in London encouraged the product's initial cultivation in the English colonies.[92] Just as royal policy failed to thwart the development of the English wine trade, it also failed to stem tobacco usage and trade. Although James I expressed extreme displeasure

---

Hyams. Vineyards in England, (953$1270218), p. 36.

(The asterisk denotes sources of which the author has been able to locate only bibliographic reviews.)

[92]Beer. The Origins..., op. cit., pp. 86-87; p. 86, footnote 2; 91-92.

displeasure at the rising English use of tobacco,[93] smoking continued its fashionable popularity.[94] By 1614, England's annual tobacco bill amounted to L200,000.[95]

Factors stimulating early colonial tobacco culture included: England's virtual curtailment of Spanish tobacco imports[96] differential duties favoring colonial tobaccos[97]

---

[93]James I. *A Counterblast to Tobacco*. London: 1604.

[94]Sarah A. Dickson. *Panacea or Precious Bane: Tobacco in Sixteenth Century Literature*, New York: New York Public Library, [Arents Tobacco Collection, publication number 5], 1954, passim.
Wright. *The Dream of Prosperity*..., *op. cit.*, pp. 53 to 55.
__________. *The Colonial Search*..., *op. cit.*, p. 33.
W. L. Grant and James Munro. (eds.). *Acts of the Privy Council*..., (908 1221133), Vol. 1, p. 191 [August 1633].
Meyer Jacobstein. "The Tobacco Industry...," (907$1271223), p. 11; p. 11, footnote 3.

[95]Wright. *The Colonial Search*..., *op. cit.*, p. 33.

[96]The complaint of Edward Bennett that "the maine decay of trade, and the chiefe cause that hindereth the importation of Bullion out of Spaine is Tobacco"* was seconded by a unanimous vote of the House of Commons (1620) that "the Importation of *Spanish* Tobacco is One Cause of the Want of Money within the Kingdom." ** The following year the House of Lords failed to concur with the decision of Commons to cut off the importation of Spanish tobacco. † Nevertheless, James I set aside his pro-Spanish leanings and restricted drastically the Spanish tobacco trade.††

- * [Edward Bennett]. *A Treatise deuided*..., (620 1261195), folio [B] ([sig. a3]).
- ** 13 March 1620 (18 James I) quoted in Jacobstein. "The Tobacco Industry...," *op. cit.*, p. 12; p. 12, footnote 1.
- † Beer. *The Origins*..., *op. cit.*, pp. 114 to 116; p. 114, footnote 2.
  Jacobstein. "The Tobacco Industry...," *op. cit.*, p. 12; p. 12, footnote 2. Dr. Jacobstein contends that Parliament approved the sanction against Spanish tobacco. He is in error.
- †† C. M. Mac Innes. *The Early English*...,

and a favorable stinted tobacco price offered by the Virginia Company.[98] Tobacco culture also promised to promote a captive market for English finished products, to create a re-export (Continental) market for colonial imports, to increase the carrying trade for English ships, and to augment the royal revenue through sale of tobacco monopolies and the imposition of tobacco duties.[99]

Given such incentives, colonists, neglecting virtually all other commodities, frantically undertook tobacco

---

(926$1270216), pp. 182-183.
Beer. The Origins..., op. cit., p. 116.

[97] Acts of the Privy Council: Colonial, I, No. 291 cited in L. C. Gray. "The Market Surplus...," (927$1281200), p. 237, footnote 49.
Beer. The Commercial Policy..., op. cit., pp. 47-48.

[98] The Virginia Company in 1618 authorized its representatives in the colony to allow 3s. for the best grades of tobacco in trade at the Company's warehouse. This stinting encouraged so much tobacco trade that the Company soon was unable to realize a profit on its offer price on the London markets. The Company, therefore, resorted to higher commodity prices in term of tobacco, discounting thereby their stinted offer price. The initial stimulus of the stinting was sufficient to introduce extensive cultivation.

[99] Richard L. Morton. Colonial Virginia, Chapel Hill: University of North Carolina Press, 1960, Vol. 1, pp. 39 to 44, 93 to 96.
Arthur Middleton. Tobacco Coast..., (953 1270681), pp. 95-96, 126-127.
Beer. The Origins..., op. cit., pp. 140, 170-171.
Jacobstein. "The Tobacco Industry...," op. cit., pp. 14 to 16, 30, 31.
Gray. "The Market Surplus...," op. cit., pp. 237 to 240.

cultivation.[100] Colonial tobacco production increased almost tenfold between 1615 and 1619 it increased threefold from 1619 to 1622 (Consult Appendix I).[101] James I and others demanded the diversification of the colonial economy (Consult Appendix II).[102] They sought to safeguard the viability

---

[100]The colonists favored tobacco cultivation, for, compared to other staple commodities, its yield per acre was higher, it was less perishable, and, when ready for shipping, its weight per unit volume was lower.* Moreover, it fetched better prices in proportion to weight than did grain.**

* Avery G. Craven. "Soil Exhaustion...," (925 1280852), pp. 30-31.
Beer. <u>The Origins</u>..., <u>op</u>. <u>cit</u>., pp. 91-92.
J. Leander Bishop. <u>History of American Manufacture</u>..., (866$1270016), pp. 348ff.
Andrews. <u>Our Earliest Colonial Settlements</u>..., (933$1270089), pp. 42-43.

** Captain John Smith asserted, "a man's labor in growing tobacco was worth fifty or sixty pounds a year, but in growing grain only ten pounds. ["Smith, p. 615" quoted in Middleton. <u>Tobacco Coast</u>..., <u>op. cit</u>., p. 95; 377, footnote 10].

[101]Appendix I lists Virginia tobacco prices and production from 1615 to 1763. The reader is referred to this Appendix for all price and production data mentioned in the text. This data is gathered to supplement L. C. Gray's ["The Market Surplus...," <u>op. cit</u>., pp. 231 to 237.] interpretation of tobacco price behavior. The quotations chosen are illustrative. They are not intended to comprise a series but only to indicate relative prices and quantities in periods of depression and prosperity.

[102]Appendix II lists supporting material relating to the encouragement of the colonial vintage, and to the conditions of tobacco prices and production. In the absence of other citations, the reader should consult this Appendix where both item and source are listed chronologically. For example, the demands of James I (1622) are contained in the writings of Iohn Bonoeil [<u>His Maiesties</u>...].

of the colony, in its contribution to royal revenue, and in its role in promoting English commodity availability. Nevertheless, the economic incentive of high tobacco prices encouraged the colonists to expand further its production. In 1629-1630, frenzied tobacco planting created a glutted market. Prices fell precipitously from their stinted levels in spite of frantic efforts by the Crown and the Virginia Company to maintain them.[103] In the 1620-1630 decade, the Virginia colony developed from exporting 40,000 pounds at 3s. per pound to producing 1,800,000 pounds valued at less than a penny per pound.[104]

King Charles I, who spoke out against the one-crop system in 1627,[105] again voiced his opposition in 1631[106] 1636,[107] and 1637.[108] His insistent instructions had little

---

[103]Gray. "The Market Surplus...," op. cit., p. 232.

[104]Consult Supra, Vol. 1, p. 227, footnote 101.

[105]Proclamations of Charles I, No. 138 (February 1627) cited in Charles D. Eaves. The Virginia Tobacco..., (945$1270206), pp. 8-9. Charles I suggested wheat, tar and pitch, soap and pot ashes, salt, iron, and grapes as worthy of attention.

[106]Consult Supra, Vol. 1, p. 227, footnote 102.

[107]Proclamations of Charles I (4 August 1636) cited in Virginia Magazine of History and Biography, Vol. 9, No. 1 (June 1901), pp. 40, 41.

[108]Virginia Magazine..., op. cit., Vol. 9, No. 2 (September 1901), pp. 176 to 178, cited in Beer. The Origins..., op. cit., p. 90, footnote 4.

effect. Unlike the Bermuda Colony,[109] Virginia continued her adherence to a single cash crop.

In 1638-1639, tobacco prices again collapsed. Despite the rather generous official rates placed on tobacco during the next two or three years, prices did not recover until the short crop of 1644. Instructions of 1638, 1639, and 1642 again ordered diversification of the colonial economy by the manufacture of staples and by the planting of vines; the colonists adhered to tobacco production.

The outbreak of civil war in England depressed tobacco prices. Illicit trade with the Dutch, however, soon sustained prices again. A tobacco depression began in the late 1650's. Except for the improvement of 1663, it continued until 1667. The unusually large crop of 1666 and the Plague in London demoralized the tobacco market. Tobacco prices

---

[109] [Silvester Jourdan]. A Plaine Description..., (613$1261115), folio [C4 verso] to f2 recto.

Beer. The Origins..., op. cit., pp. 99-100; p. 100, footnote 1.

William Hughes. The American Physitian, (672$1260190), To the Reader, passim.

The importance of the Bermuda Colony, and, more generally, of the West Indies in wine entrepot and in attempts at wine production is indicated by:

Calendar of State Papers: Colonial..., (574$1221125), Vol. 7, p. 289, item 680 [9 December 1671].

Thomas Ashe. "Carolina...," (682 1260367), p. 144.

The Colonial Records...Georgia..., (732 1241037), Vol. 2, pp. 5-6 [3 October 1732].

Calendar of State Papers: Colonial..., op. cit., Vol. 39, p. 235, item 416 [12 October 1732].

Journal of the Board of Trade..., (704 1221127), Vol. 8, p. 216 [3 December 1746], p. 255 [5 February 1747], p. 240 [7 April 1747].

hit bottom. In 1667, a great storm destroyed nearly four-fifths of the Virginia tobacco crop. This event and the destruction of twenty tobacco ships by the Dutch temporarily relieved the tobacco depression.

Agreements to cut back tobacco production in Virginia, Maryland, Carolina and other places were sanctioned and enforced in 1666, 1667, and 1668. New colonial settlements were directed to avoid sugar and tobacco culture which might further depress these commodity prices. They were ordered to concentrate on the production of silks, wines, currants, raisins and other products which England purchased from other European states.

Tobacco gluts reoccurred in 1680 to 1682, 1704 to 1710, and 1720 to 1724. During these periods, instructions were again issued "to endeavor to advance the plantation" of staple commodities. These instructions applied especially in the newly-founded colonies where land values were low and would allow extensive cultivation.

During the Stuart Era the English thus encouraged colonial viticulture in 1619-1622, 1628-1632, 1638-1639, 1642, 1662-1667, 1679-1690 and 1705. None of these intermittent trials, which occurred in response to severe tobacco gluts, ever were sustained. The encouragements and prices offered for wine were insufficient to stimulate its large-scale production in the colonies.

The failure of the English to exercise greater control in diversifying colonial manufactures was clearly the product f fiscalism. Revenues from the colonial manufacture of obacco constituted an important contribution to English oyal finance. England profited from the very outset of olonial tobacco cultivation under the Virginia Comapny. She rofited first from a tax of two and one-half percent and five ercent on all goods "trafficked bought or sold" by English itizens or foreigners, respectively; second, from the sale f monopolies which augmented royal revenue; and, finally rom the excises levied upon tobacco imports.[110]

---

[110]Mac Innes. The Early English..., op. cit., pp. 131 o 141.

George Arents. Tobacco Its History Illustrated, compiled by Jerome E. Brooks] New York: The Rosenbach ompany, Vol. 1, 1937, pp. 91 to 98.

Eaves. The Virginia Tobacco..., op. cit., p. 8.

Jacobstein. "The Tobacco Industry...," op. cit., p. 14-15.

Beer. The Origins..., op. cit., pp. 108 to 116; p. 117 to 175 [Chapter 5, "The Stuart Regulation of the obacco Industry."]

________. The Old Colonial..., op. cit., Vol. 1, p. 148, 149; Vol. 2, pp. 105-106.

________. The Commercial Policy..., op. cit., p. 47-48; p. 47, footnote 6.

In 1661, the Commissioners of the Customs reported at the colonies were beginning "to grow into Commodities f great Value and esteems, and though Some of them Continue 1 Tobacco, yet upon the Returne hither it Smells well, and aies more Custome to his Matie than the East Indies four imes ouer." [Calendar of State Papers: Domestic, Ch. II, IV, No. 12 quoted in Beer. The Old Colonial..., op. cit., ol. 2, pp. 105-106.]

> I believe the true reason is, their being so intent on their Tobacco-Plantations that they neglect all other more Noble and advantageous improvements whereof the Countrey is capable, which without doubt are many. For in their planting Tobacco they find greatest encouragement from England, by reason of the vast revenue it brings

The tobacco depression of 1724-1734, however, had a considerable influence on the colonists' decisions to shift production away from tobacco and into other crops.[111] The price depression made it increasingly difficult for planters to afford imported English goods. They yielded, therefore, to agricultural diversification and domestic industry in attempts to produce a larger portion of their own supplies. They turned, particularly, to producing grain and corn,[112]

> into the Exchequer.
>
> [Thomas Glover. An Account of Virginia..., (676 1260781), p. 12.]

> ...best Virginia [tobacco] not above sevenpence [per pound] to the Merchant, of which the King has five pence.
>
> [Dalby Thomas. An Historical Account of the Rise and Growth of the West-India Colonies, London: 1690 quoted in Arents. Tobacco..., op. cit., Vol. 2, p. 532.]

> The vicious ruinous plant of Tobacco I would not name, but that it brings more money to the Crown, then all the Islands in America besides.
>
> [William Berkeley. A Discourse... Virginia, (663$1261169), p. 2.]

[111] Diversification marked a major departure in the colonists' response to low tobacco prices. Previously, depressed tobacco quotations brought forth actual increases in tobacco acreage. The colonists attempted to offset the detrimental effects of low tobacco prices upon their total revenue by increased production. [Gray. "The Market Surplus...," (928$1281201), p. 5.]

[112] The periods of soil preparation, seed planting, and crop harvesting for tobacco coincided with those of corn and wheat. The expansion of corn and wheat production, therefore could only be achieved at the expense of tobacco production. [Craven. "Soil Exhaustion...," op. cit., pp. 30-31.]

to cultivating indigo, hemp, flax, silk and cotton in limited amounts, and to manufacturing clothing.[113] They also attempted viticulture, although such attempts were no longer in the royal favor.[114]

Soil exhaustion, too, was responsible for the rapid turnover of tobacco plantations and for the eventual decline in the profitability of tobacco culture.[115] Although exports increased until the eighteenth century, tobacco yields grew less as new lands failed, and poorer, depleted soil, was planted.[116]

The result of stabilization of tobacco exports was a leveling-off of English royal (public) revenue. To maintain the integrity of its finances, the realm promoted the distillation of brandy and spirits. This policy was designed to curb distilled spirit imports and to support the market price of English corn (wheat). Distilling, too, would

---

[113]Middleton. Tobacco Coast..., op. cit., pp. 156 to 76, especially 156-157.
Gray. "The Market Surplus...," (928$1281201), op. cit., p. 5, footnote 119.

[114]Consult Supra, Vol. 1, pp. 69 to 72.

[115]Craven. "Soil Exhaustion...," op. cit., p. 57.

[116]By 1700, the quantity of tobacco produced per individual in Maryland was reduced by one-half, although total production showed no decline. In Virginia, in spite of heavy increases in slave labor in the tobacco fields, tobacco exports remained at a fairly steady level (1710-1750), [Ibid., p. 65 to 67; p. 66, footnote 157.]

strengthen the landed interest by fostering the use of grains. It would, thereby, bolster grain prices and promote higher rents.

Parliament, accordingly, encouraged the production and consumption of spirits. It revoked the Distillers of London monopoly and granted the right to distill to anyone who gave notice to the Commissioners of Excise and paid the low excise duty. All could retail spirits without an ale house license.[117]

In 1713, Daniel Defoe argued cogently for continuing these policies:

> ...first, the corn is consum'd, which corn is our own produce, pays rent for our land, employs our people, our cattle, our shipping, etc., and secondly, the importation of foreign spirits is prevented...when markets are low abroad and no demands made for corn, that plenty which is other nations' blessing is our intolerable burthen...The distilling trade is one remedy for this disaster as it helps to carry off the great quantity of corn in such a time of plenty, and it has this particular advantage, that if at any time a scaricity happens, this trade can halt for a year and not be lost entirely as in onther trades it often happens to be...[118]

Parliament concurred. A Clause in the Mutiny Act of 1720 encouraged distilling by exempting retailer-distillers from

---

[117] The Statutues of the Realm..., op. cit., 2 W. & M., Sess. 2. c. 3; 5&6 W. & M., c. 8; 7&8 Wm. III., c. 30.

[118] Defoe. Review, 9 May 1713 quoted in M. Dorothy George. London Life..., (925$1271081), p. 29.

housing soldiers, an obligation required of those merely innkeeping or offering public accomodation.[119]

The great increase in the consumption of spirits was manifest in the exicse returns of 1721; it likewise was reflected in the Bills of Mortality. Notwithstanding, the government overlooked the "vice and debauchery among the inferior sort of people,"[120] identified in that year.[121]

---

[119]George. London Life..., op. cit., p. 29.

[120]Order Book. Westminster Sessions, April 1721 quoted in Ibid., p. 31.

[121]Vice and debauchery among the poor was identified and satirized prior to the turn of the century.* Their shift from Claret to Port drinking and their subsequent penchant for hard liquors was exalted, rather than condemned, in 1713.** Only when the radical difference in physiological effects of grape-distilled spirits and grain-distilled spirits became evident, did the poor merit concern.***

* Allen. A History of Wine, op. cit., pp. 196 to 199.
Simon. Bottlescrew Days, op. cit., pp. 15 to 20, 147.
Charles Tovey. British & Foreign Spirits..., (864 1270724), pp. 64-65.

** The Consequences of a Law..., op. cit., p. 12.
[Defoe]. An Essay..., op. cit., pp. 15-16, 30 to 34.

*** The contrast between satirizing the poor and marked concern for their plight is evident in a comparison of [Defoe]. The True Born Englishman..., [(700$1261064), folio [A recto]; p. 27], and Sir D. Dolins. Charge to the Grand Jury of Middlesex, [7 October 1725 quoted in George. London Life..., op. cit., p. 32.]

The "Lab'ring Poor...Saway, Mutinous and Beggerly"[122] had supplemented wine, beer and ale with distilled spirits.[123]

---

[122] [Defoe]. The True Born Englishman..., op.cit., p. 27.

[123] While wine, beer and ale consumption continued throughout the Gin Era (1703-1799), their relative market shares declined. Excise duties were paid on 4,947,000 gallons of domestically manufactured spirits in 1735 7,160,000 gallons were duty-paid in 1742.* Andre Simon estimates distilled spirits at 2,000,000 gallons in 1714, 11,000,000 in 1733, and 20,000,000 in 1742.** England's population in 1736 was 6,200,000.

In 1722, the production of malt for brewing beer was 33,000,000 bushels, indicating a consumption of 36 gallons per capita per annum. This figure is well below the Elizabethan estimate of 150 gallons per person [Supra, Vol. 1, p. 194, footnote 38], yet, it represents a consumption never subsequently equaled.***

Wine consumption diminished markedly. Port supplanted French wines even among the upper classes; the French wine connoisseur slowly succumbed to an improving Portuguese product.# The "notorious" adulteration of wines, particularly French wines ## lessened their relative popularity.###

* Sidney and Beatrice Webb. The History of Liquor Licensing, (963$1270719), p. 31.

** Simon. Bottlescrew Days, op. cit., p. 22.

*** Webb. The History..., op. cit., pp. 21-22 p. 22, footnote 1.

\# Simon. Bottlescrew Days, op. cit., pp. 108ff. Allen. A History of Wine, op. cit., pp. 208ff.

\#\# [Robert Walpole]. A Letter..., (733 1260309), pp. 12, 16, 21, 29, 35. Josiah Child. A New Discourse of Trade, (740$1271250), pp. iv to vi.

\#\#\# Nevertheless, wine imports continually were bemoaned. For example, consult King. The British Merchant..., op. cit., Vol. 1, p. 4; Child. A New Discourse..., op. cit., p. 189.

In 1729, and again in 1736, Parliament acted to thwart the excesses of "the drinking of Geneva and other distilled spirituous liquors...[which] hath for some years past greatly increased."[124] In place of unrestricted production and distribution, Parliament introduced a system of licensing and heavy taxation of the retail trade.[125] When the restrictions proved ineffectual, the government, in 1743, dispensed with prior restrictions and, to enhance revenue, adopted lenient, yet enforceable, policies.[126] The result was the lawful, but indiscriminate sale of liquor: 7,000 out of 12,000 quarters of wheat sold weekly in London markets in 1750 were converted into spirituous liquors.[127]

The effects of increasing spirit consumption were bemoaned not only for their social corruption,[128] but for

---

[124] Middlesex Quarter Sessions, Epiphany, 1736 quoted in Webb. The History of Liquor Licensing, op. cit., p. 28.

[125] Tovey. British & Foreign Spirits..., op. cit., pp. 53 to 57.
George. London Life..., op. cit., pp. 33 to 36.
Webb. The History..., op. cit., pp. 28 to 32.

[126] Ibid., [Webb], p. 37.

[127] Ibid., p. 43.

[128] Ibid., pp. 43-44.
Lawrence Gipson...Great Britain and Ireland, (936 1270598), pp. 68 to 73.
Ashton. Social Life..., (897$1271077), pp. 161ff.
William Hickey. Memoirs..., (767$1260662), pp. 72-73.
William Iversen. "A Short History of Toasts...," (964$1280179), p. 214.

their economic consequences. Thomas Alcock protested that, "Spirituous Liquors...consumes the Gains and Subsistence of the People, and reduces them to Poverty and Want...and makes them both unwilling and unable to Work."[129] Josiah Tucker attempted a calculation of the annual loss to "Great Britain, by drinking Gin and Spirituous Liquors."[130] Such protests, however, did not check consumption,[131] which continued until 1799 when a severe grain shortage forced all distilleries to close.[132]

The plight of England's poor attracted royal interest, both in alleviating pauperism and in employing surplus labor.[133] French Huguenots developed England's silk industry, and by the eighteenth century it was "one of the most

---

[129]Thomas Alcock. Observations on the Defects..., (752 1270636), p. 49.

[130]Josiah Tucker. An Impartial Inquiry..., (751 1270254), pp. 24 to 26.

[131]Webb. The History..., op. cit., pp. 45 to 52.
George. London Life..., op. cit., pp. 38, 39.
Patrick Colquhoun. Observations and Facts..., (795 1270736), pp. 5 to 8, 34-35; Appendix.

[132]John Sheffield. Remarks on the Deficiency of Grain..., (800 1270257), pp. 2 to 4; p. 2, footnote *. Prior prohibitions because grain shortages are discussed in George. London Life..., op. cit., pp. 38-39.

[133]D. C. Coleman. "Labour in the English Economy...," (956 1270928), pp. 280ff.
William Grampp. "The Liberal Elements...," (952$1270925), pp. 465ff.

considerable branches of the manufactures of this Kingdom,"[134] employing increasing numbers of the poor. Thus, the Crown acted both to stabilize the labor force by reducing gin consumption, and to promote colonial silk culture for home use. Neither endeavor succeeded.

To encourage silk culture in her colonies, the English aided Huguenot emigration and offered colonists bounties and differential duties.[135] England, however, strove to keep the manufacture of silk out of her colonies.[136] Her aim was to promote domestic production[137] by assuring the availability of raw silk. Colonial culture would supplement the

---

[134] Statutes at Large, Vol. 5, p. 260 (1721) quoted in Lipson. The Economic History..., op. cit., Vol. 2, p. 102.
Defoe. A Plan of the English Commerce. (1728 ed.) pp. 164, 293-294.

[135] Peter J. Hamilton. The History..., (904 1270331), pp. 43 to 47; p. 47, footnote 4.
Charles W. Baird. History of the Huguenot Emigration to America, (885$1270479), Vol. 2, pp. 299-300.
M. Charles Weiss. History of the French Protestant..., (854 1270533), Vol. 1, pp. 348 to 350.
Matthew Andrews. The Soul of a Nation..., (944 1271175), pp. 292ff.
Consult also Supra, Vol. 1, p. 172, footnote 189.

[136] Arthur H. Hirsch. The Huguenots..., (928$1270518), p. 167; p. 167, footnote 9.

[137] Weiss. History of the French Protestant..., op. cit., Vol. 1, pp. 289 to 292.
Lipson. The Economic History..., op. cit., Vol. 2, pp. 100ff.
Philip W. Buck. The Politics of Mercantilism, (942$1270941), pp. 32 to 34; p. 33, footnote 33; p. 199.
Disregarding the advice offered by D'Avenant ["An Essay on the East-India Trade," (696$1271247), p. 108] that "the stock and industry laid out on the silk manufacture, would be more usefully employed in such as are made from

intermittent foreign supply, and would free her from competing with the French, Dutch and Spanish for raw silk.[138]

Bounties fostering colonial viticulture and wine production accompanied those favoring silk culture. Encouragements of the early eighteenth century and thereafter, however, increasingly favored silk. Thus, colonial viticulture was again at a comparative disadvantage. It failed again to sustain royal interest, for silk culture, as tobacco had earlier, took priority.

Hence, while the objectives of promoting English shipping, augmenting royal (public) revenues and satisfying the royal palate had all initially advanced the wine trade, their influence in the eighteenth century was limited. The

---

materials of our own growth," the English promoted domestic silk manufacture by a series of statutes and ordinances:

Calendar of State Papers Domestic..., (689 1221120), Vol. 3, pp. 253-254, [26 April 1692].
Ibid., Vol. 4, p. 298 [1 September 1693].
Ibid., Vol. 8, p. 418 [7 October 1697].
Ibid., Vol. 9, p. 263 [21 May 1698].
Royal Instructions..., (935 1220883), p. 754 [8 Geo. I, c. 15. (1721)].
Leo Stock. (ed.). Proceedings and Debates..., (924 1221132), Vol. 4, p. 46 [26 April 1729], HC.
Ibid., Vol. 4, p. 249 [10 April 1733], HC.
Royal Instructions..., op. cit., p. 758 [20 Geo. II, c. 45. (1747)].
Stock. (ed.). Proceedings and Debates..., op. cit., Vol. 5, pp. 373 to 377 [16 January 1749/1750], HC.

[138] George. London Life..., op. cit., p. 178.

desire for greater royal revenue, which diverted English interest from wine to tobacco production in the seventeenth century, correspondingly shifted royal interest from wine to silk culture and gin manufacture in the eighteenth century. Fiscalism dominated Stuart and Hanoverian wine trade practices.

English oenological endeavors, domestic and colonial, were promoted to advance provisionment by curtailing balance of trade losses, and by developing English sources of wine supply. These trials were undertaken when wine manifested comparative advantages in production. Practices promoting royal (public) revenue, however, curtailed the commercial development of these ventures. Thus, both in England and in the colonies, individual oenological projects were only intermittently successful.

Within the context of Commodity Mercantilism, English practices highlight the provisionment-fiscalism conflict. They reveal the difficulties in promoting both the availability and balance of trade objectives of provisionment and the revenue objectives of fiscalism. These difficulties are explored further in examining the English colonial experience.

CHAPTER VI

The English Colonial Experience

English colonial attempts at viticulture and wine production were commercially unsuccessful. The accessibility of inexpensive wine imports, the fiscal needs of colonial governments and the superior short-term returns of alternative ventures all countered England's desire for wine availability and for the curtailment of balance of trade losses in her colonial and domestic wine trade. Thus, English fiscalism and colonial economic conditions primarily caused the commercial failure of oenological endeavors in the English North American colonies.

This interpretation counters currently accredited theories which stress climatic, viticultural and socio-political factors as the major causes of English failures at colonial wine production. It relies on primary sources to overwhelmingly demonstrate the dominance of economic factors. It traces non-economic theories to colonists who dismissed the economic disadvantages of wine production, and to ante-bellum viticulturists who rationalized the commercial failure of their experiments. The interpretation of Commodity Mercantilism provides a unifying theory within which English colonial oenological events are related to the mother country's wine trade practices, and more generally, to the diverse domestic and colonial practices of the European states.

Early Spanish,[1] Dutch,[2] French[3] and English[4] explorers all noted prolific vines flourishing along America's East

---

[1] Supra, Vol. 1, pp. 74 to 83.

[2] Ibid., pp. 128 to 131; p. 129, footnote 56.

[3] Ibid., pp. 148 to 150.

[4] Tracts written prior to 1600 describing the abundance of vines on the East Coast are cited Supra, Vol. 1, p. 204, footnote 60. The sources cited below exemplify the continuance of this motif in early seventeenth century exploration and colonization tracts.

John Brereton. "A Brief and True...," (602 1260128), p. 332.

________. "A Briefe Note...," (602 1260509), p. 320.

Archer. "Archer's Account...," (602 1260026), pp. 76, 77.

James Rosier. A Trve Relation..., (605$1260168), B_2 verso.

George Percy. "Percy's Discourse," (606$1260073), p. 164.

Martin Pring. "The Voyage of...," (607 1260129), p. 349.

Fernando Gorges. "Relation of a Voyage...," (607$1260130), pp. 414-415.

William Strachy. "A True Reportorie...," (610 1260512), pp. 18, 63.

John Smith. "The General Historie...," (624 1260057), pp. 300, 350.

William Hilton. "A Letter from New Plymouth," (621$1260101), p. 250.

John Robinson. "A Relation...," (622 1260070), pp. 410, 413, 436-437, 491.

[George Morton]. "A Relation...," (622 1260775), p. 97.

John Pory. "Description of Plymoutn Colony," (622$1261095), p. 42.

Graves. "A Letter Sent from New England," (630$1260878), p. 124.

Thomas Yong. "A Briefe Relation of a Voyage...," (634 1260340), p. 48.

Coast. It was particularly the English explorers, however, who wrote of the paradisical image of the vine.[5] They

---

[5]The desirable nature of America was thereby reinforced by those advocating colonization.* Although the realities of the "Starving Time" in Virginia (1607-1610)** and the hardships of early New England settlement (1622)*** countered this image, these privations were instrumental in heightening the paradisical element in the description of the colonies. To counteract the disparagement by actors, balladeers and disgruntled colonists, those fostering colonization intensified the element of plenty in their descriptions.#

* Consult Supra, Vol. 1, pp. 203 to 207.

** Edward Wingfield. "A Discourse of Virginia," (608$1260527), pp. 88 to 90.
William Simmons. "The Proceedings...," (612 1260054), pp. 127ff.
Robert Howison. A History of Virginia..., (846 1270624), Vol. 1, pp. 102 to 105.
Thomas Wertenbaker. Virginia Under the Stuarts..., (914$1270745), pp. 14 to 24.
George Willison. Behold Virginia..., (952 1270061), pp. 105ff.

***

> I confess, it hath not been much less chargeable to some of you (the Adventurers), than hard and difficult to us, that have endured the brunt of the battle: and yet small profits returned. Only, by GOD's mercy, we are safely seated, housed, and fortified...
> [Edward Winslow. "Good News...," (624$1260069), p. 514; similarly, p. 528.]

\#

> Great store of Fowle, of Venison,
> of Grapes, and Mulberries...
> There is indeed no want at all:
> but some condiciond ill,
> That wish the worke [colonization] should not goe on,
> with words doe seeme to kill.
> [R. Rich. Newes from Virginia, (610$1260788), B_2 verso.]

William Morell. "Nova-Anglia," (623$1260879), p. 128.
________. New-England..., (625 1260167), p. 14.

Famine once we had ____________

mistakenly equated the abundance of wild grapes with null or minimal capital and labor expenditures in wine production.[6] Envisioning colonial wines as virtually a "free

---

But other things God gave us in full store...
A Pleasant banquet is prepar'd for these,
Of fat things, and rich wine upon the lees;
"Eat, O my friends, (saith Christ) and drink freely,
Here's wine and milk, and all sweet spicery;
The honey and its comb is here to be had,
I myself for you have this banquet made.
[William Bradford. "A Descriptive and Historical...," (630 1260894), pp. 77, 79.]

Thomas Morton. <u>New English Canaan</u>..., (637 1261189), pp. 65, 92 to 94, passim.
Michael Wigglesworth. "God's Controversy...," (622$1260853), p. 87, stanza 5.
Louis B. Wright. <u>Religion and Empire</u>..., (943 1271269), pp. 89 to 103.

[6]Wine production was conceived as merely the barreling of a ready vintage. Hence, its production was equated to the ready manufacture of other staples.* W. Crashaw and Michael Drayton exemplify the mistaken notion that wine manufacture required no special techniques:

> Againe, they [the Indians] may spare vs <u>timber</u>, <u>masts</u>, <u>crystall</u> (if not better stones) <u>wine</u>, <u>copper</u>, <u>iron</u>, <u>pitch</u>, <u>tar</u>, <u>sassafras</u>, <u>sopeashes</u> (for all these and more, we are sure the Countrey yeeldes in great abundance) and who knowes not we wont these, and are beholden to some for them, with whom it were better for vs if we had lesse to doe.
> [W. Crashaw. <u>A Sermon Preached</u>..., (610 1261168), folio [D4 recto].]

Oft spreading vines climb up the cleeves.
Whose ripen'd clusters there
Their liquid purple drop, which drives
a vintage through the year.
[Michael Drayton. "The Muses' Elizium" [1630] quoted in Gustav Blanke. <u>Amerika</u>..., (962 1270468), p. 126.]

* Strachey. <u>The Historie of Travell</u>...,

good," they sought wine from wild grapes. The need for cultivating the wild vines soon was intimated in "Instructions for such things as are to be sente from Virginia... [send] Wyne a hoggeshead or two sower as it is...for a sample."[7] John Smith was more specific: "Of those hedge grapes, wee made neere 20 gallons of wine, which was neare as good as your French British wine, but certainely they would prove good were they well manured."[8]

A lack of oenological knowledge and skill arrested the Englishmen's cultivating the vine.[9] Accordingly,

---

(612$1260298), pp. 121-122.
"A Declaration of the State of the Colonie...," (620 1261174), pp. 4, 10.
A Briefe Relation...of New England..., (622 1261103), folio D_3 recto.
"Virginia Verger...," (625 1260516), pp. 245-246.

[7]"Instructions for Such Things...," (610 1260079), pp. 384, 385.

[8]Smith. "A Map of Virginia...," (612 1260052), p. 91.

[9]Although herbals had progressed from describing grapes by their "smooth thycke substaunce"* to delineating their botanical properties**, and had advanced from offering medicinal remedies*** to attempting systematized discussions of vine genera,# the herbals available to the colonists were void of viticultural techniques.## Similarly, garden books had not developed as instructional manuals.### Their content influenced only the court and perhaps the lesser nobility--the reading population.

Thus, English colonists were more the source than the recipients of botanical information.@ The influence of their findings with respect to wild vines is observed in comparing sixteenth and seventeenth century English herbals. The sixteenth century herbals repeatedly specify but two varieties of wild vines;@@ the herbals of the seventeenth century delineate many varieties, among them the "Virginia Vine."@@@ Such descriptions aroused the English to transplant colonial wild vines for ornamental use in their gardens.□ This use, however, did not contribute to knowledge

vinedressers and coopers were sought to promote wine availability. Robert Johnson observed:

> Wee doubt not but to make there in few yeares store of good wines, as any from the Canaries, by replanting and making tame

---

of the colonial vine. Furthermore, English tracts relating to colonial flora and fauna describe the vine, but do not prescribe successful means of colonial cultivation.@@ Thus, tracts advancing viticulture in the colonies were translations of French sources. Their unsuitability is discussed Supra, Vol. 1, p. 161, footnote 152.

* P. Treveris. The Grete Herball, (526 1270964), item Ca. ccc. lxix.

** J. Reynolds Green. A History of Botany..., (914 1270876), pp. 34, 35, 62, 63.
Julius Von Sachs. History of Botany..., (906$1270875), pp. 7 to 9, 17 to 21.
Agnes Arber. Herbals..., (935 1270399), pp. 41ff.

*** William Turner. The Seconde Parte..., (562 1270962), folio 25 recto-verso.
________. The First and Seconde Partes..., (568 1270963), folio 25 recto-verso.

\# Green. A History of Botany..., op. cit., pp. 17 to 19, 46, 50 to 53.
Eleanour Sinclair Rohde. The Old English Herbals, (922$1270161), p. 142ff.

\## Ibid. [Rohde], pp. 120 to 133.
John Gerarde. The Herball or Generall Historie of Plantes, (597$1270958), pp. 724 to 726.
Alice Lockwood. (ed.). Gardens of Colony..., (931 1270869), Vol. 1, pp. 5 to 7; Vol. 2, pp. 3 to 5.
D. Rembert Dodoens. A Niewe Herball..., (578$1270198), pp. 649 to 652.

\### Thomas Hyll. A Most Briefe..., (563 1270999), editors' preface.
John Parkinson. Paradisi in Sole..., (629$1270696), pp. 563 to 566.

@ Rodney H. True. "Beginnings of Agricultural Literature...," (920$1281220), pp. 186 to 189.
Rohde. The Old English Herbals, op. cit., pp. 133 to 137.

@@ Turner. The Names of Herbes, (548$1270160), p. 45.
Dodoens. A Niewe Herball..., op. cit.,

> the vines that naturally grow there in great abundance; onely send men of skill to doe it, and Coopers to make caske, and hoopes for that and all other uses, for which there is wood enough at hand.[10]

Correspondingly, William Strachey suggested,

> ...vnto what perfection might not these [wild vines] be brought by the art and industry of many skylfull vineroones, being thus naturally good? and how materiall and principall a Comodity this may prove either for the benefitt of such who shall inhabit there, or to be returned over hither especially where we haue Pipe-staves to make our Cask of So Cheape, and at hand, i referre yt to indifferent Iudgementes.[11]

---

pp. 651, 652.
Gerarde. The Herball..., op. cit., pp. 724ff.
@@@ Parkinson. Paradisi in Sole..., op. cit., p. 564.
________. Theatrum Botanicum..., (640 1270691), pp. 178, 1555, 1556.
Joanne Raio [John Rea]. Historia Plantarum..., (686$1270969), Vol. 1, p. 659; Vol. 2, pp. 1614 to 1617.
________. Methodus Plantarum Nova, (692$1270639), p. 46.
Philip Miller. The Gardeners Dictionary..., (741 1270988), folio UVI, openings 14-15.
▯ Ibid. [Miller].
D. J. Browne. The Trees of America..., (857$1270526), p. 135.
▯▯ William Smallwood. Natural History..., (941$1280877), pp. 8 to 21.

[10][Robert Johnson]. Nova Britannia..., (609 1260643), folio C_3 verso.

[11]Strachey. The Historie of Travell..., op. cit., p. 122.

Supporters and officials of the Virginia Company,[12] and, later, officers of the Company of Massachusetts Bay[13] reiterated similar pleas.

---

[12]"Newport's Discoveries in Virginia," related that, "the soyle is more fertill then can be well exprest. It naturally yeelds mulbery-trees, cherry-trees, vines aboundance...So the thing we crave is some skillfull man to husband, sett, plant, and dresse vynes..."* Similarly, Robert Gray asserted that, "Artificers and tradesmen must be nourished and cherished, for without...[them] a common-wealth cannot flourish nor endure."** These statements paralleled others requesting "Frenchman heere a worke to plant Vines,"*** "such as know how to plant vineyards,"# "skilfull vinearoones,"## and vinedressers.

Of the 116 "sufficient, honest and good artificers"### sought for the Virginia Plantation in 1610, fourteen were sought to promote wine production (six coopers, six vine-dressers, two presse-makers).@ In comparison, the Virginia Company sought only six blacksmiths, ten fishermen, two sope-ashe men and two silke-dressers.@@ Although artificers were dispatched to Virginia, their number was insufficient. Hence, the demand continued for vine-dressers.@@@

* Newport. "Newport's Discoveries in Virginia," (607$1260067), pp. 60, 61

** Robert Gray. A Good Speed to Virginia, (609$1260787), folio D_3 recto.

*** Strachy. "A True Repoⁿtorie...," op. cit., p. 63.

\# "Letter of Don Pedro...," (609$1260075), p. 248.

\## Governor and Council of Virginia. "Letter of...," (610 1260083), p. 409.

\### Counsell of Virginia. "A Broadside...," (610 1250081), p. 355.

@ John Stepney. "A True and Sincere...," (610$1260080), p. 353. Among the signers of the Second Charter of the Virginia Company were three vintners and The Company of Vintners. "The Second Charter...," (609 1220074), p. 226.

@@ Ibid.

@@@ John Rolfe. A True Relation..., (616 1261186), p. 34.
Pory. "Letter of John Pory...," (619 1260056), p. 284.
Patrick Copland. Virginia's God be Thanked...,

Notwithstanding the low level of oenological skills, Virginia Company colonists produced wines from uncultivated wild vines[14] and several times from vines cultivated in their

---

(622 1271178), pp. 12-13, 30.
Susan Kingsbury. (ed.). The Records..., (906 1251144), Vol. 4, p. 68 (March 28, 1623).
Wesley Craven. Dissolution of the Virginia Company, (932$1270600), pp. 101-102, 289-290. The dominance of economic motives in the Company's staples policy is discussed pp. 24ff, 92ff.

[13]"Records of the Governor...," (629 1260948), pp. 42, 43.

> It is great pittie no man sets upon such a venture [wine production], whereby he might in small time inrich himselfe, and benefit the Countrie; I know nothing which doth hinder but want to skilfull men to manage such an imployment...
> [William Wood. Nevv Englands Prospect...., (635 1260170), p. 15.]

John Winter. "Winter to...," (636$1260287), p. 86.

[14]"Instructions for Such Things...," op. cit., pp. 384, 385.
Francis Maguel. "Report of...," (610$1260082), p. 395.
Thomas Dale. "Sir Thomas Dale...," (611$1260087), p. 502.
"The New Life of Virginea," (612$1260896), p. 204.
Smith. "A Map of Virginia...," op. cit., p. 91.
Strachey. The Historie of Travell..., op. cit., p. 121.

> The Vines beeing in abundance naturally over all the Countrey: a taste of which Wine they have alreadie sent us, with hope the next yeere to send us a good quantitie.
> ["Note of the Shipping...," (621 1260514), p. 145; Kingsbury. (ed.). The Records..., op. cit., Vol. 3, p. 641 (End of May, 1622).]

own vineyards.[15] Their viticultural endeavors involved both native vines and imported scions. Such trials, with French assistance,[16] flourished in 1611, 1614, 1620, 1621 and 1622.[17]

---

[15]Vineyards were suggested as a means of improving wine quality. Even the Spanish were aware "that there is much wild growing fruit and great quantity of grapes [in Virginia], and thus it is believed, that they would try to have vineyards." [Velsasco. "Velsasco to Philip III," (611$1260085), p. 455.] Among those advocating vineyards for wine availability were:

Newport. "Newport's Discoveries...," _op_. _cit_., p. 61.
Strachy. _True Reportorie_..., _op_. _cit_., p. 63.
Strachey. _The Historie of Travell_..., _op_. _cit_., p. 122.
Iohn Bonoeil. _His Maiesties Graciovs Letter_..., (622 1261194), folio a recto, B, B_2, passim.

The Records of the Virginia Company [Kingsbury. (ed.). _op_. _cit_., Vol. 1, p. 353 (May 17, 1620); Vol. 3, p. 116(?)] also exhibit suggestions for vineyards.

[16]The inaccuracy of secondary sources relating to English colonial viticulture and wine production is virtually unbelievable. The specific dating of initial French aid to the English colonists is a classic example.

U. P. Hedrick [_The Grapes of New York_, (908$1270201), Vol. 2, p. 6] maintained that the French vinedressers dispatched to the colony in 1619 were sent in response to a 1616 appeal of Lord Delaware to the London Company. Although Dr. Hedrick correctly cites the 1611 date of _Delaware's Relation_ in the footnote [_Ibid_., Vol. 2, p. 6, footnote 1], the typographical error in the text is repeated in his _A History of Horticulture_...,[(950$1270400), p. 102] and this time without citation.

Frank Schoonmaker ["The Red Wines...," (951$1280210), p. 293] adopts this 1616 date. A. J. Winkler [_General Viticulture_, (962$1270199), pp. 11-12] inverts the final six to a nine, thus advancing the date to 1619. W. C. Strong [_Culture of the Grape_, (866$1270238), p. 21] and John Phin [_Open Air Grape Culture_..., (862 1270215), p. 23] a century earlier had suggested the year 1630.

F. R. Elliott [_Elliott's Fruit Book_..., (855 1270538), p. 232; and _The Western Fruit Book_..., (865 1270550), p. 243] contended that, "although we have record of wine being made from a native grape in Florida as early as 1564, no vineyards of note are spoken of in the United States until...about 1812." John F. von Daacke [_"Sparkling Catawba" Grape_...,

The dissolution of the Virginia Company (1624) temporarily halted efforts to revive the viticultural projects

---

(964 1211171), p. 10] totally ignores French efforts. He writes as follows: "When the first explorers and settlers came to America, they were neither interested in grapes nor grape culture...Thus few records of those early years contain any mention of grapes."

The earliest recorded date for French assistance is 1610.

> ...especially since the Frenchmen (who are with the Lord Governor) do confidently promise, that within two yeares we may expect a plentifull Vintage.
> ["A Trve Declaration...," (610 1261102), p. 23.]

[17]VITICULTURAL TRIALS UNDER THE VIRGINIA COMPANY

YEAR	TYPE OF VINE	ITEM	SOURCE
1610	native	...within two yeares we may expect a plentifull Vintage.	"A Trve Declaration...," *op. cit.*, p. 23.
1611	native	...many Vines planted in divers places...	De-La-Warre. [Lord Delaware]. "The Relation...," (611 1260053), p. 214.
	native	...allreadie 2. or 3.000 acors of cliered ground to sett corne, and plant Vines...	Dale. "Sir Thomas Dale...," *op. cit.*, p. 504.
1612	native	...soever shall... robbe any vineyard... shall be punished with death.	Strachey. "For the Colony...," (612 1261083), pp. 16-17 (item 31).
1614	native	...wilde grapes in abundance...was haue replanted in a vineyard...the quantity of three or foure Akers...	Ralph Hamor. *A True Discourse...*, (615 1260110), p. 22.
1619	imported	...skilfull Vignerons are sent, with... Vine-plants of the best sort.	"Note of the Shipping...," (619 1260513), p. 128.
	imported or native	...every householder doe yearly plant and maintaine ten vines...	Kingsbury. (ed.). *The Records...*, *op. cit.*, Vol. 3, p. 166 (July

flourishing in Virginia before the 1622 Indian massacre.

			30-August 4, 1619). "Proceedings of the Virginia Assembly...," (619$1240055), p. 265.
1620	imported	...men skilful...in ...Vines, out of France and...Rhene, and from thence... Plants of the best kindes.	"A Declaration of the Supplies...," [1620] quoted in Lockwood. (ed.). *Gardens*..., *op. cit.*, Vol. 2, p. 42.
	imported	...skillfull Vignerons...[sent], w^{th}... Vine plants of ye best Sorte.	Kingsbury. (ed.). *The Records*..., *op. cit.*, Vol. 1, p. 392 (July 7, 1620); Vol. 3, p. 279 (May 17, 1620).
1621	native and imported	[French Vignerons] ...cultivated in Virginia Vines of... those naturally growing...[and] those... from...Europe.	"Newes from Virginia...," (621 1260515), p. 151; similarly, pp. 152, 153 and Kingsbury. (ed.). *The Records*..., *op. cit.*, Vol. 3, pp. 547-548.
1622	imported (from Plimouth)	...Vines...prosper very well...	Edward Winne. "Another Letter...," (622 1260517), p. 445.
	native or imported	Vyneyeards planted... some conteyned Tenn thousant Plantes.	Kingsbury. (ed.). *The Records*..., *op. cit.*, Vol. 2, p. 349.
	native or imported	...the Vineyard our Vineyetours had brought to a good forwardnesse, bruised and destroyed...	Smith. "The General Historie...," *op. cit.*, p. 379.
1623	native or imported	...last yeare Wee had a taste of Wyne, this Yeare nothinge, (the Massacre...	Kingsbury. (ed.). *The Records*..., *op. cit.*, Vol. 4, p. 142 (May, 1623); Vol. 2, p. 349 (April 12, 1623).

Ernst and Johanna Lehner [*Folklore and Odysseys*..., (962$1270191), p. 63] allege that "the London Company sent forces of French vintners and large quantities of cuttings from European vines to the colonies for grafting." They offer no citation. John Sheffield [*Observations on the Commerce*..., (784 1270236), pp. 51-52, footnote *], however, did suggest "Perhaps to ingraft the European on the native grape..." in 1784. He apparently was unaware of such attempts in the Georgia colony. [*The Colonial Records... Georgia*..., (732 1241037), Vol. 1, p. 447; Vol. 4, p. 330.]

The greater economic incentives for producing other staples, particularly silk, tobacco and rice, diverted colonists from oenological pursuits.

Thus, in 1623, promoters of the Company directed Frenchmen to silk culture because of its relatively higher return.[18] This action followed a 1622 decision to charge part of the Company's cost in securing French vignerons to colonists receiving instructions "in the art of setting and planting of vines, and in the mystery of making wine."[19]

The withdrawal of skills and the increased cost of setting vineyards were economic deterrents to the revival of viticulture in Virginia. A 1623 statute ordering vine culture, hence, did little to increase production. Later proponents of colonial wine production attributed oenological failures under the Virginia Company to socio-political reasons. They blamed French vignerons to mask the economic disadvantages of commercial endeavors.[20]

After 1624, attempts to encourage colonial viticulture were in response to severe tobacco gluts.[21] The comparative advantage of wine production increased relative to that of

---

[18] Supra, Vol. 1, pp. 166-167; p. 167, footnote 174.

[19] R. A. Brock. (ed.). Abstract of the Proceedings..., (888 1270100), Vol. 1, p. 170 (April 3, 1622).
Kingsbury. (ed.). The Records..., op. cit., Vol. 1, pp. 627-628 (April 10, 1622).

[20] Supra, Vol. 1, p. 168.

[21] Ibid., Vol. 1, pp. 226 to 231; Appendix II.

tobacco during such periods. Yet, efforts to establish commercial production failed, as encouragements and prices for wine were insufficient to stimulate its large-scale manufacture.[22]

Despite its commercial failure, gentlemen farmers in Virginia were several times successful with viticulture during the provincial period (1624 to 1776).[23] Wine was

---

[22]Encouragements and premiums for wine production are recorded in:

Infra, Vol. 1, Appendix II.
The Statutes at Large...Virginia..., (619 1251034), Vol. 1, p. 151 [March, 1629-30]; p. 469 [March, 1657-58]; Vol. 8, p. 364f. [November, 1769].
Journal of the House of Burgesses of Virginia..., (619 1241036), Vol. 12, pp. 17-19, 98, 107 [25 May 1770].

John Phin [*Open Air Grape Culture...*, *op. cit.*, p. 23] suggests that a premium was offered for wine production in Virginia in 1651. He offers no citation. Neither does U. P. Hedrick [*History of Horticulture...*, *op. cit.*, p. 102] who quotes a 1639 Act.

Conflicting opinions on the importance of bounties in promoting the production of staples are offered by:

Emory R. Johnson et al. *History of Domestic and Foreign Commerce...*, (915 1270783), Vol. 1, p. 62.
George Beer. *The Commercial Policy of England Toward the American Colonies*, New York: Peter Smith, 1948, pp. 91 to 106. [The 1948 edition is reprinted from the 1893 monograph.]
Albert Giesecke. *American Commercial Legislation...*, (916$1270720), pp. 59 to 74, especially pp. 62-63.

[23]Robert Beverley. *The History...Virginia*, (705$1260701), pp. 134 to 137, 315.
Wright. *The First Gentlemen...*, (940$1270329), p. 90, footnote 67; p. 301; p. 301, footnote 27.
Hugh Jones. *The Present State of Virginia...*, (724 1260065), pp. 59, 139 to 141; p. 216, footnote 159; p. 263, footnote 318.
John Curtis. "Letter," (736$1260851), p. 50.
E. G. Swem. (ed.). "Brothers of the Spade...,"

produced both from wild grapes[24] and from cultivated native and imported vines.[25] The success of these and prior ventures suggests the error of theories asserting that climatic or viticultural deficiencies were the major causes of colonial oenological failures.

Early frost, high humidity and viticultural pests did cause oenological failures,[26] but were not themselves the

---

(948 1280850), pp. 170-171, footnote 85.
Philip Bruce. Economic History of Virginia..., (896 1270211), Vol. 1, pp. 471-472.

[24]William Bvllock. Virginia Impartially Examined..., (649 1261192), p. 8.
Thomas Glover. An Account of Virginia..., (676 1260781), pp. 15-16.
Francois Durand. "Voyages of One Francois...," (687 1260435), p. 126.
Beverley. The History...Virginia, op. cit., pp. 134, 282.
William Byrd. William Byrd's Natural History..., (737 1260772), p. 33.
Bruce. Economic History of Virginia..., op. cit., pp. 410-411.

[25]Hearty native varieties were more successful than imported vines. Albeit, both native and imported vines were cultivated successfully and used for producing wine.

Beverley. The History...Virginia, op. cit., Bk. II, pp. 19, 21; Bk. IV, p. 46 [in 1705 edition].
Jones. The Present State of Virginia..., op. cit., pp. 59, 139-140.
Swem. (ed.). "Brothers of the Spade...," op. cit., pp. 170-171, footnote 85.
Lewis C. Gray. History of Agriculture..., (941$1270207), Vol. 1, pp. 188-189.
Hedrick. A History of Agriculture..., op. cit., pp. 102 to 104.

[26]"A Perfect Description...," op. cit., p. 109.
Beverley. The History and Present State of Virginia,

major causes. The poor selection of sites and, more precisely, the poor choice of soils induced these damaging effects. They caused, "the grapes generally [to] burst before they are fully ripe which...[was] occasioned by their having too much nourishment."[27]

Thus, it was a lack of knowledge, rather than environmental conditions, that was responsible for viticultural failures.[28] This deficiency was a direct consequence of economic factors, that is, proponents of wine production failed to offer sufficient remuneration to attract skilled viticultural workers. For example, emigrating Huguenots,

---

op. cit., p. 135.
Jones. *The Present State of Virginia...*, *op. cit.*, p. 140.
Byrd. "Letters Relative to Plants...," (739 1260767), p. 196.

27Miller. *The Gardeners Dictionary...*, *op. cit.*, folio ꝹVI, openings 14-15.
Consult also:
[Edward Williams]. *Virginia's Discovery...*, (650 1261193), p. 34.
Bruce. *Economic History of Virginia...*, *op. cit.* pp. 238-239.

28The oenological success of the Spanish and the French in their colonies [*Supra*, Vol. 1, pp. 76 to 89; pp. 150f.], and that of their nationals in English colonies [*Supra*, Vol. 1, pp. 252, 253; pp. 170f.] suggest a direct correlation between viticultural skill and the achievement of commercial wine production. Dutch and English oenological failures further substantiate this relationship. [*Supra*, Vol. 1, pp. 131, 132; *Infra*, Vol. 1, pp. 258ff.]
The return on Dutch and English wine production ventures was not sufficient to warrant the marshaling of skilled labor. Thus, George Sandys admonished: "Encourage the Frenchmen to stay, if not forever, at least 'till they have taught our people their skill in silk and vines." ["Letter to Mr. Ferrar," (August, 1623) quoted in Alexander Brown. *The First Republic...*, (898$1070090), p. 562.]

transported to the colonies for their oenological skills, were induced to cultivate other crops because of their higher return. Except for wine production from wild grapes,[29] these Huguenots abandoned oenological pursuits.[30]

In the province of Maryland, too, the scarcity of labor limited wine production. The author of the "Relation of the Successful...Plantation in Maryland" conjectured,

> ...if wee had Vessells and skill, wee might make many a tonne of Wine, euen from about our Plantation; and such Wine...is as good as the Wine of Spaine.[31]

The colonists' instructions, however, were to "imploy their servants in planting of sufficient quantity of corne and other provision...and...not...to plant any other commodity whatsoever before that be done."[32]

Thus, few colonists attempted viticulture or wine production with the wild grapes[33] growing abundantly in the

---

[29]Durand. "Voyages of One Francois...," op. cit., p. 126.
Beverley. The History...Virginia, op. cit., pp. 282, 315-316.

[30]Supra, Vol. 1, pp. 173, 174.

[31]"Relation of the Successful...Plantation in Maryland," (634 1260325), p. 31.

[32]Lord Baltimore. "Instructions to the Colonists...," (633 1270276), p. 23.
Archives of Maryland..., (636 1241030), Vol. 1, p. 34 [February-March 1638/39], p. 97 [October 1640], p. 135 [29 July 1642].

[33]Bernard C. Steiner. "Beginnings of Maryland...," (903$1280919), p. 97.
John Ogilby. America..., (671 1271109), pp. 187-188.

province.[34] As early as 1635, prospective immigrants to Maryland were advised to transport "Wine, Sugar, Prunes, Rasins...with which hee may procure himselfe cattell there."[35]

Maryland followed Virginia in adopting a single staple (tobacco) economy.[36] She turned to wine imports to an even greater extent than did Virginia.[37] At times when tobacco gluts reduced her revenue and fostered demands for colonial diversification, Maryland encouraged silk, flax, hemp and iron, though not wine.

---

[34] Baltemore. A Declaration..., (633 1261179), p. 5.
Andrew White. "A Brief Relation...," (634 1260277), pp. 40, 45.
"A Relation of Maryland," (635$1260278), pp. 79, 82.
John Hammond. "Leah and Rachel...," (656 1260280), p. 291.
Nathaniel Shrigley. "A True Relation of Virginia and Mary-Land...," (669 1261106), pp. 4-5.

[35] "A Relation of Maryland," op. cit., pp. 97-98.

[36] "Virginia and Maryland...," (655$1260279), p. 200.
George Alsop. "A Character...," (666$1260281), pp. 68 to 71.
Margaret Morriss. Colonial Trade of Maryland..., (914$1210780), pp. 24ff.

[37]

> Medera-Wines, Sugars, Salt, Wickar-Chairs, and Tin Candlesticks, is the most of the Commodities they bring in...
> [Alsop. "A Character...," op. cit., p. 72.]

Morriss. Colonial Trade of Maryland..., op. cit., pp. 81-82, 145.
Archives of Maryland..., op. cit., Vol. 3, p. 177 [19 January 1646]; Vol. 2, p. 296 [March-April 1671]; Vol. 7, p. 44 [October-November 1678]; Vol. 27, p. 371 [17 December 1708]; Vol. 39, p. 79 [3 April 1733]; Vol. 44, p. 168 [14 September 1745]; Vol. 52, p. 178 [7 July 1755], p. 325 [11 March 1756]; Vol. 55, pp. 697-698 [6 May 1758]; Vol. 32, p. 24 [11 December 1761].

Yet in 1662, during a severe tobacco glut, Lord Charles Baltimore, son of the grantee of the province, planted three hundred acres with vines. He made wine "as good as the best Burgundy" and sold it in large quantities.[38] John Ogilby noted his efforts:

> The Ground doth naturally bring forth Vines in great quantities, the quality whereof being something corrected by Industry, (as there have been several trials thereof already made there) may no doubt produce good Wine, to the great encouragement and advantage of The Undertakers.[39]

Notwithstanding the viticultural success of Lord Baltimore, which again emphasizes the environmental feasibility of colonial viticulture, the industry did not gain as a major staple because of economic factors. The continued availability of inexpensive wine imports, the accessibility of domestic brews[40] and the encouragement of other commodities[41] discouraged extensive commercial wine production in Maryland.

---

[38]Edward R. Emerson. _The Story of the Vine_, (902$1270387), pp. 161-162.
Hedrick. _The Grapes of New York_, _op_. _cit_., p. 9.
________. _A History of Horticulture_..., _op_. _cit_., p. 104.

[39]Ogilby. _America_..., _op_. _cit_., pp. 187-188.

[40]_Ibid_.
Hammond. "Leah and Rachel...," _op_. _cit_., p. 292.
Archives of Maryland..., _op_. _cit_., Vol. 2, p. 267-268 [17 April 1671]; p. 296 [March-April 1671].

[41]Examples of encouragements to promote silk, flax, hemp and iron are found in the _Archives of Maryland_..., _op_. _cit_., Vol. 2, p. 300 [March-April 1671]; Vol. 26, p. 632 [18 April 1706]; Vol. 28, p. 484 [29 May 1750].

Similar factors influenced the colonies of New England. Again, it was not adverse climatic or viticultural conditions, but rather the accessibility of wine imports, the superior return of alternative labor uses and the fiscal needs of the colonies which discouraged oenological attempts in Massachusetts, New Hampshire and Connecticut.

Unquestionably, the greatest discouragement was the accessibility of inexpensive wine imports. While early tracts emphasized the abundance of wild vines and suggested their culture for wine production,[42] such writings became fewer in number when foreign and colonial commerce afforded a cheap and readily available wine supply. The contrast is evident, for example, in William Bradford's History of Plimoth Plantation, wherein he remarked on the change in colonial wine supply between 1624[43] and 1646:

> ...how ye Lord doth chaing times & things; for what is now more plentifull then wine? and that of ye best, coming from Malago, ye Cannaries, and other places, sundry ships lading in a year. So as ther is now more cause to complaine of y^e^ excess...then of any defects or wante of y^e^ same.[44]

---

[42]"The Planters' Plea...," (630 1260645), p. 15. Iohn Smith. Advertisements..., (635 1260664), p. 43. Wood. Nevv Englands Prospect..., op. cit., p. 15.

[43]James Sherley. "Letter," (624$1260102), p. 191.

[44]Bradford. History of Plimoth Plantation, (624$1260835), p. 191, footnote /.

This unabated supply of wines and other beverages "made wine...very plentiful, and cheap, in the country."[45] William Hubbard, in relating "Various occurrents in New England, from 1646 to 1651," complained that, "too much indulgence... opened a door of encouragement to wine merchants, who have since filled the country with that commodity, to the over-flowing of luxury and other evils."[46] Similar complaints were voiced in 1675, 1676 and 1686.[47]

Wine, however, continued as a major import the eighteenth century. Hence, the accessibility of inexpensive wine imports through increased participation in triangular trade[48]

---

[45] James Hosmer. (ed.). Winthrop's Journal..., (630 1260336), Vol. 2, p. 93.

[46] William Hubbard. "A General History...," (682 1260900), p. 520.

[47]

> ...for the Merchant to increase his gains... comes in with a walking Tavern, a Bark laden with the Legitimate bloud of the rich grape, which they bring from Phial, Madera, Canaries...when Wine in their guts is at full Tide, they [the fishermen] quarrel, fight and do one another mischief, which is the conclusion of their drunken compotations.
>
> [John Josselyn. "An Account...," (675 1260273), pp. 161-162.]

Benjamin Tompson. "Prologue to New-Englands Crisis," in Jay B. Hubbell. American Life..., (936$1270002), p. 38.

"Commercial Orders...," (686$1260270), p. 174.

[48] Hosmer. (ed.). Winthrop's Journal..., op. cit., pp. 92-93.

J. Leander Bishop. A History of American Manufactures...," (866$1270016), p. 269.

Bernard Bailyn. The New England Merchants..., (955$1270739), pp. 83ff.

Samuel Morison. The Maritime History...,

discouraged domestic wine production. The triangular trade also was instrumental in shifting colonial wine taste toward sweet wines.[49] This further discouraged colonial wine production, as the manufacture of sweet wines from native or imported wines was impossible in New England.[50]

Notwithstanding the accessibility of wine imports, New England colonists attempted viticulture and wine production. These trials followed the proposed development of New England as a source of staple commodities for the mother country.[51]

(941$1270702), p. 19.

William Weeden. Economic and Social History of New England..., (890 1270606), Vol. 2, p. 586.

Herbert Bell. "The West India Trade...," (917 1280907), pp. 272 to 275.

Charles Andrews. "Colonial Commerce," (914$1280766), pp. 54ff.

Richard Pares. Yankees and Creoles..., (956 1270905), pp. 31 to 36, 46, 133 to 138.

Acts of the Privy Council...Colonial Series, (908 1220751), Vol. 1, pp. 273, 282, 283, 293; Vol. 2, pp. 105-106, 759.

[49]Imports shifted from French and Spanish wines, initially transhipped to the colonies through direct trade with the mother country, to the sweet wines of Madeira and the Wine Islands. This shift was particularly noticeable after passage of the Navigation Acts which excluded Madeira wine and, in practice, the vintages of the Wine Islands from the restrictions and taxation imposed upon European wines. The Acts increased the accessibility of sweet wines and thereby established for them a colonial price differential which favored them over the dry wines of the Continent.

[50]The climatic conditions of New England, specifically the limited growing season, rendered impossible the culture of high-sugar-content grapes. This, in turn, prevented the manufacture of sweet wines, produced by adding high-proof wine distillates to the vintage before all the plentiful grape sugars convert to alcohol.

[51]Infra, Vol. 1, pp. 288-289.

Thus, on February 26, 1628, William Sherman, an emigrant, was allowed "fourteen days to fetch his vines in Northampton"[52] before embarking for Massachusetts; on March 16, 1629, the Massachusetts Bay Company requested "Men skilful in making of pitch, of salt, Vine-planters."[53] The Reverend Higgeson noted in 1629 that, "Excellent vines are here up and down in the woods. Our governor has already planted a vineyard with great hope of increase."[54] John Winthrop's vineyard on an island in Boston Harbor had its rent fixed in 1634 by the General Court at "a hogshead of the best wyne that shall grow there to be paide yearly."[55]

At the mouth of the Piscataqua River, on the borders of the present state of Maine, Ambrose Gibbons, in 1620, founded a plantation "to cultivate the vine, discover mines...and trade with the natives."[56] By 1631, settlers of the Pascataway Grant were transporting vines for wine

---

[52]"Records of the Governor...," _op_. _cit_., p. 43.

[53]_Ibid_., p. 42.

[54]"New England's Plantation...," (630 1260644), p. 7. M. Higgeson. "New Englands Plantation," (629$1260155), Vol. 1, p. 119.

[55]The decree of the General Court is quoted in Bailey. _Sketch of the Evolution_..., _op_. _cit_., p. 12.

[56]_Ibid_., p. 13.

production.[57] Elsewhere in New England, Dr. Robert Child attempted to set vines to establish a wine industry about 1646.[58]

These auspicious attempts, however, did not mature.[59] Colonists explained their failure to engage in wine production, not in terms of climatic or viticultural deficiencies, but that,

---

[57]"The Great Council...," (631 1260295), pp. 145-146.
Provincial, Town, and State Papers...New-Hampshire, (623 1241013), Vol. 29, p. 40 [3 November 1631], p. 48 [5 December 1632], p. 52 [13 July 1633]. The first wine imports to the area are mentioned May 5, 1634 [Ibid., Vol. 29, p. 56.]
Jeremy Belknap. The History of New-Hampshire, (813$1271096), Vol. 1, pp. 25-26.
William H. Fry. "New Hampshire as a Royal Province," (908$1280860), p. 21.

[58]In 1645, before embarking for New England, Dr. Child wrote to Governor Winthrop the following:

> I have sent you 5 or 6 sorts of [French] vines in a cask...I desire you that they may be carefully planted with all expedition, and I am confident in 3 years wine may be made as good as any in France.
> [Robert Child. "Letter," quoted in Lockwood. Gardens of Colony..., op. cit., Vol. 1, p. 171.]

Dr. Child's endeavors are discussed further in:

Morison. Builders of the Bay Colony, (930$1270147), pp. 245 to 247.
Bailyn. The New England Merchants..., op. cit., p. 107.

[59]The failure of commercial wine production in New England, despite many reports describing the prolific vine there, baffled U. P. Hedrick and L. H. Bailey, noted authorities on the history of American viticulture. Their conclusions based on inadequate research, were as follows:

> In New England the seventeenth century notices of the wild grape are even more

> ...as yet either skill is wanting to cultivate and order the roots of those wild vines, and reduce them to a pleasant sweetness, or time is not yet to be spared to look after the culture of such fruits.[60]

Thus, they acknowledged labor scarcity[61] and the inadequate return of wine production, given the high level of wine

---

> numerous than similar records to the south but they are briefer and the northern observer did not recognize the possibilities of their domestic use and of bringing them under cultivation.
> [Hedrick. The Grapes of New York..., op. cit., p. 34.]

> ...the New Englanders appear not to have given great attention to wine-making, either from the native grape or from plantations of introduced vines...we must look farther south for the early evolution of the American grape. Probably every important settlement in what is now New England made an especial effort to grow the grape...But all of them sooner or later failed, and we shall not, therefore, pursue the history further.
> [Bailey. Sketch of the Evolution..., op. cit., pp. 3, 13.]

[60]Hubbard. "A General History...," op. cit., p. 23. Similarly, Thomas Dudley ["Gov. Thomas Dudley's Letter...," (631 1260646), p. 3] declared, "wee purpose to send the next yeare sooner, to make some small quantitie of wine...wee not haueing yett any leasure to plant vineyards."

[61]Hosmer. (ed.). Winthrop's Journal..., op. cit., p. 112.

J. F. Jamesson. (ed.). Johnson's Wonder-Working Providence..., (637$1260337), pp. 247-248.

Robert E. Moody. A Proprietary Experiment..., (930$1270014), p. 13.

imports. While yet cognizant of the bountiful vine,[62] they increasingly adopted rum and domestic brews.[63]

---

[62]The Connecticut Colony on its first seal about 1644 represented a vineyard "of fifteen vines, supported and bearing fruit. Above the vines a hand issuing from clouds holds a label with the motto SUSTINET QUI TRANSTULIT."* The motto translates he who transplanted continues to sustain; it expressed and colonists' belief in Divine sustaining power of the colony.**

* George Shankle. (ed.). State Names, Flags, Seals..., (938 1270938), p. 185; p. 185, footnote 9.

** Ibid., p. 159.
Charles Hoadly. "The Public Seal of Connecticut," (860$1280873), pp. 251 to 255.

[63]James Baxter. (ed.). Documentary History..., (884 1270282), p. 303, note 2.
John Winter. "Winter to...," (639$1260290), p. 174.
Daniel Gookin. "Historical Collections...," (674 1260880), p. 151.
Josselyn. "An Account...," op. cit., pp. 161-162.
John Dunton. "Letters from New-England," (686$1261084), p. 132.
"An Account of the Present State...," (696 1260895), pp. 126, 129.
[Edward Ward]. "A Trip to New England," (699$1261184), p. 52.
Pares. Yankees and Creoles..., op. cit., pp. 29 to 36.
Charles F. Adams. Three Episodes of Massachusetts History, (829$1270916), pp. 785 to 791.
Wertenbaker. The First Americans..., (929$1270532), pp. 196 to 202.
George Marlowe. Coaching Roads..., (945 1270661), p. 162.
Alice M. Earle. Stage-Coach..., (915$1270658), pp. 100 to 137.
________. Home Life in Colonial Days, (937$1270659), pp. 162 to 164.
Elise Lathrop. Early American Inns..., (926$1270660), pp. 25ff.
Hedrick. A History of Horticulture..., op. cit., pp. 38 to 40.
Bishop. A History of American Manufactures..., op. cit., pp. 245ff.
Margaret E. Martin. "Merchants and Trade...," (938 1280856), p. 5.

The Rhode Island colony was an important exception to this pattern. To this New England colony alone, the Crown promised "from time to time [to] give all fitting encouragement to the planting of vineyards (with which the soil and climate seem to concur) and discovery of fishing banks."[64] Although English records and Rhode Island colonial statutes do not reveal any act specifically encouraging the French Huguenots who settled in Rhode Island,[65] such Frenchmen did develop Narraganset County as a viticultural center. The wine they produced from 1685 until their expulsion in 1692 compared favorably to Bordeaux claret.[66]

The success of the Huguenots in Rhode Island spread beyond the boundaries of the colony. In 1700, when the suitability of New York state for commercial wine production was questioned, Lord Bellomont suggested: "The French you speak of will easily judge, or in a short time finde, whether that country of New York or any other place in those parts be proper for the production of wines."[67]

Lord Bellomont was hopeful that the abundance of wild vines in the state was "an index in these Plantations that

---

[64]Calendar of State Papers: Colonial..., (574$1221125), Vol. 5, pp. 148 to 150, item 512 [[8 July] 1663].

[65]Contrast this to the English Crown's position encouraging Huguenots who emigrated to Carolina. Supra, Vol. 1, pp. 171-172.

[66]Ibid., Vol. 1, pp. 170-171.

[67]"Lord Bellomont...," (700$1260381), pp. 787-788 [November 28, 1700].

points to us what may be done in that by the help of art."[68] His motivation was "propagating vines in these plantations to supply all of the dominions of the Crown."[69] The failures of the Dutch,[70] and the disappointing results that Richard Nicolls, the first English governor of New York, experienced in attempting to foster commercial wine production,[71] appeared not to sway Lord Bellomont's conviction that the colony could develop as an important English source of wine supply.

His aspirations to develop commercial wine production, however, were never realized. Alternative ventures offering greater returns attracted colonists away from wine manufacture. The most direct of these competitive projects was stimulated by the 1700 "Act for Incouraging Brewing of Beer

---

[68] Ibid., p. 787.

[69] Ibid.

[70] Supra, Vol. 1, pp. 131, 132.

[71] On January 10, 1664, Richard Nicolls granted Paul Richards a monopoly of viticulture and wine production in New York state. The grant stipulated that Richards could sell all of his wine production free of impost. It further allowed him to tax any person planting vines in the colony five shillings per acre. The monopoly, granted for thirty years, unwittingly discouraged commercial wine production when Jean Richards' trials on Long Island failed.

The grant is quoted in Hedrick. The Grapes of New York, op. cit., pp. 11-12; p. 11, footnote 2. It is discussed in Hedrick. A History of Horticulture..., op. cit., pp. 58-59 and in Emerson. The Story of the Vine, op. cit., pp. 195 to 198.

and Making of Malt."[72] This Act lessened the potential wine market, for it stimulated home production of beer by levying an excise on its import.

The development of fruit beverages in the colony competed, as well, with commercial wine production endeavors. Fruit beverages became popular because of the ease of producing them, the availability of raw materials on account of the proliferation of orchards, and the incentive of evading the levies on imported wines and liquors.[73]

In the Colonies of the Delaware, grain distillates, as well as fruit beverages and beer, competed with colonial wine manufacture.[74] Distillates offered colonists the advantage of lower transport costs per unit value than wine or its competitive products. Hence, the English colonists did not sustain the successful oenological trials of the Swedes

---

[72]The Colonial Laws of New York..., (664 1241021), Vol. 1, pp. 439-440 [2 November 1700].
Journal of the Legislative Council of...New York..., (691 1241022), Vol. 1, p. 151 [21 October 1700], p. 153 [29 October 1700].

[73]Percy Bidwell and John Falconer. History of Agriculture..., (925 1270205), pp. 16-17, 100.
Hedrick. A History of Agriculture...New York, (933$1270486), pp. 225 to 227.
________. A History of Horticulture..., op. cit., pp. 59 to 61.

[74]J. Franklin Jameson and B. B. James. (eds.). Journal of Jasper Dankaerts..., (679 1260335), pp. 245-246.
"The Present State...West-Jersey...," (681 1260343), p. 191.
Irving S. Kull. New Jersey..., (930$1270886), pp. 278 to 282.
The History of Applejack. (954$1270202), pp. 11, 12.

in the Delaware River basin.[75] They relied, instead, on imported wines and on the import and manufacture of substitute beverages.

Pennsylvania, under the proprietorship of William Penn (1681-1718), differed from the other Colonies of the Delaware in the importance assigned to viticulture and wine production. At the inception of the proprietorship, William Penn suggested, "the Commodities that the country is thought capable of...[as] silk, flax, hemp, wine, cider."[76] In 1685, he proposed that Pennsylvania had "prospect for Staples of Trade...[in] Wine, Linnen, Hemp, Potashes and Whale Oyle."[77] The Council Records of Germanton instituted its own seal, a trefoil, in 1691. Daniel Pastorius described the seal:

> On one of the leaves a grape-vine is represented, on another a flax-blossom and on the third a weaver's spool, with the inscription: <u>Vinum</u>, <u>Linum</u> <u>et</u> <u>Textrinum</u>, to signify that one may in this place maintain himself by cultivating the vine, by growing flax, or by manufactures, to the satisfaction of God and his honor.[78]

---

[75] <u>Supra</u>, Vol. 1, p. 130, footnote 57; p. 132, footnote 61.

[76] William Penn. "Some Account...," (681 1260323), p. 124.

[77] Penn. "A Further Account of Pennsylvania," (685$1260347), p. 273.

[78] Francis D. Pastorius. "Circumstantial...Description of Pennsylvania," (700 1260352), p. 415.

Similarly, the obverse of the Great Seal of the Province of Pennsylvania displays grape vines and corn encircled by the motto, "Truth, Peace, Love, and Plenty."[79]

Lavish descriptions of native vines,[80] attempts at their cultivation,[81] the importation of French and Spanish vines,[82] the hiring of French vignerons,[83] and continued

---

[79] Charter to William Penn..., (676 1241028), pp. ii, iv.

[80] Pennsylvania Archives..., (664$1241026), Vol. 1, pp. 68, 69 [30 May 1683].
Penn. "Letter from William Penn...," (683 1260345), pp. 227-228.
Supra, Vol. 1, p. 171, footnote 186.
Robert Burton. [pseud. for Nathaniel Crouch]. The English Empire in America..., (739 1271090), p. 107. Burton's description of the vines native to Pennsylvania is a verbatim plagiarism of the "Letter from William Penn," above.

[81] Penn. "Letter from William Penn...," op. cit., p. 228.
________. "A Further Account...," op. cit., p. 265.
Gabriel Thomas. "An...Account of Pensilvania...," (698 1260351), p. 322.
Penn. "Letter to Marquis of Halifax," [December 9, 1683] quoted in Bishop. A History of American Manufactures..., op. cit., p. 273.
Hedrick. A History of Horticulture..., op. cit., pp. 75-76. Hedrick errs in stating "Unfortunately, Penn seems to have tried planting only the European grape." [Ibid., p. 76.]

[82] Penn. "Letter from William Penn...," op. cit., p. 228.
Pastorius. "Circumstantial...," op. cit., p. 398.
Lockwood. (ed.). Gardens of Colony..., op. cit., Vol. 1, p. 333.

[83] Penn. "Letter from William Penn...," op. cit., p. 227; p. 227, footnote 1.
________. "A Further Account...," op. cit., p. 265.
Nicholas More. "A Letter from Doctor More," (687$1260348), p. 287.
Thomas. "An...Account of Pensilvania...," op. cit., p. 322.
Stevenson W. Fletcher. Pennsylvania Agriculture...,

efforts to establish commercial wine production[84] all demonstrate William Penn's avid interest in oenological pursuits. Many colonial tracts record his success in producing wine from both domestic and imported vines.[85] His absence from the colony (1684-1699; 1701-1718)[86] and the temporary suspension of his proprietary rights (1692-1694)[87] were important in the ultimate decline of wine production ventures.

(950$1270485), p. 223.
Joseph S. Davis. Essays in the Earlier History..., (917 1270631), p. 44.

[84]Pennsylvania Archives..., op. cit., Vol. 1, p. 127 [30 November 1699].
Pastorius. "Circumstantial...," op. cit., pp. 383, 408.
Penn. "A Further Account..., op. cit., p. 273.
________. "Letter to James Harrison," [1686] quoted in Rayner Kelsey. "Description...of Early Agriculture in Pennsylvania," (920 1280915), p. 286; and, Fletcher. Pennsylvania Agriculture..., op. cit., p. 223.
Leo Stock. (ed.). Proceedings and Debates..., (924 1221132), Vol. 2, p. 200, footnote 79.

[85]More. "A Letter from Doctor More," op. cit., p. 287.
David Lloyd. "A Letter from David Lloyd," (686$1260349), p. 291.
Richard Frame. "A Short Description of Pennsylvania...," (692 1260350), p. 301.
Pastorius. "Circumstantial...," op. cit., p. 398.
Joseph Serviere. Der Theoretische und Praktische..., (828 1270743), p. 194.

[86]Bishop. A History of American Manufactures..., op. cit., p. 274.
Kelsey. "William Penn," in Dictionary of American Biography, Vol. 14, pp. 433 to 437.

[87]Leo Stock. (ed.). Proceedings and Debates..., op. cit., Vol. 2, p. 200.
William S. Shepherd. History of Proprietary Government in Pennsylvania, (896$1210777), pp. 5ff.
Andrews. "American Colonial History...," (898$1281202), pp. 52-53.
Herbert L. Osgood. "The Study of American Colonial History," (898$1281203), p. 67.

The declining involvement of Pennsylvanians in wine production was evident by 1722 when an ordinance was passed encouraging beer production.[88] Wine production had succumbed to imports, competitive beverages and the relative production advantages of other commodities.[89] These advantages stemmed from English bounties encouraging silk, hemp, flax and naval stores in the colonies. They attracted the scarce labor resource away from wine production. Accordingly, Peter Kalm inquired "of Mr. Bartram why they did not plant vineyards or press wine from the grapes of the wild vine. He answered that the chief objection to that was the same as to the erection of a silk factory--the necessary

---

[88] The Statutes at Large of Pennsylvania..., (700 1241024), Vol. 3, pp. 291 to 295 [12 May 1722]. In the following year a bounty was offered for "all proof spirits distilled...which shall be exported and carried out to sea." [Ibid., Vol. 3, p. 415]. The relative success of these bounties is suggested in the Minutes of...Council of Pennsylvania..., [(683 1241025), Vol. 3, p. 391 [6 January 1730/31]]. Therein, the colony is described as exceeding all its neighbors in "fineness of its flower and bread and goodness of its Beer, which are the only produce of its grain."

[89] Penn. "Letter from William Penn...," op. cit., p. 233.
Thomas Paschall. "Letter of Thomas Paschall," (683$1260346), p. 253.
Penn. "A Further Account...," op. cit., p. 267.
Thomas. "An...Account of Pensylvania...," op. cit., p. 323.
Peter Kalm. "Travels in North America," (770$1260441), pp. 47, 51-52.
Earle. Stage-Coach..., op. cit., p. 104.
Bidwell and Falconer. History of Agriculture..., op. cit., p. 17.
Bishop. A History of American Manufactures..., op. cit., pp. 274-275.

labor was too scarce."[90] In the interim from the dissolution of the royal province (1715) to 1751, therefore, Pennsylvania increasingly experienced the withdrawal of vine dressers to alternative employs and a deficiency of oenological skills similar to that of most other colonies.

The attraction of skilled vignerons and vintners was recognized immediately as essential to the oenological prospects of the Southern Atlantic colonies. The English Crown repeatedly encouraged Huguenot emigration to the plantations of Carolina. Such encouragements paralleled attempts to establish commercial wine production as a staple of the North and South Carolina colonies.[91]

---

[90]Kalm. "Travels in North America," op. cit., p. 67. Peter Kalm maintained that "the true reason undoubtedly is that the wine...is sour and sharp." [Ibid.]

[91]Wine production was a major objective of the following: the Albemarle Point settlement of 1670;* the 1674 migration of dissatisfied Dutch settlers from New York;** the 1679 dispatchment of French refugees under Charles II;*** the similar 1690 arrangement under William;# the 1736, 1739, 1741 and 1743 South Carolina Acts encouraging Protestant settlement;## the 1761 establishment of New Bordeaux.###

* William Powell. (ed.). Ye Countie of Albemarle..., (958 1270429), p. xv ff. Bishop. A History of American Manufactures..., op. cit., p. 271. Lockwood. (ed.). Gardens of Colony..., op. cit., p. 197.

** Ibid. [Lockwood]

*** Supra, Vol. 1, pp. 171-172.

\# Bishop. A History of American Manufactures..., op. cit., p. 271.

\## The Colonial Records of South Carolina..., (736 1241041), Vol. 1, p. 49 [7 December 1736], p. 70 [15 December 1736]; Vol. 2, p. 124 [14 December 1739]; Vol. 3, p. 260 [27 October 1741]; Vol. 4, p. 346 [30 March

The reports of the Huguenot immigrants paralleled those of other colonists in extolling the abundance of wild vines[92] and the success of early oenological trials.[93] The Huguenots

---

1743], p. 404 [7 May 1743].
David Wallace. The History of South Carolina, (934$1270752), pp. 45 to 47.
A. S. Salley. "The Settlement of New Bordeaux," (937$1280854), pp. 38, 39.
Herbert Adams. (ed.). Johns Hopkins...Studies ...South Carolina..., (895 1280393), p. 62; p. 62, footnote 4.

[92]"A 1649 Account...," (649$1260425), p. 14.
Francis Yeardly. "Description of...Carolina," (654$1260426), p. 15.
William Hilton. "A Relation...," (664$1260364), pp. 44, 47.
Robert Horne. "A Brief Description...," (666 1260365), p. 68.
Thomas Ashe. "Carolina...," (682 1260367), p. 144.
Samuel Wilson. "An Account...," (682$1260368), p. 174.
John Archdale. "A New Description...," (707 1260371), p. 290.
John Oldmixon. "Oldmixon's British Empire," (708$1260372), p. 360. [a verbatim plagiarism of Archdale's "A New Description."]
John Lawson. "A New Voyage to Carolina...," (714 1260428), pp. 63, 104, 115.
Byrd. William Byrd's Histories..., (727 1260498), p. 194, item 12.
The Colonial Records of North Carolina..., (662 1241038), Vol. 2, pp. 792, 794, items 12, 20 [14 December 1729].
Peter Purry. "Proposals...," (731$1260396), pp. 126-127, 131.
Bartram. "Travels Through North and South Carolina...," (741 1260439), pp. 208-209.
Mark Catesby. The Natural History..., (754 1261112), p. xxii.

[93]Peter Carteret. "Letter to Mr. Carterett...," (665$1260430), pp. 7, 8.
John Colleton. "Letter to Mr. Carterett...," (665$1260431), p. 9.
________. "Letter to Peter Carteret...," (666$1260432), p. 12.
Ogilby. America..., op. cit., p. 205.

predicted favorable vintages, and thus began cultivating both native vines and imported seeds and cuttings.[94] The wine they produced was "very good in colour and taste,"[95] but the quantity was insufficient for commercial sale.

Although encouragements were offered to stimulate production,[96] they were insufficient to attract the skills and capital necessary for commercial wine manufacture in the

---

[94]Ashe. "Carolina...," op. cit., p. 144.
Wilson. "An Account...," op. cit., pp. 174-175.
Thomas Newe. "Letters of Thomas Newe," (682$1260369), p. 182.
Lawson. "A New Voyage to Carolina...," op. cit., p. 115.
The Colonial Records of North Carolina..., op. cit., Vol. 4, p. 6 [12 December 1734], p. 16 [12 September 1735], p. 919 [1749?]; Vol. 5, p. 316 [1755?].
William Stork. (ed.). A Description..., (769 1261107), p. 29.

[95]Wilson. "An Account...," op. cit., p. 174.

[96]"Charter to the Lords Proprietors...," (663 1220421), p. 82.
"Charter to the Lords Proprietors...," (665 1220422), p. 98.
The Colonial Records of North Carolina..., op. cit., Vol. 1, p. 51 [1663?], p. 101 [2 June 1665]; Vol. 4, p. 16 [12 September 1735].
"A Brief Description...," (666$1260322), p. 120.
Francis L. Hawks. History of North Carolina, (858$1270436), pp. 107 to 109.
The Public Laws..., (790$1241039), p. vii [20 June 1694].
The Statutes at Large of South Carolina..., (682 1241040), Vol. 2, p. VIII, 78 ["Ratified 20 June 1694. Expired. The original act not now to be found."]
The Colonial Records of South Carolina..., op. cit., Vol. 1, p. 624 [9 February 1738/39]; Vol. 2, p. 35 [20 November 1739]; Vol. 4, p. 553 [27 January 1743/44]; Vol. 8, p. 105 [3 March 1748], p. 383 [28 June 1748]; Vol. 9, p. 89 [12 May 1749].
Requests for encouragements exceeded those offered. John Hamilton, for example, petitioned for a tract of

Carolinas. When John Oldmixon was asked, "...[if] the Climate is so proper, since Grapes are so plentiful, and the Wine they make so good, why is there not more of it?" he replied, "That the Inhabitants either think they can turn their Hands to a more profitable Culture, or impose upon us in their Reports; for I would not think them so weak, as to neglect making good Wine, and enough of it, if they could, and thought it worth their while."[97] Thus, by 1708, colonists had found that higher and more immediate returns on labor and capital investment were possible from pitch, tar and rice production.[98]

200,000 acres for about 140 Protestant families. He sought land "well adapted to the Culture of Vineyards for Wine... and several other Commoditys very advantagious to the Trade and Commerce of England."
[Acts of the Privy Council..., op. cit., Vol. 3, pp. 572-573 [21 July 1737].]

[97]Oldmixon. "Oldmixon's British Empire," op. cit., p. 371.

[98]The Humble Address..., (698 1260797), p. 442, item 11, 12.

Edward Randolph. "Letter of Edward Randolph," (699$1260370), p. 207.

"State of the British Plantations...," (721 1270385), p. 610.

Neil Franklin. "Agriculture in Colonial North Carolina," (926$1280885), p. 556. Mr. Franklin's 1735 date for initial rice Culture in North Carolina is in error. John Oldmixon ["Oldmixon's British Empire," op. cit., p. 360], for example, mentions rice exports from Carolina in 1708. Mr. Franklin again errs in confusing wild grape culture for the totality of viticultural attempts in North Carolina. He also misrepresents the Moravians as interested in wild vines for fruit. [Franklin. "Agriculture...," op. cit., p. 560, footnote 115.] Further study in Adelaide L. Fries' Records of the Moravians in North Carolina..., [(752 1260884)] reveals that the Moravians attempted viticulture [Ibid., Vol. 1, p. 180] and wine production from native vines [Ibid., Vol. 2, p. 1189].

Several other economic factors diverted the colonists from oenological endeavors. Inexpensive wine imports from Madeira and the Wine Islands lowered the price and the prospective return for colonial wines.[99] The author of "A Description of South Carolina" reasoned that,

> The Woods are full of wild Vines...but for want of Vine-dressers, &c. scarce any Wine is drank there but what comes from Madera, which are indeed cheap, for a Bottle of excellent Wine cost last Winter but 2s. Carolina Money to those who bought by the Hogshead.[100]

Increasing rum imports similarly discouraged wine production.

Oenological trials, nevertheless, continued in the Carolinas. The changing wine tastes of colonists and Englishmen[101] resulted in a shift from French vine varieties to vines and seeds of Madeira and the Canaries.[102] The English again sought to redress unfavorable trade balances by promoting the production of wines popular at home and in the colonies.

---

[99]Nathaniel Johnson, et al. "Letter," (708$1260792), p. 234.
The Colonial Records of North Carolina..., op. cit., Vol. 5, p. 317 [1755?].
"A Description of South Carolina," (761$1260397), p. 231.
John Hinton. "A Short Description...South Carolina...," (763 1260398), p. 482.
"Instructions to Joseph West...," (670$1260796), p. 351.

[100]"A Description of South Carolina," op. cit., p. 131.

[101]Supra, Vol. 1, pp. 220 to 224; p. 221 footnote 90.

[102]The sequential reading of the following tracts delineate this shift:
Carteret. "Letter to Mr. Carterett...," op. cit.,

The reinstitution of significant viticultural trials in the Carolinas resulted from the 1761 encouragements to the French Huguenots and from the 1768 arrival of Louis de Mesnil de St. Pierre in Charlestown. The French Huguenots--both those arriving in 1764 and those accompanying M. St. Pierre--successfully attempted viticulture and wine production in South Carolina.

Accordingly, M. St. Pierre petitioned the Board of Trade for 20,000 acres of land in Georgia to expand his viticultural pursuits.[103] He testified in 1772 that, "he had now 100,000 vines planted, and above 20 French Protestants, all vinedressers, ready to embark with him for the

---

p. 8.
Colleton. "Letter to Mr. Carterett...," _op_. _cit_., p. 9.
________. "Letter to Peter Carteret...," _op_. _cit_., p. 12.
"Copy of Instruccons...," (669 1260795), pp. 343, 344.
W. J. Rivers. _A Sketch_...._South Carolina_..., (856 1270791), p. 174.
Ashe. "Carolina...," _op_. _cit_., p. 144.
Wilson. "An Account...," _op_. _cit_., p. 174.
Lawson. "A New Voyage...," _op_. _cit_., p. 117.
Calendar of State Papers: Colonial..., _op_. _cit_., Vol. 39, p. 235, item 416 [12 October 1732].
"A Description of South Carolina," _op_. _cit_., p. 248.
Stork. (ed.). _A Description_..., _op_. _cit_., p. 29.

[103] _Journals of the Board of Trade_..., (704 1221127), Vol. 1768-1775, p. 271 [15 November 1771].

colony."[104] He requested "publick encouragement"[105] for the development of a wine industry in the Carolinas but the Board of Trade referred his latter request to the Lords of Treasury, saying that, in awarding M. St. Pierre 5000 acres of land in South Carolina,[106] "they have done...all was fit for them to do."[107]

A shortage of capital forced M. St. Pierre to curtail his oenological pursuits; the Huguenots consequently pursued projects promising more immediate returns.[108] M. St. Pierre, however, continued to advocate colonial viticulture and wine

---

[104] Ibid., Vol. 1767-1775, p. 291 [18 March 1772].
Edward Barry [Observations Theoretical..., (775 1271181), p. 476] suggests that "Captain St. Pierre... [in 1772] carried...three hundred vignerons from different parts of Europe." He dispatched with M. St. Pierre cuttings from his vineyard in England for trial in the colonies.

[105] Ibid., Vol. 1767-1775, p. 292 [18 March 1772].

[106] Ibid., Vol. 1767-1775, p. 275 [18 December 1771].

[107] Ibid., Vol. 1767-1775, p. 297 [4 April 1772].

[108] John Rutherford. "The Importance of the Colonies...," (761$1260726), pp. 110 to 113.
[Scotus Americanus]. "Information Concerning... North Carolina," (773 1260727), pp. 438-439.
Alexander Hewit. An Historical Account..., (779 1260066), pp. 38, 386, 425, 437-438.
John Drayton. "Beschreibung von Sud-Carolina," (802 1260904), pp. 253 to 271.
B. R. Carroll. (ed.). Historical Collections of South Carolina, (836$1270394), p. 323.
South Carolina..., (883 1270440), p. 13.
Salley. "The Settlement of New Bordeaux," op. cit., p. 53.
Wallace. The History of South Carolina, op. cit., pp. 387-388.

production. In his book, The Art of Planting and Cultivating the Vine..., "compiled for the Use of such as intend to prosecute that beneficial and national Branch of Commerce and Agriculture in AMERICA, and particularly for that of the Colony at NEW BORDEAUX,"[109] he argued against those who blamed his oenological failures on climatic or viticultural factors:

> Wine has been made in America. Unless any man will say that the soil that produced one pipe may not as easily produce a million...The Soil; the climate; the Vine growing spontaneous every where; nay Wine actually made, and a ready market for much larger quantities than you can for many years be supposed able to make with the utmost activity, call aloud: in a word, honour, independance, wealth, stretch out their hands to us!
> ...we have every inducement to move us to set about this important and national enterprize. Nor should the jealousy of any allies deter us from so noble a pursuit.[110]

Advocates of commercial wine production in Georgia expressed even stronger sentiments. Rev. Mr. Samuel Wesly [Wesley] proclaimed in doggerel verse:

---

[109]Louis[de Mesnil]de St. Pierre. The Art of Planting..., (772 1270251), title page.

[110]Ibid., pp. xxii, xxiii. Mark Catesby [The Natural History of Carolina..., op. cit., p. xxii] detailed the "vicissitudes of weather" and ill effects of "too much wet" on viticultural trials in Carolina. His remarks were adopted by Alexander Hewit. [An Historical Account...South Carolina and Georgia, op. cit., pp. 437-438.] Both writers concluded that viticultural skills would overcome readily these impediments to commercial wine production. M. St. Pierre, being skilled, experienced no difficulty.

> Now bid thy Merchants bring thy Wine no more
> Or from the Iberian or the Tuscan Shore;..
> Behold! at last, and in a subject Land,
> Nectar sufficient for they large Demand:
> Delicious Nectar, powerful to improve
> Our hospitable Mirth and social Love:[111]

He also extolled silk culture,[112] envisioning Georgia as especially adapted to wine and silk production. These commodities were advocated as the colony's staples to enhance their availability in England and to redress English balance of trade losses.[113] Because of their commercial failure in

---

[111]Samuel Wesly [Wesley]. "Georgia, and Verses upon Mr. Oglethorpe's Second Voyage...," quoted in Pat Tailfer, and Hugh Anderson et al. A True and Historical...Georgia, (960$1260148), p. 15.

The author of "An Impartial Inquiry...," [(741 1260622), p. 164.] was more explicit in extolling the benefit of wine production in the Georgia colony:

> If wine can be made...This will not interfere with the products of our other plantations...it would be a vast profit to Georgia as well as them. They might purchase it at a cheaper rate than they do from Spain and the Canaries. They would not be liable to be interrupted in the purchase of it in a time of war between us and the nations, which now supply them; and the money, which they are to pay for it, will still remain among the subjects of Great Britain.

Similarly, the author of "A State of the Province of Georgia...," [(740 1260641), p. 10.] advocates the "staple of the country of Georgia...to be principally silk and wine." These staples would not "interfere with what other English plantations have produced."

[112]Wesly. [Wesley]. "Georgia, and Verses...," op. cit., p. 15.

[113]Robert Mountgomry. "A Discourse...of a New Colony to the South of Carolina...," (717 1260640), p. 13.

[Benjamin Martyn]. "A New and Accurate Account...," (733 1260620), pp. 67 to 72.

The Colonial Records...Georgia..., op. cit., Vol. 1,

other colonies, they would find a ready market. The established staple trade of other colonies would be protected from infringement by the Georgia colony's adoption of these noncompetitive staples.

Thus, the objectives of the Georgia settlement were fulfilled in initial attempts at silk and vine culture. Such endeavors relieved English unemployment, enhanced trade balances and erected a buffer against Spanish or Indian incursion.[114] They also fostered legislative provisions during early colonization which made Georgia distinct from all other settlements. They prohibited selling imported rum and distilled spirits and using imported Negro slaves.[115] The latter prohibition was especially detrimental to vine and silk culture, as it intensified the colony's labor shortage.

---

p. 364 [23 January 1739/40].
"A State of the Province of Georgia...," _op_. _cit_., p. 10.
Benjamin Martyn. "An Account Showing the Progress... of Georgia...," (742 1260642), p. 41.
"An Impartial Inquiry...," _op_. _cit_., pp. 162 to 164.
Reba Strickland. "The Mercantile System...Georgia," (938$1281206), pp. 161-162.

[114] Albert B. Saye. _New Viewpoints in Georgia History_, (943$1270774), pp. 9 to 50.
James R. McCain. _Georgia as a Proprietary Province_, (914$1271217), pp. 17 to 19.
E. Merton Coulter. _A Short History of Georgia_, (933$1270531), pp. 15 to 18.

[115] McCain. _Georgia as a Proprietary Province_, _op_. _cit_., pp. 171 to 181.
Walter Cooper. _The Story of Georgia_, (938$1270528), pp. 163, 164.
The repeal of these laws is discussed by Albert R. Saye [_New Viewpoints_..., _op_. _cit_., pp. 70 to 74] and E. Merton Coulter [_A Short History_..., _op_. _cit_., pp. 61 to 65].

As the economic objectives of silk and wine production were so steadfastly advanced, colonists bypassed direct wine production from abundant wild vines[116] and immediately began domesticating these vines[117] and cultivating imported varieties. Madeira and Portuguese cuttings received particular emphasis,[118] because of an increased demand for sweet wines.

---

[116]Mountgomry. "A Discourse...," op. cit., p. 7.
[Martyn]. "A New and Accurate Account...," op. cit., pp. 50-51.
"To James Oglethorpe...," (734 1261209), p. 64.
Baron Von Reck. "Journal," quoted in Cooper. The Story of Georgia, op. cit., p. 144.
"An Impartial Inquiry...," op. cit., pp. 163, 191, 195.
Boltzius. "Extract out of the Journal...," (741 1260647), p. 19.
Francis Moore. "A Voyage to Georgia...," (744 1260621), p. 116.

[117]"To the Honourable James Oglethorpe...," (734 1261210), p. 66.
"A State of the Province...," op. cit., pp. 4, 5.
The Colonial Records...Georgia..., op. cit., Vol. 5, p. 347, item 5, 6 [9 May 1740], p. 500, item 14 [22 April 1741]. James C. Bonner [A History of Georgia Agriculture..., (964$1270144), p. 159; p. 227, footnote 56] states that "the native grapes were neglected by early settlers in favor of imported varieties." He falsely ascribes the statement "sad stuff, and bitter, rather the juice of the stalk than of the grape" to imported vines. Rather, this description refers to native vines which Col. William Stephens cultivated [The Colonial Records...Georgia..., op. cit., Supplement Vol. 4, pp. 135, 155, 165].

[118]A public garden was established on the Savannah River in 1733. The garden was a general nursery "Vines and vine cuttings were sent in great tubs and were wet in the public garden till private vineyards were made ready for them." [Bertha Hart. "The First Garden of Georgia," (935$1280903), p. 328.] The vines of the garden were mostly of the Malmsey and Madeira varieties. [The Colonial Records...Georgia..., op. cit., Vol. 1, p. 98; Vol. 2, pp. 5-6 [3 October 1732]; Earl of Egmont. The Journal of

Despite the economic merit of the project, commercial wine production in Georgia did not mature. Captain John Mordaunt satirized the oenological failure of the colony in 1740:

> two things proposed by the colony was to raise silk and wine...as to wine, he believed it would be well to give it to the inhabitants for their own drinking, and wished them good luck with it, for it would be all would ever be seen of their wine, and if the people of the place drank no other, they would be the soberest subjects in the world.[119]

He did not indicate that successful viticultural trials had been conducted during the prior decade.[120] Neither did he

---

the Earl of Egmont, (737$1260482), p. 243.] Despite the efforts of William Houston, a botanist employed by the Trustees, the garden fell into "a sad confusion" by 1738. [Hart. "The First Garden...," op. cit., pp. 329 to 332.]

Other mentions of foreign vine imports include:

Calendar of State Papers: Colonial..., op. cit., Vol. 39, p. 235, item 416 [12 October 1732].

[Martyn]. Reasons for Establishing... Georgia..., (733 1261188), p. 13.

"An Impartial Inquiry...," op. cit., p. 164.

The Colonial Records...Georgia..., op. cit., Vol. 1, p. 475 [28 October 1745].

[119] John Mordaunt. "A Speech Before the House," [6 February 1739/40] quoted from Egmont's Diary, III, 112-113 in Stock. (ed.). Proceedings and Debates..., op. cit., Vol. 5, p. 28.

[120] The Colonial Records...Georgia..., op. cit., Vol. 1, p. 362 [16 January 1739/40].

"An Impartial Inquiry...," op. cit., p. 164.

"A State of the Province...," (742$1261211), p. 71 [10 November 1740].]

Tailfer and Anderson et al. A True and Historical..., op. cit., p. 61, note 96.

Bailey. The Evolution..., op. cit., pp. 14 to 16.

Bishop. A History of American Manufactures..., op. cit., p. 275.

specify that the Trustees failed to honor their oenological encouragements,[121] nor that capital shortage, insufficient labor and Spanish harassment of the infant colony caused the capitulation of attempts at viticulture and wine production.[122]

---

[121]Tailfer and Anderson et al. A True and Historical..., op. cit., pp. 61-62, note 98; p. 62; p. 62, note 100.

James Oglethorpe. "General Oglethorpe to the Trustees...," (738 1261214), p. 59.

________. "General Oglethorpe to the Trustees...," (739 1261215), pp. 89, 90.

[122]The author of "A State of the Province of Georgia...," [(740 1260641), op. cit., p. 12] called attention to capital scarcity. He advocated "that a bounty be settled...by which means the planter so assisted might be able to live, whilst at the same time he propagates vines...from which he can expect no immediate benefit before they come to some maturity."

A letter to the Trustees of Georgia, pleading for the repeal of the ban on Negro slaves, advised of insufficient labor in the colony:

> We do not in the least doubt, but that in time Silk and Wine may be produced here... but since the Cultivation of Land with White Servants only, cannot raise Provisions for our Families...it is likewise impossible to carry on these Manufactures.
> [The Colonial Records...Georgia..., op. cit., Vol. 3, p. 423 [9 December 1738].]

Even after the introduction of Negro slavery to Georgia, labor scarcity remained a discouragement to oenological trials. [Consult Stork. (ed.). A Description..., op. cit., p. 29 quoted Supra, Vol. 1, p. 174.]

Colonists who sought to dismiss the economic disadvantages of wine production in Georgia stressed socio-political factors. The Earl of Egmont, for example, argued that it was not the failure of the Trustees to honor their encouragement to Abraham De Leon that motivated him to leave the colony. It was rather that "this man ran away for fear of the Spaniards." [Tailfer and Anderson et al. A True and Historical..., op. cit., p. 62, note 100.] Similarly, General Oglethorpe pictured Spanish hindrance to viticultural attempts in Georgia:

> We shall certainly succeed in Silk and Wine in case the planters are supported by the

The failure of wine as a staple commodity in Georgia reflected, as well, the greater English demand for raw materials necessary for defense and industrial development.[123] The comparative production advantages of other commodities suited for manufacture in Georgia is inferred in this failure.

In retrospect, these same causal factors held true for all the American colonies. In each colony, wine was envisioned as a principal staple, but became subordinate to staples more aligned with the domestic endowment of individual colonies. Thus, regional specialization manifested itself in developing fishing, naval stores and lumber industries in New England, in flourishing grain production in the Middle Atlantic colonies, in extensive tobacco cultivation

---

> Publick in those attempts. This Province bridles the Spaniards in America & covers the English Frontiers. The poor people that are here have been so harrassed by their threats & so constantly under arms that they have not been able to make that Provision for their subsistence which was necessary though it was far from want of Industry in them.
>
> [Oglethorpe. "General Oglethorpe...," (738 1261212), p. 49.]

He repeated this assertion on February 12, 1743, in a letter to the Trustees of Georgia. [Oglethorp. "General Oglethorpe...," (743 1261216), p. 144.]

[123] Strickland. "The Mercantile System...," <u>op</u>. <u>cit</u>., pp. 160 to 168.

Cooper. <u>The Story of Georgia</u>, <u>op</u>. <u>cit</u>., pp. 282 to 284.

in the Colonies of Chesapeake Bay, and in naval stores, rice, indigo and silk production in the Southern Atlantic colonies.[124] The success that wine experienced as a competitive

---

[124]Virginia exemplifies the changing role envisioned for wine production in each colony. A sequential reading of the following tracts delineates the shift in English thought relating to wine as a major staple. At first, sources suggest that wine be a primary staple in the Virginia colony.* Beginning with Bvilock,** Englishmen question the economic feasibility of commercial wine production. They examine capital and labor investments, noting the time factor between investment and return.*** Later sources continue to discuss commodity availability, but no longer consider wine an important commodity.# Finally, Englishmen again advocate colonial wine production, stressing that a change in comparative costs and returns make it once more feasible and economically rewarding.##

* Richard Hakluyt. "Inducements...," (585 1270028), p. 104, item 6; p. 107, item 24; p. 108, item 31; pp. 109 to 111.
Thomas Herriot. "A Brief Extract...," (585 1260031), pp. 117, 119.
Newport. "Newport's Discoveries...," quoted in Wertenbaker. <u>The Planters of Colonial Virginia</u>, (922$1270111), p. 15.
Andreas de Prade. "New Britain," (609 1260076), pp. 265, 268.
Edward Neill. "Virginia, Vestusta," (609$1260077), p. 313.
Kingsbury. (ed.). <u>The Records</u>..., <u>op</u>. <u>cit</u>., Vol. 3, p. 22, item 29; p. 30 [May 1609].
Smith. "Description of Virginia...," in Louis Hacker and Helenes Zahier. (eds.). <u>The Shaping of the American Tradition</u>, New York: Columbia University Press, 1947, p. 84.
"Newes from Virginia...," <u>op</u>. <u>cit</u>., pp. 151 to 153.
"A Declaration...Virginia," <u>op</u>. <u>cit</u>., pp. 4, 6, 10.
Pory. "Letter of John Pory...," (619 1260056), p. 283.
Smith. <u>The Generall Historie</u>..., <u>op</u>. <u>cit</u>., Vol. 1, pp. 61, 288-289; Vol. 2, pp. 17-18.
"Virginias Verger...," <u>op</u>. <u>cit</u>., pp. 239, 245-246, 249.

**

> These are fine commodities...but not to be the Staples that must do the work.
> The next...will be Wine, Reisens...

staple was commensurate to capital and skilled labor investment devoted to wine production. These investments, in turn, were a function of anticipated returns.

The ascendancy of other domestic beverages and of inexpensive wine imports lowered anticipated returns to wine production in all colonies. In New England, cider and rum

---

the time and money spent before they can be brought to perfection, may happily make the poore Planter with the horse starve whilst the grasse grows.

Yet I confesse all these are very good to be brought on by degrees, without prejudice to the main Designe.
[Bvllock. Virginia Impartially Examined..., op. cit., p. 32.]

*** [Williams]. Virginia's Discovery..., op. cit., pp. 31-32, 33.
Gorges. A Briefe Narration..., (658 1261105), pp. 52-53.
Jones. The Present State..., op. cit., p. 140.
[John B. Bordley]. Necessaries; Best Product of Land; Best Staple of Commerce, Philadelphia: James Humphreys, 1776, pp. 16-17.
John B. Bordley. Essays and Notes on Husbandry and Rural Affairs, 2nd Ed. Rev., Philadelphia: Budd and Bartram, 1801, pp. 245, 254-255.

\# J. Evelyn. "Navigation and Commerce...," (674 1260139), pp. 38, 96-97.
William Keith. The History of the British Plantations..., (738 1271091), pp. 181-182.

\#\# John Locke. The Works of John Locke, (679 1260629), Vol. 10, p. 326.
"Report of Board of Trade...," (709 1260383), p. 88.
"An Essay on the...Decline of the Foreign Trade," (750 1260141), p. 216.
The Statutes at Large...Virginia, op. cit., Vol. 8, pp. 364 to 366. [November 1769].
John Bartram. "Letter to Jared Eliot," in Jared Eliot. Essays Upon the Field Husbandry..., (748$1260229), p. 200.
Timothy Pitkin. A Statistical View..., (817 1271222), pp. 11, 12.

discouraged oenological efforts; in the Middle Atlantic colonies, beer and grain distillates complemented extensive cider production to the virtual neglect of wines; in the Colonies of the Chesapeake Bay and in the Southern Atlantic colonies, inexpensive wine imports and rum forced down colonial wine prices. In all the colonies, the tendency toward stronger liquors curtailed wine demand and, consequently, colonial wine production.

More important than these factors were the superior returns to alternative ventures. These alternative investments competed for scarce capital and labor in the colonies.[125] They diverted skilled workers from oenological

---

[125]Few observers agreed with Samuel Hartlib that "planting Vines [involved] small labour, little cost, long enduring."* John Bonoeil, for example, sensed a scarcity of labor and, therefore, suggested the enslavement of Indians for viticultural trials.** William Alexander recommended that Indians be taught "to plant Corne, Wine, and Oyle."*** Edward Williams attributed the miscarriage of French aid to their having been "compelled to labour in the quality of Slaves." Later colonists similarly attested to the detrimental effects of skills and labor shortages on viticultural endeavors.##

* Samuel Hartlib. <u>The Reformed Virginian Silk-Worm</u>..., (655 1271177), p. 16, item 3.

** Bonoeil. <u>His Maiesties Graciovs Letter</u>..., <u>op. cit</u>., pp. 85-86.
Almon W. Lauber. <u>Indian Slavery</u>..., (913 1271221), pp. 105-106.
Stanley Johnson. "John Donne and the Virginia Company," (947$1280753), p. 132; p. 132, footnote 21.

*** William Alexander. <u>An Encouragement to Colonies</u>, (624$1261170), p. 38.

\# E[dward] W[illiams]. <u>Virginia</u>..., (650 1261196), p. 17.

\## William Berkeley. <u>A Discourse</u>...<u>Virginia</u>,

pursuits. Without these vignerons, the climatic and viticultural impediments to commercial wine production could not be overcome. The fluctuating returns to alternative ventures, however, prompted intermittent oenological trials. As establishing commercial wine production required continued investment over a period of years (during which time the vines mature to productive capacity), these sporadic attempts to promote the wine staple were deficient. They could not sustain commercial wine production.

The prolonged period of non-remunerative investment restricted wine from competing with other staples on a short-term basis. Similarly, colonists failed to recognize that long-term discounted net returns to wine production could equal or exceed current or anticipated returns to other

---

(663$1261169), p. 4.
Byrd. "Letters Relative to Plants...," op. cit., p. 196.
John de Crèvecoeur. Sketches of Eighteenth Century America, (769$1260759), pp. 134-135.
American Husbandry, (775$1260228), pp. 96, 126-127, 192 to 195.
M. Chaptal. A Treatise Upon Wines, [translated from French by John H. Sargent] Charleston: John H. Sargent, 1811, p. v.
S. I. Fisher. Observations..., (834 1270520), p. 42.
Wertenbaker. The Founding of American Civilization..., (938 1270500), pp. 18-19.

colonial staples.[126] Jared Eliot had "no doubt Wine would turn to a good Account" yet he observed that the raising of hemp was preferred as it "comes Sooner to Market to turn the Penny than Vines."[127] Similarly John Sheffield noted "the reason why the people have not attempted to make vineyards is, because the ground with easy cultivation produces an immediate profit, and it takes six or seven years to bring a vineyard to yield any considerable profit."[128] Bounties and encouragements were insufficient to suggest a rate of return to oenological ventures equaling or exceeding that to other staples.

The fiscal importance of wine and other alcoholic beverages in the colonies also hindered the development of commercial wine production. As Colonies increasingly turned to wine imports as a source of Revenue,[129] their interest

---

[126]Wright. Religion and Empire..., op. cit., pp. 93-94.
Alexander Whitaker. Good Newes from Virginia, (613$1261104), p. 32.
Wilson. "Good News...," op. cit., pp. 514-515.
Smith. Advertisements..., op. cit., p. 13.
Charles de Rochefort. Récit de l'estat present des célèbres colonies..., (681 1261166), p. 7.
Joshua Gee. The Trade and Navigation of Great-Britain..., (729 1271251), pp. 106, 109.

[127]Jared Eliot. Essays upon Field Husbandry..., op. cit., p. 216.

[128]Sheffield. Observations..., op. cit., pp. 50-51, footnote *.

[129]Giesecke. American Commercial Legislation..., op. cit., pp. 18 to 28.
Johnson et al. History of Domestic and Foreign Commerce..., op. cit., Vol. 1, pp. 56 to 59.
Davis Dewey. "Economic Organization...,"

in colonial wine manufacture waned. Imposts were a more direct and controllable means of taxation than were sales, consumption or turnover levies on home production.

Colonial fiscalism further discouraged commercial wine production by giving bounties and encouragements to competitive staples whose manufacture indirectly enhanced colonial revenue.[130] These incentives strengthened the comparative advantage of other commodities and, therefore, further restrained wine production.

Although the relative importance of the economic factors discouraging wine production differed markedly among colonies, it was, none the less, these factors in each colony which thwarted the development of commercial wine production. The current prevailing opinion, however, is that climatic, viticultural or socio-political elements

---

(927$1280778), pp. 437, 438.

Nelson P. Mead. Connecticut as a Corporate Colony, (906$1270868), pp. 32 to 34.

Edwin Tanner. "The Province of New Jersey...," (908$1280862), pp. 535-536.

Edgar Fisher. "New Jersey as a Royal Province...," (911$1280863), p. 289.

Percy Flippin. The Royal Government..., (919$1280864), pp. 230ff.

[130]Giesecke. American Commercial Legislation..., op. cit., pp. 59ff.

Johnson et al. History of Domestic and Foreign Commerce..., op. cit., Vol. 1, pp. 60 to 62.

Beer. The Commercial Policy..., op. cit., pp. 91 to 104.

Bishop. A History of American Manufactures..., op. cit., p. 269.

Thiebaut De Berneaud. The Vine-Dresser's...Manual..., (829 1270917), p. 26.

were the primary causes for the failure. This notion originated with colonists who dismissed the economic disadvantages of wine production, and was also voiced by ante-bellum viticulturists who rationalized their own failures in climatic terms.

A few colonists suggested that harassment by foreign powers impeded oenological endeavors. They viewed these encroachments as primarily socio-political rather than as economic. They failed, therefore, to interpret their harassment as the thwarting of an industry which might compete with a principal export of European states.

Several colonists blamed climatic and viticultural deficiencies for oenological failures. Their complaints suggested inadequate economic rewards to colonial wine producers, that is, promoters did not offer sufficient incentives to attract the skills pre-requisite to commercial oenological success.

Ante-bellum viticulturists who experimented widely with both native and imported varietals also failed to sustain commercial wine production.[131] Like their colonial

---

[131]Philip Wagner. A Wine-Grower's Guide, (945$1270487), pp. 21 to 23.
________. "Wine from American Grapes," (933$1280908), pp. 362 to 365.
Bishop. A History of American Manufactures..., op. cit., pp. 266-267, 274ff.
Hedrick. A History of Horticulture..., op. cit., pp. 180-181, 208 to 211, 224 to 226, 285, 286, 434 to 439.
________. The Grapes of New York, op. cit., pp. 40 to 59.
Bailey. The Evolution of Our Native Fruits, op. cit., pp. 21ff.

predecessors, they, too, explained their failure in climatic and viticultural terms.[132] Again, it was capital shortages, insufficient skill and inadequate economic returns to successful commercial vintages that limited their endeavors.[133]

Later horticultural authorities, seeking to explain American oenological failures, turned to these ante-bellum sources and to a small sample of colonial tracts. Their biased and confused compilations were imbued with ante-bellum climatic and viticultural rationales; they ignored the economic causation of colonial oenological failures.

---

[132] Bernard McMahon. The American Gardener's..., (806 1270539), p. 227.
J. S. Kecht. Der verbesserte praktische..., (828 1270546), p. v.
William Prince. A Short Treatise on Horticulture..., (828$1270545), pp. 70-71.
C. S. Rafinesque. American Manual of the Grape Vines..., (830 1270870), p. 42, item 9.
George Lindley. A Guide to the Orchard..., (846 1270549), p. 155.
William Chorlton. The American Grape Grower's Guide..., (856 1270243), pp. 11-12.
Charles Downing. The Fruits and Fruit Trees..., (857$1270551), p. 302.
James S. Lippincott. "Climatology of American Grape Vines," (863$1280591), pp. 196, 197.
James L. Denman. The Vine and its Fruit..., (864 1270219), pp. 297-298.

[133] Thomas Jefferson. "Letter...," (808$1260405), p. 375.
Wagner. A Wine-Grower's Guide, op. cit., pp. 22-23.
De Berneaud. The Vine-Dresser's..., op. cit., pp. 26 to 28.
Fisher. Observations..., op. cit., pp. 42-43.
Alden Spooner. The Cultivation of American Grape Vines..., (846 1270637), pp. 10, 12, 66-67.
Robert Buchanan. "Letter to Mr. Charles Cist," (849$1281156), pp. 616, 617.

Peyton Boswell, for example, proclaimed:

> It occurred to no one to domesticate these indigenous grapes...so as to improve their quality...The wild grapes grew in profusion, so why wouldn't the European varieties... the soft roots of Europe's vines were consumed by the tiny devouring worms of the phylloxera.[134]

L. H. Bailey explained the "disastrous failures" of early attempts to grow the European grape as a "result of an obscure sickness which caused the leaves to die and drop, and the grapes to rot."[135] Philip Wagner was more resolute, but no more correct in his interpretation:

> All sorts of reasons, except the right one, were put forward to explain the failures. The vinedressers proved to be lazy, or were scalped, or ran away; a more attractive crop, such as tobacco, lured the proprietor. The truth is that invariably 'a sickness took hold of the vines.'[136]

More critical than such misinterpretations were those failing to grasp the economic significance of oenological trials in the American colonies. Undaunted, John von Daacke proposed:

> When the first explorers and settlers came to America, they were neither interested in grapes nor grape culture. The grapes that were growing here were wild; in this

---

[134] Peyton Boswell. *Wine Makers Manual*..., (935 1271172), p. 31.

[135] Bailey. *The Evolution of Our Native Fruits*, *op. cit.*, p. 88.

[136] Wagner. "Wine from American Grapes," *op. cit.*, p. 361.

> state, grapes tend to be small and almost unnoticeable. Thus few records of those early years contain any mention of grapes.[137]

U. P. Hedrick categorically stated that, although there were few explorers of the Atlantic seaboard who did not mention grapes in their tracts, "none saw intrinsic value in these wild vines." Almost two decades earlier, Dr. Hedrick had avowed that "the value of the native grapes as a source of food and for wine was recognized by the first settlers in practically all of the colonies...their possibilities as cultivated plants were considered by some of the colonizers."[139]

The amendment of these currently accepted theories is a major facet of the Commodity Mercantilism approach. It argues that it was a lack of economic incentives and a dearth of capital and skilled labor which allowed climatic and viticultural factors to influence adversely the success of oenological ventures in the colonies. This interpretation views economic incentives to wine production within the

---

[137]Von Daacke. "Sparkling Catawba" Grape..., op. cit., p. 10.

[138]Hedrick. Manual of American Grape-Growing, (924$1270263), p. 5. Even the earliest tracts advocating colonial wine production conflict with Dr. Hedrick's surmise. Richard Hakluyt, for example, suggested that in the colonies "in setting your vine plants this year, you may have wine within three years, and it may be that the wild vines growing there already, by orderly pruning and dressing at your first arrival, may come to profit in shorter time." [Hakluyt. "Inducements to the Liking...," op. cit., p. 109.]

[139]Hedrick. The Grapes of New York, op. cit., p. 36.

context of rewards to alternative colonial staples. It suggests that such rewards were related to England's domestic and colonial mercantile practices, and more specifically, to her desires for wine availability, favorable trade balances and royal revenue. As wine-producing European states pursued these same objectives, and thus acted to discourage England's oenological trials, their practices, too, thwarted commercial wine production in the English colonies.

Conclusion

This dissertation has focused on the role of wine production in attempts by European states to solve the problems of provisionment and fiscalism. It has demonstrated the uniformity of their mercantile practices and offered a synthesis of them under the title, Commodity Mercantilism.

Commodity Mercantilism stresses the ready availability of commodities and the maintenance of favorable trade balances as criteria for successful mercantile policy. It emphasizes, as well, the importance of fiscalism in determining the commercial practices of the European states. The examination of the fishing trade and of the naval store, drug, spice and silk industries has suggested the uniform <u>means</u> by which European states improved their strength and value through trade and colonization. The economic motivations and consequences of such <u>means</u> parallel Spanish, French, Dutch and English commercial practices advancing oenological attempts in the colonies.

Spain and France, as wine producers, restricted the colonial production of wine and other commodities which would affect adversely their export trade. They attempted to control colonial trade and to augment royal revenue by taxing the sale of wine and other commodities. To supply the needs of home industry, they promoted the colonial production of naval stores, spices, drugs and silk. The channeling of capital and labor into these alternative ventures and the promotion of imported wines discouraged colonial viticulture and wine production.

The Dutch, having a copious supply of wine through entrepot trade, did not encourage colonial wine production. Similarly, Dutch colonists had little incentive to promote the industry. They turned rather to wine imports as a source of colonial fiscalism, finding it convenient to finance almost their entire colonial regime by wine and liquor imports, excises and sales taxes.

The English promoted domestic and colonial oenological trials to thwart balance of trade losses and to develop sources of wine supply. The popularity of wine in England prompted these efforts, as well as measures to stem the foreign wine trade and to curb wine prices. Thus, while promoting English shipping, augmenting royal (public) revenue, and satisfying the royal palate all advanced the wine trade, the desire for still greater revenue diverted English interests from wine to tobacco production, silk culture and gin manufacture. Viticulture was promoted only when it manifested comparative advantages in production. Hence, both in England and in the colonies, individual oenological projects were only intermittently successful.

This economic interpretation conflicts with the current prevailing opinion that climatic, viticultural or socio-political elements were the primary causes for the failure of commercial wine production in the English North American colonies. It argues instead that it was a lack of economic incentives and a dearth of capital and skilled labor which allowed climatic and viticultural factors to influence adversely the success of oenological ventures in the colonies. It interprets socio-political encroachments as attempts by European states to thwart an industry which might compete with one of their principal exports.

APPENDIX I

Tobacco Prices and Production: Virginia

DATE	PRICE PER POUND	(POUNDS) QUANTITY	SOURCE*
[1598 to 1619--London Prices]			Beer. The Origins..., pp. 86-87; p. 86, footnote 2.
1615-1616	-	2,300 1/2	Mac Innes. The Early English Tobacco..., p. 150.
1616-1617	-	19,388	Ibid. Beer. The Origins..., p. 109.
1617	-	20,000	Beer. The Origins..., p. 87. Arents. Tobacco..., Vol. 1, p. 88, footnote 4.
1618	"best at 3s., rest at 18d."	-	Arents. Tobacco..., Vol. 2, p. 141.
1619	2s. 11d. at auction	-	Beer. The Origins..., p.92, footnote 4.
	3s.	20,000	Jacobstein. "The Tobacco Industry...," p. 23.
	3s. "best" 18d. "second best"	-	Arents. Tobacco..., Vol. 1, p. 88, footnote 4.
	"stinted at" 3s.	-	Ibid., Vol. 2, p. 144.
	-	20,000	Keynes and Macgregor (eds.). "The Consumption...," Vol. 1, p. 58.
	-	20,000	Mac Innes. The Early English Tobacco..., p. 134.

*For bibliographic references to the sources of Appendix I, consult Infra, Vol. 1, pp. 311, 312.

DATE	PRICE PER POUND	(POUNDS) QUANTITY	SOURCE
1619	"less than half 10s."	-	Gray. "The Market Surplus...," p. 232; p. 232, footnote 4.
1620	-	40,000	Keynes and Macgregor (eds.). "The Consumptioh...," Vol. 1, p. 58.
	-	40,000	Mac Innes. The Early English Tobacco..., p. 134.
	8s.	-	Stock. Proceedings..., Vol. 1, p. 28.
	3s.	-	Arents. Tobacco..., Vol. 1, p. 102, footnote 5.
1621	8s.	-	Stock. Proceedings..., Vol. 1, pp. 30, 39.
	8s. to 10s.	-	Va. Co. Proceedings...., Vol. 1, p. 34.
	3s. "be it good or badd"	-	Arents. Tobacco..., Vol. 1, p. 96, footnote 7.
	-	55,000	Keynes and Macgregor (eds.). "The Consumption...," Vol. 1 p. 58.
	-	55,000	Mac Innes. The Early Englis Tobacco..., p. 134.
1621-1622	3s.	-	Arents. Tobacco..., Vol. 1, p. 101, footnote 4.
1622	3s. offered ("a great inducement")	-	Tatham. An Historical..., pp. 147-148.
	-	60,000	Keynes and Macgregor (eds.). "The Consumption...," Vol. 1, p. 58.
	-	60,000	Mac Innes. The Early Englis Tobacco..., p. 134.

DATE	PRICE PER POUND	(POUNDS) QUANTITY	SOURCE
1623	"depreciation of tobacco prices [from 3s.] commences"	-	Arents. Tobacco..., Vol. 1, p. 102, footnote 5.
	1s.	-	Beer. The Origins..., p. 93; p. 93, footnote 2.
c. 1625	3s. [discounted by higher prices of commodities purchased with tobacco]	-	Arents. Tobacco..., Vol. 1, p. 101, footnote 4.
1626	-	500,000	Keynes and Macgregor (eds.). "The Consumption...," Vol. 1, p. 58.
	-	500,000	Mac Innes. The Early English Tobacco..., p. 134.
1627	-	500,000	Beer. The Origins..., p. 87.
1628	-	500,000	Middleton. Tobacco Coast..., p. 95.
	-	369,254	Mac Innes. The Early English Tobacco..., p. 150.
	3d.	-	Jacobstein. "The Tobacco...," p. 23.
1629	"there comes...such abundance...it is not worth bringing home"		Smith. The True Travels..., folio G2 recto, verso.
	-	1,500,000	Keynes and Macgregor (eds.). "The Consumption...," Vol. 1, p. 58.
	-	1,500,000	Mac Innes. The Early English Tobacco..., p. 134.
1627-1638	on average not more than twopence	-	Beer. The Origins..., p.159.

DATE	PRICE PER POUND	(POUNDS) QUANTITY	SOURCE
1630	-	1,800,000	Keynes and Macgregor (eds.). "The Consumption...," Vol. 2, p. 58. Mac Innes. The Early English Tobacco..., p. 134.
	2d. ["lowest level between 1620 and 1640"]	-	Arents. Tobacco..., Vol. 1, p. 102, footnote 5.
	"less than a penny"	-	Calendar of State Papers: Colonial, Vol. 1, pp. 117, 124.
			Beer. The Origins..., p. 93, footnote 5.
1631	6d.	-	Jacobstein. "The Tobacco Industry...," p. 23.
	-	1,300,000	Keynes and Macgregor (eds.). "The Consumption...," Vol. 1, p. 58.
			Mac Innes. The Early English Tobacco..., p. 134.
1634	6d. offer; no bid	-	Keynes and Macgregor (eds.). "The Consumption...," Vol. 1, p. 158.
1635	6d. best	-	Arents. Tobacco..., Vol. 1, p. 102, footnote 5.
	4d. medium grade	-	Ibid.
1636	2d. low price for tobacco	-	Beer. The Origins..., p. 94, footnote 1.
1637	-	1,500,000	Keynes and Macgregor (eds.). "The Consumption...," p. 60.
1638	-	3,100,000	Ibid

DATE	PRICE PER POUND	(POUNDS) QUANTITY	SOURCE
1638-1639	"so low that planters could not subsist"	-	Gray. The Market Surplus..., p. 233.
1639	-	1,400,000	Keynes and Macgregor (eds.). "The Consumption...," p. 60.
	-	1,500,000	Middleton. Tobacco Coast..., p. 95.
1639-1640	around 3d.	-	Arents. Tobacco..., Vol. 1, p. 102, footnote 5.
1640	"'by reason of excessive quantities made,' that the planters cannot subsist by it"		Beer. The Origins..., pp. 96-97.
		1,300,000	Keynes and Macgregor (eds.). "The Consumption...," p. 60.
	12d.	-	Arents. Tobacco..., Vol. 1, p. 103.
1641	2s.	-	Ibid.
			Gray. The Market Surplus..., p. 233; p. 233, footnote 16.
	-	1,300,000	Beer. The Origins..., p. 97, footnote 1.
1642	-	1,300,000	Ibid.
1644	-	"short crop"	Arents. Tobacco..., Vol. 1, p. 103.
c. 1649	"would not yield in England 2d. cleare"	-	Bullock. Virginia Impartially..., pp. 96-97.
1649-1662	fluctuated between 1/2d. and 3d.	-	Beer. The Old Colonial..., Vol. 2, p. 116.

DATE	PRICE PER POUND	(POUNDS) QUANTITY	SOURCE
1662	1d.	-	Ibid.
1664	3d. to 3 1/2d.	-	Arents. Tobacco..., Vol. 1, p. 128, footnote 5.
1665	1d.		Ibid., Vol. 1, p. 128.
	1d.		Jacobstein. "The Tobacco Industry...," p. 23.
1667	"temporarily advanced prices"	-	Arents. Tobacco..., Vol.1, p. 129.
1676	15s./100 wt. [1.8d.]	-	Beer. The Old Colonial..., Vol. 2, p. 145, footnote 3.
1677	"rated at 8s./ 100 wt. ... commonly sold at twice that" [2d.]	-	Ibid., pp. 147-148.
1680	-	market over-stocked	Arents. Tobacco..., Vol. 1, p. 130.
1681 12 Dec.	"speedy and certain ruin of the Colony, is the low price of tobacco."	"market is over-stocked... tobacco enough... to last five years"	Calendar of State Papers: Colonial..., Vol. 11, p. 156 item 319.
1688	-	18,157,000	Jacobstein. "The Tobacco Industry," p. 23.
1689	-	14,392,635	Keynes and Macgregor (eds.). "The Consumption...," Vol.1, p. 61.
1689-1709		Annual average London import 28,000,000	Ibid.
1690	2d.	-	Jacobstein. "The Tobacco Industry...," p. 23.

DATE	PRICE PER POUND	(POUNDS) QUANTITY	SOURCE
1690-c.1700	1 1/2d. to 2d.	-	Arents. Tobacco..., Vol. 1, p. 133, footnote 3.
1700	-	28,000,000	Beer. The Commercial Policy..., p. 51.
1704	2d.	-	Ibid., p. 49; p. 49, footnote 2.
1704	"hogsheads on consignment brought no return whatsoever."	-	Gray. "The Market Surplus...," p. 235.
c. 1705			
	"marriage license 20s. or 200 lbs. tobacco" [1.2d.]	-	Arents. Tobacco..., Vol. 3, p. 42.
1709-1710	-	23,350,735	Mac Innes. The Early English Tobacco..., p. 150.
1710	"nominally rated at 1d. ...large quantities unsalable"	-	Gray. "The Market Surplus...," p. 235.
1722	3/4d.	-	Jacobstein. "The Tobacco Industry...," p. 23.
	"2 1/2d. best Virginia"		Arents. Tobacco..., Vol. 3, p. 138.
c. 1724	"market... in a depressed state"	-	Ibid., Vol. 4, p. 443.
1737	-	50,196,181	Keynes and Macgregor (eds.). "The Consumption...," Vol. 1, p. 61.
1738	-	40,103,449	Ibid.

DATE	PRICE PER POUND	(POUNDS) QUANTITY	SOURCE
c. 1738	12d.	-	Arents. *Tobacco...*, Vol. 3, p. 275.
1753	2d.	53,862,000	Jacobstein. "The Tobacco Industry...," p. 23.
1758	-	22,050,000	*Ibid*.
1763	2d.	-	*Ibid*.

APPENDIX I: BIBLIOGRAPHY

Arents, George. Tobacco Its History Illustrated by The Books, Manuscripts and Engravings in the Library of George Arents, Jr. [compiled by Jerome E. Brooks] New York: The Rosenbach Company, Vol. 1 to 5, 1937 to 1953.

Beer, George L. The Commercial Policy of England Toward the American Colonies. New York: Peter Smith, 1948. [A reprint of Studies in History, Economics and Public Laws, Vol. 3, No. 2 (1893).]

________. The Old Colonial System 1660-1754. New York: The Macmillan Company, 1913, [reprinted Gloucester, Mass.: Peter Smith, 1958], Vol. 1, 2.

________. The Origins of the British Colonial System 1578-1660. New York: Macmillan Company, 1908, [reprinted Gloucester, Mass.: Peter Smith, 1959].

Bvllock, William. [Bullock, William]. Virginia Impartially Examined, and Left to Publick View. London: John Hammond, 1649.

Gray, L. C. "The Market Surplus Problems of Colonial Tobacco," in William and Mary Quarterly. Second series. Vol. 7, No. 4 (1927).

Great Britain. Public Record Office. Calendar of State Papers, Colonial Series, America and the West Indies. Vol. I, II.

Jacobstein, Meyer. "The Tobacco Industry in the United States," in Studies in History, Economics and Public Law, Vol. 26, No. 3 (1907).

Keynes, J. M., and Macgregor, D. H. (eds.). "The Consumption of Tobacco Since 1600," in Economic History (A Supplement to the Economic Journal), London: Macmillan Company, 1929, Vol. 1.

Mac Innes, C. M. The Early English Tobacco Trade. London: Kegan Paul, Trench, Trubner and Company, 1926.

Middleton, Arthur P. _Tobacco Coast A Maritime History of Chesapeake Bay in the Colonial Era._ Newport News, Virginia: The Mariners' Museum, 1953.

Smith, John. _The True Travels, Adventures and Observations of Captain J. Smith in Europe, Asia, Africa and America 1592 to 1629..._ London: J. H., 1630.

Stock, Leo F. _Proceedings and Debates of the British Parliaments Respecting North America._ Washington: The Carnegie Institution, Vol. 1 to 5, 1924 to 1941.

Tatham, William. _An Historical and Political Essay on the Culture and Commerce of Tobacco._ London: T. Bensley, 1800.

Virginia Company of London. _Abstract of the Proceedings of the Virginia Company of London, 1619-1624._ Richmond: The Virginia Historical Society, 1888-1889.

APPENDIX II

English Encouragements for Crop Diversification, Particularly Viticultural Expansion

DATE	ITEM	SOURCE
1619	"daiely husbandtrie--sum to clering ground for corn and tobacko, sum to building houses sum to plant vines and mulberie trees"	Ferdinando Yate, quoted in Brown. The First Republic..., (898$1270090), p. 374.
1619-1620	Instructions to augment tobacco with "corn, wine, silke, hempe"	Orders and Consti- tvtions..., (619 1251173), p. 21.
1621	"instructions recently received from England; en- couraging the cultivation of other commodities than tobacco"	Governor Wyatt, quoted in Brown. The First Republic..., op. cit., p. 458.
1622 12 April	"By encouraging only tobacco and sassafras, other commod- ities have been neglected, and 8 or 10 ships going to Virginia in one year have all returned empty."	Calendar of State Papers: Colonial..., (574$1221125), Vol. 1, p. 29, item 4.
1622	James I instructs the diversification of the Virginia economy "Commanding the Present Setting Vp of Silke Works, and Planting of Vines in Virginia"	Iohn Bonoeil. His Maiesties..., (622 1261194), title page, folio a, [b], pp. 1 to 3, and passim.
1616-1623	Unfruitful attempts to diversify the Virginia economy and to allay tobacco production.	Andrews. Our Earli- est Colonial..., (933$1270089), pp. 42-43.
1624	Virginians "purchasing their food and rayment from England in exchange of Tobacco...[the] Countrey [was] before this time for Wine, Oyle, Wheate,..."	William Alexander. An Encouragement..., (624$1261170), pp. 29-30.

DATE	ITEM	SOURCE
1624 ? July	James I asserts the colonies will not prosper if they rely upon tobacco alone and neglect other crops of greater consequence.	Calendar of State Papers: Colonial..., op. cit., Vol. 1, p. 63, item 16.
1625	"[England] to tolerate the use of tobacco of the growth of those plantations for a time, until by more solid commodities they be able to subsist otherwise"	Rymer. Foedera, xvii. 668, quoted in Lipson. The Economic History..., (961 1271271), Vol. 3, p. 181.
1625	"the only Commodity for Marchandizes in booth the Plantations is at this day no other than Tobacco"	Colonial Papers, III, 32, quoted in Beer. The Origins..., (922$1271268), p. 87.
1626 19 April	"That whereas y^e tobacco falleth every day more and more to a baser price, Wee require y^u to use y^e best endeavours to y^e raising of more staple comodities"	Colonial Entry Book, LXXIX, quoted in Beer. The Origins..., op. cit., p. 91, footnote 1.
1627	"The King [Charles I] is much troubled...that this plantation is wholly built upon smoke"	Calendar of State Papers: Colonial..., op. cit., Vol. 1, p. 86. [Similarly: Ibid., pp. 125, 239, 250.]
1628	Charles I instructs "to have especial care that the oils, potashes, soaps, and other commodities they are about to undertake the manufacture of, be really perfect, and that none pass out of the country without examination"	Calendar of State Papers: Colonial..., op. cit., Vol. 1, p. 95, item 65.

DATE	ITEM	SOURCE
1628 26 March	Governor, Council and Burgesses of Virginia reply to Charles I: "Tobacco... to which nevertheless they are not so much wedded as wholly to neglect the raising of staple commodities...pitch, and tar... they conceive that the planting of vines will prove a commodity both beneficial and profitable."	"Answer of the Governor...," in Virginia Magazine of History and Biography, Vol. 7, Number 3 (January, 1900), p. 262.
1628 30 April	"the people making great quantities of tobacco... and neglected the corn... [a means sought] to manage Tobacco and to oblige the planting of corn"	Minutes of the Council..., (622 1241035), p.10.
1628 6 August	"And wheras your Tobacco falleth everie day more and more to a baser price, we require you to...cause... everie Plantation to plant a proportion of Vines, answerable to theire numbers, and to plant mulbury trees, and to attend silke wormes."	W.L. Grant and James Munro. (eds.). Acts of the Privy Council..., (908 1221133), Vol. 1, pp. 127-128.
1631-1632	"the cultivation of a certain number of vines was enjoined upon each settler."	Hening. The Statutes At Large...Virginia, (619 1241034), Vol. 1, pp. 161, 162, 192 cited in Beer. The Origins..., op. cit., p. 248; p. 248, footnote 2.
1631 ? Jan.	"the king marvels that they apply themselves wholly to tobacco, and requires them not to plant so much as they leave hitherto done. Every planter to have his proportion limited."	Calendar of State Papers: Colonial..., op. cit., Vol. 1, p. 125, item 2.

DATE	ITEM	SOURCE
1631	"the King is careful to encourage and support the Plantation and he has long expected some better fruit than tobacco and smoke to be returned from thence."	Calendar of State Papers: Colonial [1631] quoted in Mac Innes. The Early English Tobacco..., (926$1270216), p.133.
1638 ?	"Acts to be passed...for planting vines, mulberry trees, and apple and pear slips, and also hemp, flax, and other staple commodities."	Calendar of State Papers: Colonial..., op. cit., Vol. 1, pp. 268-269, item 98.
1638/9 Jan.	"Tobacco falling every year to a baser price [since the discontinuation of price "stinting" in 1637]...[ordered] to raise staple commodities as hemp and flax, rape seed and madder, pitch and tar, and to plant vines and white mulberry trees and to attend to silk worms. The price of tobacco to be left free and the Merchant to be allowed to make his own bargain for his goods."	"Instructions to Sir Francis Wyatt." quoted in Virginia Magazine of History and Biography, Vol. 11, No. 1 (June 1903), p. 56.
1639	"Whereas the excessive quantity of tobacco of late years planted in the colony, and the evil condition and quality thereof being principally occasioned thereby, have debased the commodity to so vile esteem and rate...[subscribers agree to "absolutely destroy and burn" 1639 tobacco crop except for 40/100 pounds of the best tobacco to be saved and distributed according to planting.]	William Tatham. An Historical and Political Essay on the Culture and Commerce of Tobacco. London: T. Bensley, 1800, pp. 151, 152.
1640-1641	A limit on tobacco planting proposed.	Ibid., p. 153.

DATE	ITEM	SOURCE
1642	"Where yor Tobacco falleth every day more and more unto a baser price....We require you to use yor best endeav^r to cause ye people to apply themselves to the raising of more staple commodities as Hemp and Flax, Rape Seed and Madder, Pitch & Tar for Tanning of Hides and Leather. Likewise every Plantation to plant a proportion of Vines, answerable to their numbers, and to plant white Mulberry Trees, and attend to Silk Worms."	"Instructions to Berkeley...," in _Virginia Magazine of History and Biography_, Vol. 2, No. 3 (Jan. 1895), p. 287.
1657	"Encouragement for Staple Commodities...first...two tunne of wine raized out of a vineyard made in this collonie shall have given him...ten thousand pounds of Virginia tobacco."	Hening. _The Statutes at Large... Virginia_, _op. cit._, Vol. 1, pp. 469-470.
1662 [May 14]	"the great evils of planting vast quantities of tobacco...to remedy which ...resolved...to prohibit the planting of any tobacco in Virginia and Maryland after 1st June 1663, which will encourage the more staple commodities of silk, flax, hemp, pitch, potashes..."	_Calendar of State Papers: Colonial..._, _op. cit._, Vol. 5, p. 90, item 301. [Similarly: _Ibid._, Vol. 5, p. 98, item 332; p. 103, item 345; p. 110, item 368, 369.]
1663 30 Aug.	"the land [is] proper to bear commodities not yet produced in other Plantations, as wine, oil, currants, raisins, silks, &c., the planting of which will not injure other Plantations which may very well happen if there were a very great increase of sugar works or more tobacco..."	"The Lords Proprietors of [North] Carolina...," quoted in _Calendar of State Papers: Colonial..._, _op. cit._, Vol. 5, p. 157, item 547. [Similarly: _Ibid._, Vol. 5, pp. 125-126, item 427; pp. 154-155, item 536.]

DATE	ITEM	SOURCE
1664 25 Nov.	"Order for all hemp, pitch, and tar from Virginia and Maryland to be custom free for five years, in order to encourage the planters to apply themselves to commodities more beneficial than tobacco."	Calendar of State Papers: Colonial..., op. cit., Vol. 5, p. 257, item 865.
1666-1668	Agreed in Virginia, Maryland, Carolina and other places not to plant tobacco.	Mac Innes. The Early English Tobacco..., op. cit., p. 139. Arents. Tobacco Its History Illustrated... New York: The Rosenbach Company, 1937, Vol. 1, p. 128.
1666	"on this vicious weed of tobacco, which at length has brought them to that extremity, that they can neither handsomely subsist with it, nor without it."	Berkeley. quoted in Beer. The Old Colonial..., (912$1271267), p. 119.
1667 29 Sept.	To stimulate production of silks, wines, currants, raisins...English customs duties waived for a seven-year period. The new settlement was expected to avoid such products as sugar and tobacco in order not to depress further their price. [Consult Item 30 Aug. 1663, above.]	Colonial Records of North Carolina, Vol. 1, p. 108 cited in Beer. The Old Colonial..., op. cit. p. 178; p. 178, footnote 2.
1671	Navigation Acts responsible "that wee cannot add to our plantacon any Commodity that growes out of itt [Europe], as oliue trees, Cotton or Vines, besides this wee Cannot procure any skilfull Men..."	Berkeley. quoted in Beer. The Old Colonial..., op. cit., p. 113.

DATE	ITEM	SOURCE
1672 20 Jan.	"Cannot question the growth of a good sort of tobacco, which may surpass the fame of Virginia, but conceives most worthy of their thoughts wine, oil, and silk..."	"Dalton to Lord Ashley," [Charlestown] quoted in Calendar of State Papers: Colonial..., op. cit., Vol. 7, p. 319, item 736.
1673	"the low and contemptable price [for tobacco] is occasioned cheifely by the greate quantityes yearely made."	Hening. The Statutes at Large...Virginia, op. cit., Vol. 2, p. 306.
1674	Virginia should desist from growing tobacco and plant instead mulberry trees, vines and olives as was done in Carolina.	Carew Reynell. The True English Interest, London: 1674, pp. 32 to 35.
1679-1683	"moved to put some restraint on the planting of tobacco in that our colony."	Royal Instructions..., (935 1220883), p. 695, item 964.
1679-1690	"Encourage Raising Other Crops Than Tobacco...particularly endeavor to advance the plantation of vines, silks, hemp, flax, pitch, and potashes..."	Ibid., p. 696, item 965.
1680-1682	Proposals to again restrict tobacco planting [1666-1668]; these proposals not followed.	Mac Innes. The Early English Tobacco..., op. cit., p. 139.
1680	Carolina beneficial: "the likelyhood of Wines, Oyls and Silks, and the great Variety of other Natural Commodities."	Beer. The Old Colonial..., op. cit., Vol. 2, p. 188; p. 188, footnote 2.
1681 13 May	"Our most formidable enemy, poverty, is falling violently on us through the low value, or rather no value, of tobacco..."	Calendar of State Papers: Colonial..., op. cit., Vol. 11, pp. 47-48, item 104.
1682	"The low price of tobacco was at this time termed a calamity, 'the sad resentment of which would force blood from any loyal Christian subject's heart.'"	Beer. The Old Colonial..., op. cit., Vol. 2, p. 153; p. 153, footnote 1.

DATE	ITEM	SOURCE
1696	"tobacco swallows up all other things, every thing else is neglected, and all markets are often so glutted with bad tobacco, that it becomes a mere drug, and will not clear the freight and custom."	"An Account...," (696 1260895) p. 127.
1705	"Colonial authorities, as well as Parliament, tried to induce the colonists to substitute other crops for tobacco. Flax, hemp, cotton and silk were tried but these yielded an inadequate return."	Beverley. History of Virginia, p. 233 [(705 1260701)] cited in Jacobstein. The Tobacco Industry..., (907$1271223), p. 22; p. 22, footnote 2.
1706	"Never was so great a quantity of tobacco come from the Plantations in one year, as is expected in England this summer, nor was there ever so dismall a prospect of a market."	"Colonel Quarry to Board of Trade," quoted in Middleton. Tobacco Coast..., (953 1270681), p. 127.
1708	low price of tobacco "so low that for some years it hath not been sufficient to purchase Cloaths for the Makers thereof."	Executive Journals... Virginia, (680 1241033), Vol. 3, p. 194.

VITA

David Joel Mishkin was born on January 29, 1937, in Brooklyn, New York. He was awarded a Bachelor of Arts degree from Queens College in 1958 and an Artium Magister from Columbia University in 1960. Both degrees were granted in economics. In September, 1960, Mr. Mishkin assumed two positions: Investment Analyst at Bache and Company, an international stock brokerage firm; and, Instructor in economics at Fairleigh Dickinson University. He maintained both positions until February, 1962, when he was employed as an Economic Consultant by Standard Financial Corporation, a major commercial loan company. Mr. Mishkin left this position to embark upon doctoral studies at the University of Illinois in September, 1962.

As a student at the University of Illinois, Mr. Mishkin was awarded a teaching assistantship (1962-1964), a National Science Foundation Fellowship (Summer, 1963), a Freedom Committee Grant (1964-1965), and an H. B. Earhart Foundation Fellowship (1965-1966). His article, "The Credit Rationing Artifact in Light of an Expanded Price Rationing Theory," was selected in a national competition to be the lead article in _The American Economist_, of Winter,

1964. *The Journal of Economic History* published an abstract of this dissertation, the abstract being a summary of Mr. Mishkin's Invited Dissertation speech at the 25th Annual Meeting of the Economic History Association, at Yale University, September 1-3, 1965. His prior publications include "A Practical Solution to the Silver Problem," *The Commercial and Financial Chronicle*, October 19, 1961; and, "Outlook for the Finance Industry under Tightening Credit," *The Magazine of Wall Street*, November, 1961.

Mr. Mishkin has been elected to *Who's Who in American Universities and Colleges*, 1957-1958, *American Men of Science*, 1962-1963, and *Who's Who in the Midwest*, 1966-1967. He is a member of Omicron Delta Epsilon--National Honor Society in Economics, the American Finance Association and The Wine Institute.

Dissertations in American Economic History

An Arno Press Collection

Adams, Donald R., Jr. **Wage Rates in Philadelphia, 1790-1830.** (Doctoral Dissertation, University of Pennsylvania, 1967). 1975

Aldrich, Terry Mark. **Rates of Return on Investment in Technical Education in the Ante-Bellum American Economy.** (Doctoral Dissertation, The University of Texas at Austin, 1969). 1975

Anderson, Terry Lee. **The Economic Growth of Seventeenth Century New England:** A Measurement of Regional Income. (Doctoral Dissertation, University of Washington, 1972). 1975

Bean, Richard Nelson. **The British Trans-Atlantic Slave Trade, 1650-1775.** (Doctoral Dissertation, University of Washington, 1971). 1975

Brock, Leslie V. **The Currency of the American Colonies, 1700-1764:** A Study in Colonial Finance and Imperial Relations. (Doctoral Dissertation, University of Michigan, 1941). 1975

Ellsworth, Lucius F. **Craft to National Industry in the Nineteenth Century:** A Case Study of the Transformation of the New York State Tanning Industry. (Doctoral Dissertation, University of Delaware, 1971). 1975

Fleisig, Heywood W. **Long Term Capital Flows and the Great Depression:** The Role of the United States, 1927-1933. (Doctoral Dissertation, Yale University, 1969). 1975

Foust, James D. **The Yeoman Farmer and Westward Expansion of U. S. Cotton Production.** (Doctoral Dissertation, University of North Carolina at Chapel Hill, 1968). 1975

Golden, James Reed. **Investment Behavior By United States Railroads, 1870-1914.** (Doctoral Thesis, Harvard University, 1971). 1975

Hill, Peter Jensen. **The Economic Impact of Immigration into the United States.** (Doctoral Dissertation, The University of Chicago, 1970). 1975

Klingaman, David C. **Colonial Virginia's Coastwise and Grain Trade.** (Doctoral Dissertation, University of Virginia, 1967). 1975

Lang, Edith Mae. **The Effects of Net Interregional Migration on Agricultural Income Growth:** The United States, 1850-1860. (Doctoral Thesis, The University of Rochester, 1971). 1975

Lindley, Lester G. **The Constitution Faces Technology:** The Relationship of the National Government to the Telegraph, 1866-1884. (Doctoral Thesis, Rice University, 1971). 1975

Lorant, John H[erman]. **The Role of Capital-Improving Innovations in American Manufacturing During the 1920's.** (Doctoral Thesis, Columbia University, 1966). 1975

Mishkin, David Joel. **The American Colonial Wine Industry:** An Economic Interpretation, Volumes I and II. (Doctoral Thesis, University of Illinois, 1966). 1975

Oates, Mary J. **The Role of the Cotton Textile Industry in the Economic Development of the American Southeast:** 1900-1940. (Doctoral Dissertation, Yale University, 1969). 1975

Passell, Peter. **Essays in the Economics of Nineteenth Century American Land Policy.** (Doctoral Dissertation, Yale University, 1970). 1975

Pope, Clayne L. **The Impact of the Ante-Bellum Tariff on Income Distribution.** (Doctoral Dissertation, The University of Chicago, 1972). 1975

Poulson, Barry Warren. **Value Added in Manufacturing, Mining, and Agriculture in the American Economy From 1809 To 1839.** (Doctoral Dissertation, The Ohio State University, 1965). 1975

Rockoff, Hugh. **The Free Banking Era: A Re-Examination.** (Doctoral Dissertation, The University of Chicago, 1972). 1975

Schumacher, Max George. **The Northern Farmer and His Markets During the Late Colonial Period.** (Doctoral Dissertation, University of California at Berkeley, 1948). 1975

Seagrave, Charles Edwin. **The Southern Negro Agricultural Worker:** 1850-1870. (Doctoral Dissertation, Stanford University, 1971). 1975

Solmon, Lewis C. **Capital Formation by Expenditures on Formal Education, 1880 and 1890.** (Doctoral Dissertation, The University of Chicago, 1968). 1975

Swan, Dale Evans. **The Structure and Profitability of the Antebellum Rice Industry:** 1859. (Doctoral Dissertation, University of North Carolina at Chapel Hill, 1972). 1975

Sylla, Richard Eugene. **The American Capital Market, 1846-1914:** A Study of the Effects of Public Policy on Economic Development. (Doctoral Thesis, Harvard University, 1968) 1975

Uselding, Paul John. **Studies in the Technological Development of the American Economy During the First Half of the Nineteenth Century.** (Doctoral Dissertation, Northwestern University, 1970) 1975

Walsh, William D[avid]. **The Diffusion of Technological Change in the Pennsylvania Pig Iron Industry, 1850-1870.** (Doctoral Dissertation, Yale University, 1967). 1975

Weiss, Thomas Joseph. **The Service Sector in the United States, 1839 Through 1899.** (Doctoral Thesis, University of North Carolina at Chapel Hill, 1967). 1975

Zevin, Robert Brooke. **The Growth of Manufacturing in Early Nineteenth Century New England.** 1975